ra

LEARNING LINGO™

the art and science of programming
with MacroMedia® Director®

LEARNING LINGO™

the art and science of programming with MacroMedia® Director®

Michael Callery

Addison-Wesley Publishing Company

Reading, Massachusetts • Menlo Park, California • New York
Don Mills, Ontario • Wokingham, England • Amsterdam
Bonn • Sydney • Singapore • Tokyo • Madrid • San Juan
Paris • Seoul • Milan • Mexico City • Taipei

Library of Congress Cataloging-in-Publication Data

Callery, Michael.
    Learning Lingo : the art and science of programming with
    Macromedia Director / Michael Callery.
        p.   cm.
    Includes bibliographical references and index.
    ISBN 0-201-87043-6
    1. Lingo (Computer program language)   2. Multimedia systems.
I. Title
QA76.73.L22C35   1996
006.6—dc20   95-36230
                                                                  CIP

Sponsoring Editors: Martha Steffen and Mary Treseler
Project Manager: Sarah Weaver
Production Coordinator: Erin Sweeney
Cover design: Ann Gallager
Text design: Michael Callery
Set in Times, Industria, Courier, and Gill Sans Condensed.

2 3 4 5 6 7-MA-0099989796
Second printing, March 1996

Addison-Wesley books are available for bulk purchases by corporations, institutions, and other organizations. For more information please contact the Corporate, Government, and Special Sales Department at (800) 238-9682.

Find us on the World-Wide Web at: http://www.aw.com/devpress/

For Robert Beardsley, Kathleen Tracey, and, most of all, Helen Koritz—colleagues in my first teaching appointment in the joined Biology Department of Manhattan College and the College of Mount Saint Vincent. Bob, Sister Kathleen, and Helen saw the potentials of computers in education a decade before most educators, and they didn't seem to mind an ecologist morphing into a computer person. With their support, encouragement, and collaboration, a career was born.

Table of Contents

Introduction

This is not a book about how to use MacroMedia Director—about how to import files into the cast, how to arrange these cast members in the score, how to use all the gizmos in the Paint Window, and so on. I expect you know how to do all this. You want Director to do more than move a crawling worm across the screen; you want to create a multimedia spectacle, an interactive *Birth of a Nation* for the '90s.

This is a book about doing cool things with MacroMedia Director.

Cool things like an adventure game where you are stranded in an apparently exit-less dungeon until you find the key to release you, or a carnival arcade game where you can shoot at the targets to win that big pink teddy bear ... if you don't run out of bullets. And lots more!

To do these things with Director—to move beyond film loops, Tempo Channel commands, and color cycling—you must master Lingo, the programming language of Director.

Why Lingo?

Interactivity, by definition, demands that your movie respond to the user; he or she—not you—determines the course of events. You provide the possibilities.

You may have experimented with Director's Tempo Channel to make your movie stop and wait for the user to press a key or click the mouse. You can do the same thing with a simple Lingo command. With a little more Lingo programming, you can make buttons to allow the user to jump around in a movie depending upon where he or she clicked.

By delving more deeply into Lingo, you can create dynamic animations that are different each time the movie is run, buttons that change shape, and links between text (hypertext). You can also open more than one movie, or do almost anything your imagination dreams up.

Lingo is the key—freeing you from the frame-by-frame rigidity of the score to let you make truly interactive movies.

Why This Book?

The documentation that comes with Director is a logical place to start learning Lingo. These manuals, however, are intended to explain how the program works, not to teach you programming. Most books about Director focus on the basics—using the score, the cast, the tools, and so on. Discussion of Lingo, if there is one, is often limited to making simple buttons. That's not enough depth to do cool things. Which is why I wrote this book.

I've watched hundreds of students struggle with Lingo over the last several years. When I first started using computers, I had to learn to program; there were few general-purpose applications, save for a handful of text editors. With the microcomputer revolution of the late '70s and '80s, programming became less important; applications allowed us to do our work merely by entering (or drawing or scanning or ...) the needed data. We've come full circle, and, at least for now and the foreseeable future, you must program to create interactive movies and to take full advantage of Director.

I needed a book my students could use when I'm not around. But I did not want a book of "canned" solutions to specific needs. What happens if the canned solution does not work? I want my students to understand what's going on underneath, to be able to generalize from a specific situation to a broader context so that their movies do what they really want them to do.

Lingo is a computer programming language. To go beyond canned solutions or the examples in the Director documentation, you must learn about programming principles and constructs as well as Lingo's command language. This way, you'll be able to build on what you know and create *new* Director applications that work.

How This Book Is Organized

Learning Lingo's first three sections cover a cluster of related programming concepts. Within each section, the chapters detail specific programming techniques in small Director movies. The sections culminate in a large project showing the commands, structures, and techniques you learned in action.

Section One focuses on the basics: loops, conditionals, and basic use of variables. The Section Project is a simple dungeon adventure game.

Section Two takes these concepts one step further, exploring puppets—objects controlled entirely by Lingo, rather than by the score. The Section Project is an arcade game.

Section Three centers on data—words, numbers, lists, and files. The Section Project is a hypertext movie featuring cross-referenced words and a glossary.

Section Four differs from the preceding sections in that each chapter is devoted to an advanced topic too diverse for a Section Project. The topics include working with digital video, working with menus, windows, and other interface items, and working with external commands.

Finally, a set of appendices offers reference information, including a list of all objects and their properties, suggestions for how to structure and organize a movie for the outside world, a quick reference for HyperCard programmers who are converting to Director, and an annotated list of references and sources.

I have tried to make each chapter stand alone as much as possible; however, explanations in later chapters **do** depend on those in earlier ones. I've cross-referenced all important topics.

One of the most important aspects of Director programming is the look and feel of your movies. Where appropriate, I'll comment on user-interface issues as they apply to the specific movie we're developing.

How to Use This Book

This book is meant to be used with a computer. As you read, type in and experiment with the scripts and handlers. All Lingo pragrams are printed in the `Courier typeface`. Code you must type is **boldfaced**.

You may find that a specific script doesn't work as it is being developed, but **how** it doesn't work is the crux of the learning experience. By the end of a chapter, everything **will** work as advertised. You should use the Save as... command to save intermediate versions of developing movies.

At the end of each chapter, you'll find a command summary detailing the syntax of each command introduced in the chapter. You may want to refer to these summaries when a command is introduced. The Lingo Dictionary, part of the Director documentation, provides a more detailed examination of each command. You may also find the on-line Director Help useful to see the full syntax of a command as well as some examples.

Look for these icons to cue you to important ideas:

 Marks sections dealing with good user-interface principles.

 Marks sections dealing with common, potential sources of bugs or errors.

 Marks sections dealing with nuts-and-bolts programming issues, things you really want to master.

 or Marks version-specific (Mac or Windows) information—changes that make a difference in how your movie will work when run under a different version of Director.

A Note on Programming Style

All programming languages, Lingo included, allow a problem to be solved in a variety of ways. In writing the code for this book, I have tried to create the most readable scripts, opting to emphasize understandability over elegance. Therefore, I use the long form of a statement over a shorter form, avoid cleverness where it's not really necessary, use more variables than necessary, and so on.

On the other hand, I use comments sparingly—this book provides the documentation for the code. As you develop your programming skills, you'll discover more economical ways to achieve your goals and, I hope, you'll comment your code so generously that you (or a colleague) can understand what a script is doing six months after you've written it.

Using the Companion CD-ROM

All movies in the book are included on the companion CD-ROM—most of them in both their unprogrammed and fully-programmed forms. In the early chapters of this book, I explain how to construct a movie, but as the movies become more complex, you'll be instructed to open specific movies from the CD as a starting place. The movies are organized in folders or subdirectories according to chapter number.

> *A special note to Macintosh users: I have used PC DOS naming conventions for the files on the companion CD-ROM so that our compatriots, working on the PC platform, can use these movies too.*

If you have sufficient space, you may want to copy the book-specific folders to your hard disk. Some movies will not run properly from locked media, such as CD-ROM. These movies are flagged in the text. The folder structure is also important for some movies. If you copy a movie to your hard disk, copy the entire folder or subdirectory.

In addition to the book-specific movies, I've included a number of extras in the Goodies Folder. Some of these provide additional examples for you to model your work on, others illustrate specific Director features beyond the scope of this book. Start by opening the ReadMe file for specific information on these additional movies.

Acknowledgments

Thanks to my students at The New School, New York University, and Parsons School of Design. I developed most of the movies in this book in response to their problems, questions, and challenges.

Thanks to Roberta Schwartz, Pat Schiller, and Jane Willson, who read early versions of this book and helped me immeasurably as it took shape.

Thanks to Carole Lowenstein and Jim Lambert, designers of beautiful books, for their guidance and expert suggestions.

Thanks to the folks at Addison-Wesley: Martha Steffen and Mary Treseler, who had the faith to start me up and keep me going; Sarah Weaver, Erin Sweeney, and John Webber, who guided the production of this book; Nancy Hayes Clune, who kept my ellipses (and other grammatical idiosyncrasies) under control; and Ian Cotler, who watched my Lingo-istics.

Section 1 ◆ Interactivity 101

Where to get started learning Lingo? With basic interactivity: menus, rollovers, moveable sprites, and other fun stuff. This section will introduce you to the basics of creating an interactive Director movie. We end with an adventure game, allowing the user to explore a world you've made. It's not MYST, but, then, I'll leave it to you to expand this project into the grandest adventure game ever!

1 ◆ On the Menu

Menus are the most commonly used feature in interactive Director movies. I'm not talking here about the Menu Bar, but full-frame menus. (We'll customize the Menu Bar in Chapter 15.) Like a menu in a restaurant, a movie's menu allows the user to choose what he or she wants to do.

A simple Director movie starts at the beginning and runs through the end of the movie. In a menu system, however, the movie must stop so that the user can decide where to go next by clicking on a word or graphic. You may have used the Tempo Channel options to stop the playback head, but this method will not work for menus. That is because with Tempo Channel options you cannot control where the movie goes after the mouse or keyboard event—it always goes to the next frame. Further, if you want your menu to include animation, the Tempo Channel options won't work.

Fortunately, Lingo features a go to command that allows you to jump— or in programmer's parlance, "branch"—to another frame in the movie. Later on, you'll use this same command to branch to a different movie, even branch to a specific frame of another movie, and come back to where you left off. But we're getting ahead of ourselves here....

Let's start by making a movie of two simple animations: a circle moving left to right and a box moving up and down.

Fire up Director and start a new movie. Open the Score Window and click on channel 1, frame 10.

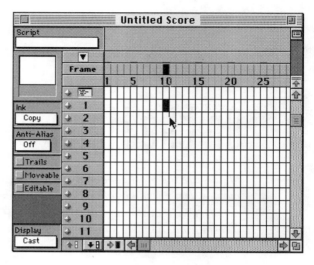

Then open the Tools Window and draw a circle on the stage.

Now, copy and paste your circle from frame 10 to frame 20:

On the stage, drag the circle in frame 20 to the desired location, frames 10 to 20, and choose In-Between Linear from the Score Menu.

Repeat these actions to create a box moving up and down in frames 30 to 40.

Your final score should look something like this:

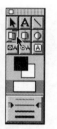

The Tools Menu

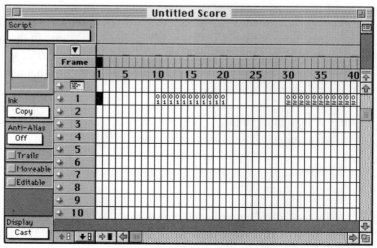

Now let's add the programming to make the playback head stop.

You may be wondering why we've left frames 21 through 30 empty. When you are making an interactive movie, you're controlling the movement of the playback head, so the frames need not be contiguous. We'll "jump over" the blank frames.

Double click on the Script Channel in frame 1. This opens the script editor, which looks like this:

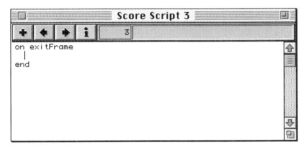

Director scripts are composed of handlers. Each handler begins with the keyword "on" and concludes with the keyword "end," like bookends. Handlers respond to messages. Director itself sends a bunch of messages as things happen in your movie. Much of your work in Lingo involves creating handlers to respond to these messages. See the sidebar "Message Central" to learn more about messages.

There's more to it than just creating handlers; you must place these handlers in the right place. In the movie we are developing here, we want to stop the playback head, so the logical place to put the script is in the Script Channel of the score. As part of the score, the Script Channel receives the exitFrame and enterFrame messages. Other places where you can put scripts (like on buttons) don't receive this message.

Notice that Director thoughtfully creates a handler for you—an exitFrame handler. This is the message we most often want to trap when creating a Score Script. That is, we want the action to take place **after** the current frame is displayed. The companion message, enterFrame, can also be used here, if you want something to happen **before** the frame is displayed (e.g., play a sound). However, you'll have to type the "on enterFrame" and "end" yourself or delete exitFrame and replace it with enterFrame. You can even have handlers for both messages in one script. The important thing is to be sure the object you're scripting **receives** the message. If so, the handler will execute.

Message Central

The key to all Lingo programming is understanding the flow of messages. Director constantly sends messages as events occur when a movie plays. These messages fall into four categories: frame events, mouse events, keyboard events, and movie events. You can script responses to any of these events, but you must place your handler in the right place to receive the event. If no handler is present for an event, the message is passed on; if a handler is present, the message is "trapped" (processed and discarded).

Frame events include enterFrame and exitFrame. These events are triggered when the playback head passes into and out of a frame, respectively. These messages are passed to the Script Channel of the score, then, if no handler traps them, to the Movie Script.

Mouse events include mouseDown and mouseUp. These events are triggered when the user presses the mouse button and releases it, respectively. These messages are passed to the Sprite Channel, the Cast Member Script, the Script Channel, and, finally, to the Movie Script.

Keyboard events include keyDown and keyUp and follow the same path as mouse events.

Movie events include startMovie, stopMovie, idle, and timeOut. StartMovie and stopMovie are triggered when a movie is played or stopped, respectively. Idle is sent when nothing else is happening, when no other events are occurring. Finally, timeOut is sent when Director's built-in timer runs out. You must start the timer for this message to be generated. Movie messages are sent only to the Movie Script.

The real power of Lingo lies in that you can create your own messages and send them pretty much where you want to. You can "trigger" your own event simply by using its name. As long as you have a handler to trap it, you're in business. The handlers for these user-defined messages should always be placed in the Movie Script.

This scheme may seem unnecessarily complicated, but it is quite logical. Why should a cast member receive a startMovie message? As you work your way through this book and begin to master Lingo, where to place your scripts will become increasingly obvious.

While it may seem logical to put enterFrame before exitFrame, the order in which handlers appear in a Script Window does not make a difference. Director responds to events; if you program a handler for the event, it will happen regardless of where it appears in the Script Window.

You'll notice that the insertion point is automatically located between the on and end lines—you can just start typing. Enter this script:

```
on exitFrame
  go to frame 1
end
```

Close the Script Window.

Director "looks" at programming when you close a Script Window and will flag incorrect syntax at this point. Get into the habit of closing Script Windows before trying your animation.

If you want to try your animation, do so. Nothing exciting will happen, however. The playback head will stay on frame 1, which is completely blank. If you get an error message when you try to play this movie, see the sidebar "Dealing with Errors."

If you've perused the Help File or the Lingo Dictionary, you know that Lingo also has a pause command that stops the playback head on a frame. See the sidebar "The Pause That Refreshes" for information about when you should use this command.

In programming parlance, you've created a **loop**—an endless loop. You have to stop the animation to "get out of" the loop.

Be sure to stop the animation before continuing. Director doesn't cope well with a change in programming while a movie is running.

Compare this behavior with what happens when you use Wait for Mouse Click or Key in the Tempo Channel instead of using the Script Channel. Using the Tempo Channel, the playback head continues after the mouse click, showing the blank frames 1–10 and 20–30.

Dealing with Errors

You can make two basic types of errors when you are programming: syntax errors and logical errors.

Syntax errors are the simplest to deal with, as Director will stop and inform you of the error in a dialog box like this:

Stop and read this dialog. Lingo is telling you what "doesn't compute." Granted, the error messages you receive may not be as clear as this one, but it is your first, and only formal, message telling you what's wrong.

In this case, Lingo is telling you that it can't find a handler named "goto." But Lingo, you say, has a go to command! Yes, but the command is really "go," and "to" cannot be "glued" to it. That is, "goto" doesn't compute, whereas "go to" does.

Click the Script Button, and Director will open the Script Editor, placing the insertion point on the line it didn't "understand." You can then edit the line, close the Script Window, and replay the movie. If you've corrected the error, your movie will play; otherwise, you'll get another error message.

If you have several syntax errors in a handler, Lingo will find only the first one, fixing it will uncover error 2, and so on. Just don't panic. Read your handlers carefully, and remember that Lingo's syntax and grammar are fixed and inflexible. Eventually, you'll get it right.

The hardest type of error to fix is a logical error, a mistake in *how* the handler works. You can, for example, have an "off-by-one" error where a handler works but "misses" the first or last item. Or maybe you've placed a handler where it never receives the message it's programmed for. Or maybe you are testing for a condition that never occurs. Fixing these kinds of errors is the reason programmers have a reputation for drinking Jolt Cola late into the night.

Let's create similar loops for each of our animations. In the Script Channel of frame 20, enter:

```
on exitFrame
  go to frame 10
end
```

and in the Script Channel of frame 40, enter:

```
on exitFrame
  go to frame 30
end
```

If you want to try out your new loops, move the playback head to the appropriate frame and play your movie. Unlike the case in frame 1, you can watch the playback head loop back to the start of the animation.

Now we'll add buttons to frame 1 to give us access to the animations.

We could use the Tools Window to create two button cast members—one to access the moving circle and another to access the moving rectangle. However, in Director anything on the stage can be a button. Let's reuse the circle and square for our buttons.

Move the playback head to frame 1 and drag your circle from the Cast Window onto the stage. Repeat the process with your rectangle. Your score should look like this:

The Pause That Refreshes

At first glance, the pause command seems an ideal way to stop a movie to wait for user input. But pause possesses a fatal flaw for most interactive uses: The movie actually stops. Because the playback head is not moving, a lot of things you might want to do from a script cannot be performed—playing music under Lingo control, for example, or doing a rollover. (Chapter 2 is all about rollovers.)

To demonstrate the difference, change your frame 1 Script Channel script to read:

```
on exitFrame
  pause
end
```

When you run your movie, it will play as it did before the change. Stop the movie and edit your new script to read:

```
on exitFrame
  beep
  pause
end
```

Then play your movie. You'll hear only one beep as the playback head has stopped. Return to your original script, but add the beep command, like so:

```
on exitFrame
  beep
  go to frame 1
end
```

When you play this version of your movie, you'll hear a continuous series of beeps as the playback head is moving, although you don't see it moving in either the Score or Control Panel Windows.

If you know that no activity or animation will take place on a frame, then use the pause command, but for most interactive uses, I think you'll prefer a loop.

Buttons—sprites that contain "click on" scripts—can be programmed in two places: on the cast member itself and on the score. If you program the cast member, every use of this cast member "inherits" the programming; if you program the score, the button will "work" only in the frame(s) you've programmed.

What if you programmed both the cast member and the score? The score will have priority. Messages sent by Director follow a defined path called a "hierarchy." Unless you explicitly pass the message onward, it is "trapped" and disposed of by the score sript.

For these buttons, we'll program the score.

Click on channel 1, frame 1. Click on the script pop-up at the upper left-hand corner of the Score Window and choose New.

A new Script Window will appear, but note the subtle difference between this script—on a sprite—and the script you placed in the Script Channel.

In Lingo programming, "sprite" refers to the animation channels of the score. Thus, you can have 48 sprites in any frame.

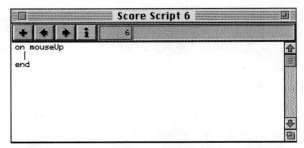

This time, instead of exitFrame, Director has automatically created a mouseUp handler. Director generates two messages relating to mouse button activity—mouseUp and mouseDown. MouseUp is sent when the mouse button is released, whereas mouseDown is sent when the mouse button is first pressed. Think about how buttons work in the Macintosh or Windows interface; things happen when you release the mouse button, not when you press it. MouseUp, then, is the message you most often want a button to respond to, although we'll see some important uses of mouseDown as well. Enter the script:

```
on mouseUp
  go to frame 10
end
```

Click on channel 2, frame 1. Open a new Script Window. Enter the script:

```
on mouseUp
  go to frame 30
end
```

You should now have seven cast members, five of which are scripts.

Try your animation. You now have a working menu system, with a slight problem: Once you've gotten to the circle or rectangle animation, you can't get back!

There are lots of ways to provide a way back. Let's make a Menu Button.

Move the playback head to frame 10. From the Tools Window, choose the rectangular button tool.

Draw a button on the stage and position it where it looks good and doesn't obscure your animations. When you draw a button, Director automatically switches into text mode to allow you to label or resize your button.

Reposition the button by dragging on the thick edges of the button; resize your button by dragging on the handle at the right edge. You can also color it from the Tools Window and change many text properties from the Text Menu. Label this button "Menu." Mine is shown at the right.

Because this button will always take you back to the menu (frame 1), we'll put the programming on the cast member rather than on the score.

If you've followed these instructions, your button is cast 8. Click on the button in the Cast Window and then click on the purple Script Button at the top of the Cast Window.

Once again, Director creates an empty mouseUp handler. In this Script Window, enter the script:

```
on mouseUp
  go to frame 1
end
```

All that remains is in-betweening this button so that it is seen in all the frames. Shift click to frame 10 to frame 40. Choose In-Between Linear from the Score Menu. Your Score Window should look like this:

The Rectangular Button Tool

My Menu Button

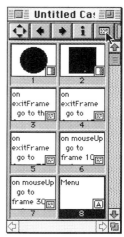

Programming Cast 8

You may want to delete the button in frames 21 to 29, but leaving those frames there will have no effect on your movie. Our scripting ensures that the playback head never reaches these frames.

Play your movie. You now have a complete, working movie with two simple animations, a menu to get you to either of the animations, and a button to get you back to the menu.

Label It

The scripting we've done in this simple movie is OK. But it could be better. Suppose you decide, after all the scripting is done, that you want an animated menu instead of our static, unmoving one. You might need more than the 9 empty frames we have now. It's easy to insert frames (from the Score Menu), but in doing so, frame 10 will become frame 11 and your scripting will no longer work properly.

The Marker Channel is located directly above the playback head in the Score Window. By placing markers in this channel, you can label important frames. The markers will move when you insert or delete frames.

To create a marker, drag from the triangular icon at the far right of this channel horizontally to the desired frame. Then type an appropriate name.

Label frame 10 "Circle" and frame 30 "Square."

To move a marker, just drag it. To delete a marker, drag it up or down, out of the Marker Channel.

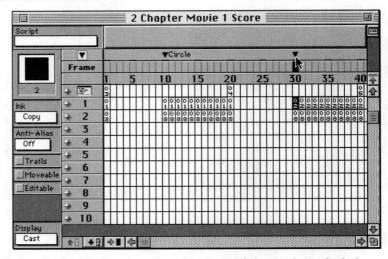

Now let's edit the handlers to take advantage of the markers. Switch to the Cast Window and open the first script (cast 3 if you've followed my

directions exactly). Choose Find/Change from the Text Menu. The following dialog box should appear:

```
┌──────────────────────────────────────────────────────────┐
│                                                            │
│   Find/Change                                              │
│                                                            │
│       Find: │ 10                          │   ╭─────────╮  │
│                                               │  Find   │  │
│  Change to: │ "Circle"                    │   ╰─────────╯  │
│                                               ╭─────────╮  │
│             ☒ Whole Words Only                │ Change  │  │
│             ☒ Wrap-Around Search              ╰─────────╯  │
│             ☒ Search All Cast Members         ╭─────────╮  │
│                                               │Change All│ │
│                                               ╰─────────╯  │
│                                               ╭─────────╮  │
│                                               │ Cancel  │  │
│                                               ╰─────────╯  │
│                                               ╭─────────╮  │
│                                               │  Help   │  │
│                                               ╰─────────╯  │
└──────────────────────────────────────────────────────────┘
```

Enter "10" in the Find field and "Circle" in the Change To field. Note the
quotation marks! Click on Change All. In this simple movie, it's safe to
choose Change All, but in a more complicated movie, you'd probably
want to choose Find and then Change if the instance found is OK to change.

If you're coming from a background in publishing, don't type curly quotes
("smart quotes")! Director will not interpret these characters as quote
marks.

> *How do you know when to use quotes? Quotation marks define liter-
> als—data you want Director to take word for word or letter for letter.
> So when you are referring to a marker in a script, you **must** use quo-
> tation marks. In the Marker Channel, however, you are labeling a
> frame, so you don't type the quotation marks. After markers, file
> names are the other items most commonly quoted in scripts.*

The two scripts (the exitFrame and the mouseUp handlers) that read "go
to frame 10" should now read "go to frame "Circle"."

Repeat the Find/Change command for "30" and "Square."

Try your movie. It should work exactly as before, with several added ben-
efits: You can insert and delete frames; you can jump immediately to a
section of your movie by using the Marker Window (Windows Menu);
and, perhaps more important, you can tell, by looking at the score, what's
happening at frames 10 and 30. We'll be using markers extensively in this
book, and you should use them in any original movies you create.

A Final Polish

From a programmer's perspective, it seems somewhat inefficient to "hard code," or individually script, each loop in our movie. If we had 40 loops, we'd have to have 40 "loop back" scripts. There's got to be a more efficient way to do this.

Our menu buttons must branch to specific places in the score, so these cannot be easily optimized. But the two exitFrame handlers that loop back to the Circle and Square markers are doing essentially the same thing—looping back to the marker immediately "behind" them in the score.

Select frame 20, Script Channel, and ask for a new handler by choosing New from the script pop-up menu. Enter the following script:

```
on exitFrame
  go loop
end
```

Place this new handler on frame 40 too. You need only select the Script Channel of frame 40 and choose the handler from the script pop-up:

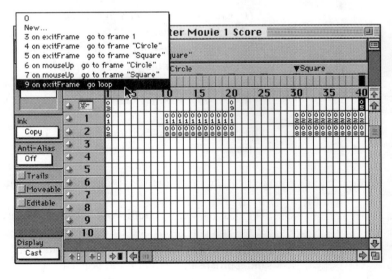

Notice that only the Score Scripts are included in the script pop-up. The Menu Button script—a Cast Script—does not appear here.

If you label frame 1, you can use your new go loop script in the Script Channel of frame 1 too:

Try your modified movie. It should work as it did before, even though the Script Channel handlers in frame 1, frame 20, and frame 40 are the same! We've made one handler do the work of three.

The go loop command makes the playback head bounce back to the marker immediately "behind" it in the score. "Behind" here means in a lower-numbered frame.

By the way, Director version 3 lacks the go loop command, so go marker(0) performed this function.

Why is this better? Because it's more efficient. Efficiency in programming can be defined in many ways, but most definitions include economy—don't create two scripts when one will do. This rule can be especially important in Director as you may find yourself fighting for every byte to fit a movie on a single diskette. Admittedly, eliminating a few hard-coded go to commands will do little to reduce the size of your movie. But as our examples grow more complicated, it becomes more important to write code that you can apply to many situations rather than writing scripts to handle every specific situation that might arise.

Divide and Conquer

Another aspect of efficiency is in your construction of large projects. If you attempt to make a monolithic movie—10, 15, maybe even 20 MB—you'll find Director slowing down as it has to pause to load cast members from the disk. Appendix B deals specifically with some of these issues. However, there is a very simple way you can resolve some of these problems: Segment your large movies into smaller ones and use the go to command to control the loading and unloading of movies.

For example, a simple résumé movie might be divided into three movies: main menu, credentials, and portfolio. When the user is looking at your portfolio, the cast members for the main menu and for the credentials don't need to occupy memory.

Let's start by making two new movies, using the simple circle and rectangle movie we already made as our main menu. Make one new movie that animates a rectangle in some way and another that animates the circle in some way. My movies are shown on the left.

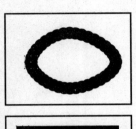

My Circle and Rectangle Movies

In the score, I turned "trails" on so that you could see the animations—the circle travels in an oval, and the rectangle travels along a rectangular path. I've called the first "Circle Movie" and the second "Rectangle Movie."

Don't forget to make your movies loop by placing the following script in the Script Channel of the last frame in each movie:

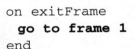

```
on exitFrame
  go to frame 1
end
```

You could use the control panel Loop Button to make each movie loop, but if you make your movies into projectors, this button will be ignored. You must use Lingo if you want your projectors to loop.

Return to your first movie and edit the scripts of your buttons on frame 1 to read:

For the Circle Button:

```
on mouseUp
  go to movie "Circle Movie"
end
```

Be sure to use the full name of the movie inside the quotation marks. Also, you must be sure all movies are in the same folder. It's not too hard to tell Director to look somewhere else for a movie, but let's keep it simple for now.

For the Rectangle Button:

```
on mouseUp
  go to movie "Rectangle Movie"
end
```

Save your movie and play it. Try the buttons. They work, but they have the same problem we had with our simple movie: Once you get to your animation, there's no way to get back to the menu.

Let's make a Menu Button to return us to the main menu. Open your Circle Movie and create a menu button just as we did earlier in this chapter. Position it so that it doesn't overlap your animation, and add the following script to this button cast member:

```
on mouseUp
  go to movie "Menu"
end
```

Or whatever your Menu Movie is called.

You can copy and paste this button into the Cast Window of your Rectangle Movie. One of the advantages of Cast Scripts is that they travel with the cast member. This would be even handier if Director allowed you to open more than one movie, but for now, you must save and close the first movie, then open the other movie to accomplish the copy and paste.

When you have the buttons on both the Circle and Rectangle Movies, try them. Reopen your Menu Movie and test your buttons.

Director supports a special movie, which must be named "Shared.dir," allowing you to share cast members of all kinds in any movies saved in the same folder (subdirectory). We'll see this powerful feature in action later on.

There's little advantage to creating three movies for such simple animations; in fact, there's a disadvantage. There is a noticeable pause, depending on the size of your movie and the speed of your disk drive and computer, as Director closes the Menu Movie and opens the Circle or Rectangle Movie. But in movies with large casts, this technique can make managing movies simpler and allow individual movies to run faster and more efficiently.

Notice, however, that the movies always start at the beginning. For many purposes this is OK, but suppose you needed a movie to jump to a specific frame of another movie, as our simple menu system in the first part of this chapter did.

In that case, you'd edit your Circle and Rectangle Scripts to read something like:

```
on mouseUp
  go to frame 10 of movie "Circle Movie"
end
```

and

```
on mouseUp
  go to frame 10 of movie "Rectangle Movie"
end
```

Try it. Instead of jumping to the beginning of the sub-movies, you'll jump to frame 10. As in the earlier examples in this chapter, you could also jump to a labeled frame.

For many movies, you **do** know where you are jumping to and can therefore include a direct, hard-coded, jump to a frame as we did here.

But what if you don't know where you are jumping to? What if you are jumping to the place where the user last was? In a typical résumé movie suite, for example, imagine that the user is looking at your portfolio and decides to check your credentials. Maybe you want to provide a button that will jump back to the portfolio, to the same frame the user left. Such a button is often labeled "Back." I call this function "bookmarks."

Bookmarks

To make a bookmark, we have to save where we were (as a frame number or name) so that the bookmark can be used from movie to movie.

There are a couple of ways to save information in Director. Text cast members, for example, provide an ideal place to stash information. We'll be using text cast members a lot in this book for just this purpose. But this method wouldn't work given the way our current movies are structured. After all, when we jump from the Menu Movie to the Circle or Rectangle Movie, the Menu Movie's cast is flushed from memory and is no longer accessible.

You can also stash information in a variable. Variables are a little harder to conceptualize as they don't have a physical presence in the cast. When you create a variable, you have access to the information stored there for the duration of the current handler. Take this little handler as an example:

```
on mouseUp
  put 10 into x
end mouseUp
```

The Lingo verb "put" tells Director to store the information included, by name, in memory. The name of the variable in this example is "x," and the information stored to this name is "10."

To retrieve the information, you need only use the variable's name, like so:

```
on mouseUp
  put 10 into x
  go to frame x
end mouseUp
```

When the "x" is used in the second line of this handler, Director retrieves the value stored and uses this information as if it were hard-coded, in this case as if the line were "go to frame 10."

Using variables correctly is central to mastering Lingo, so you'll be seeing a lot of them in this book.

You can name a variable anything you want as long as it is one word (but not the same as an existing Lingo word). You could not, for example, name a variable "frame," as this is already a Lingo keyword, but you could use "aFrame" or "theFrame" or "the_frame." Choose a name that means something. In my example above, "x" is not really a good choice. This might be better:

```
on mouseUp
  put 10 into whichFrame
  go to frame whichFrame
end mouseUp
```

Director is case-insensitive, meaning that "whichFrame" is the same as "WHICHFRAME" or "Whichframe" or even "WhIcHfRaMe." By convention we capitalize in a way that makes the most sense.

All you have to do, then, to make the Circle and Rectangle Movies start where they left off is find a way to have Director remember which frame was on stage when the movie was stopped. Director has a verb, the frame, which reports the current frame number. We can use this verb to learn the frame that was on stage when the user pressed the Menu Button ... save the frame number in a variable, then use it to jump back. Edit your Menu Button in the Circle Movie to read:

```
on mouseUp
  put the frame into whichCircleFrame
  go to movie "Menu"
end
```

Edit your Menu Button in the Rectangle Movie to read:

```
on mouseUp
  put the frame into whichRectFrame
  go to movie "Menu"
end
```

Edit your Circle and Rectangle Buttons in your Menu Movie to read:

```
on mouseUp
  go to frame whichCircleFrame of movie ¬
  "Circle Movie"
end
```

and

```
on mouseUp
  go to frame whichRectFrame of movie ¬
  "Rectangle Movie"
end
```

Don't type the "¬" character. This symbol indicates the line continues below.

Try it. It doesn't work. **Variables are maintained only in the handler in which they were created.** We have three movies here, so simple variables won't work.

To make Director maintain a variable over a series of movies, you must declare the variable to be global. Global variables (or, simply, "globals") are retained until you quit Director (or exit a projector). This feature is both good and bad.

It's good because globals allow you to pass information from one movie to another as you must to get our menuing system working.

It's bad in that you can accidentally change the value of a global by careless coding, resulting in what programmers call "side effects." In other words, your program is OK, but an accidental change to a global variable causes it to behave incorrectly. These are among the toughest bugs to find. Global variables, as you might imagine, also eat up precious memory. However, unless you go really overboard and make lots of complex globals, their use of memory is not usually a problem.

For these movies we'll need two globals—one to hold the bookmark for the Circle Movie and one to hold the bookmark for the Rectangle Movie.

To make our menuing system work, edit the Menu Buttons in the Circle and Rectangle Movies to read:

```
on mouseUp
  global whichCircleFrame
  put the frame into whichCircleFrame
  go to movie "Menu"
end
```

```
on mouseUp
  global whichRectFrame
  put the frame into whichRectFrame
  go to movie "Menu"
end
```

Notice that you need only refer to the particular global you want to work with in a handler. Director maintains the value of whichRectFrame in the Circle Movie; however, you don't need to work with it. Therefore, you don't need to refer to it in the global declaration.

Now edit your Circle and Rectangle Buttons in your Menu Movie to read:

```
on mouseUp
  global whichCircleFrame
  go to frame whichCircleFrame of movie ¬
  "Circle Movie"
end
```

and

```
on mouseUp
  global whichRectFrame
  go to frame whichRectFrame of movie ¬
  "Rectangle Movie"
end
```

And that's it. Well, that's almost it. If you try the Menu Movie, you'll get a Lingo error message telling you that whichCircleFrame or whichRect-Frame has no value. Actually Lingo says the value is "<void>." Remember that variables are actually little pieces of RAM to which you've assigned a name. Lingo is telling you that you haven't yet given a value to the variable.

Add this startMovie handler to your Menu Movie:

```
on startMovie
  global whichCircleFrame, whichRectFrame
  put 1 into whichCircleFrame
  put 1 into whichRectFrame
end
```

Notice here that you are giving both variables initial values and therefore must include **both** variable names in the global statement.

In programmer's parlance, this is called "declaring a variable." Some programming languages require you to declare **all** the variables you use in a program. Lingo does not require you to declare any variables, but it's usually a good practice to do it anyway. You should also give these variables initial values so that you don't get the dreaded <void> error.

If you try this movie, you'll discover that it still starts the Circle and Rectangle Movies at frame 1. Here's the solution:

```
on startMovie
  global whichCircleFrame, whichRectFrame
  if whichCircleFrame < 0 then put 1 into ¬
  whichCircleFrame
  if whichRectFrame < 0 then put 1 into ¬
  whichRectFrame
end
```

Chapter 2 introduces the if statement. For now, just know that the if statement ensures that both whichCircleFrame and whichRectFrame have valid values.

You now have the core programming needed to make everything from simple to complex menuing systems involving one movie or many movies.

Command Summary

beep *{numberOfTimes}*

Generates a system beep—the sound the user has set in the Sound Control Panel.

Examples:

```
beep
beep 10
```

go *{to}* *{frame}* *frameNumberOrName*
go *{to}* **movie** *movieName*
go *{to}* *{frame}* *frameNumberOrName* **of movie** ¬
                    movieName

Moves the playback head to the specified frame in the current movie or another movie. If no frame is specified in the other movie, it starts playing at frame 1.

Examples:

```
go frame 1
go to frame 10
go to frame "Menu"
go to frame "Menu" of movie "Main Menu"
go to movie "Main Menu"
```

go loop|next|previous

Moves the playback head one marker back, one marker ahead in the score, or two markers back.

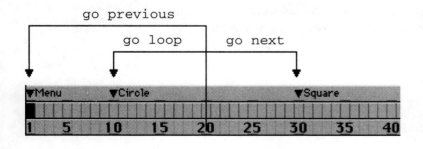

Examples:

```
go loop
go next
go previous
```

Equivalent to go to marker(0), go to marker(1), and go to marker(-1) in Director version 3.

*Note: These commands do **not** depend on the playback head encountering a marker; they cause the playback head to jump to the appropriate marked frame, in order, as shown in the Score Window.*

pause
Stops the playback head.

Example:

```
pause
```

The movie can be reactivated by a continue or go command.

put *expression* {into *variable*}
put *expression* into | before | after *textobject*
Stores information (a calculation, i.e., 2 + 2, or a value, hard-coded or variable) into the specified object—either a variable or text objects created with the Tools Menu.

If no variable or text object is specified, the information is placed in the Message Window.

Examples:

```
put "Hello" into greeting
put 2 + 2 into total
put "Hello" into cast 12
put "Hello " before cast "Student Name"
put studentName after cast "Greeting"
```

Note: Using put to store the result of a mathematical operation into a text field converts the numerical answer into a string, into text.

HyperCard programmers should note that many Lingo programmers use the set command to assign a value to a variable something that HyperTalk does not allow. (Set will be covered in Chapter 2.)

Command Summary Typographic Conventions

Director is, for the most part, case-insensitive, which means you can type a command in either uppercase or lowercase, and Director won't care. Lingo programmers have adopted a convention that all words are typed in lowercase. Where two or more words are "glued" together (e.g., mouse-Up), the second (or third or fourth or ...) word is capitalized.

go {to} {frame} *frameNumberOrName*

Plain text denotes a required word.
Words in curly brackets are optional.
Words in italics are placeholders for values; don't type the word shown, substitute an appropriate value or variable.

For this command, then,

```
go 10
go to 10
go to frame 10
```

are all equivalent.

go loop|next|previous
A vertical line separator denotes alternatives. In this case, you must use one of these words, but any will do (depending, of course, on what you want to achieve).

2 ◆ Rollin' Along

Rollovers are perhaps the simplest way to add zip to your movies. Using the rollOver function, you can make something happen when the pointer is on top of a sprite: A small animation, a help message, or a new cursor may appear, for example.

Unlike the go to command, rollOver() is a function. That means you cannot just use this word, by itself, in a script. Functions do something **and** return a value, while commands just do something. You must **use** the value in some way, or Director will stop and give you an error message.

You can easily differentiate between functions and commands. Functions have parentheses; commands do not.

RollOver(), like many Lingo functions, returns one of two values: true or false. The value is true if the pointer is on top of a specified sprite and false if it is not. The sprite—or channel number—is specified in parentheses. For example:

```
rollOver(1)
```

would generate a true if the pointer were on top of sprite 1 and false if it were not. The value within the parentheses is called the function's "argument."

Rollovers are most often used with the if/then keywords. If/then allow you to issue differential commands based upon a true or false test. Incidentally, "if" and "then" are called "keywords" because they are part of Lingo, but in and of themselves they don't create or change data (functions) or cause anything to happen (commands).

The simplest form of the if/then keywords looks something like this:

```
if test then command
```

where *test* is a Lingo statement that generates a true or false and *command* is a valid Lingo command. If the test is true, the command is executed; if the test is false, Director continues to the next statement in the handler, ignoring the command.

Because you want rollOver functions to be called frequently, as the playback head moves, you don't find them in Cast (button) Scripts. Instead, they are most often used in the Script Channel of the score.

Let's make a simple movie to see how rollOvers can be implemented.

Create a new movie.

With the tools menu, draw a rectangle on the stage. Your score should look like this:

Let's make a loop so the playback head moves but stays on frame 1. In the Script Channel of frame 1, enter the following script:

```
on exitFrame
  go to frame 1
end
```

Now we've got a working movie—not a very exciting one, but one that does work. Let's add the rollOver.

Open the Script Channel of frame 1 again and edit the script to read:

```
on exitFrame
  if rollOver(1) then beep
  go to frame 1
end
```

When you play this movie, Director will beep when you move the pointer over the box. If you move the pointer away, the beeps will stop.

The "1" in the rollOver function is the sprite number. Recall that a sprite is simply a channel. When this function evaluates to true, Director executes the command after the "then" keyword and beeps. When this function evaluates to false, Director ignores the beep command and continues on to the next statement, looping back to frame 1.

This simple form of a rollOver is of limited use. Let's expand it to a more powerful version.

Cast Switching

Add a circle to your movie by choosing the circle tool in the Tools Window and drawing it on the stage. Be sure the circle "resides" in cast 2, or the scripts in this section won't work. Here's the revised score and cast.

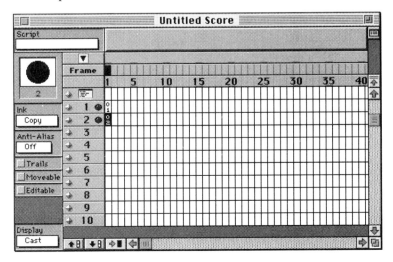

Now delete the circle from the stage but **not** from the cast.

Revise your frame 1 Script Channel script to read:

```
on exitFrame
  if rollOver(1) then set the castNum ¬
  of sprite 1 to 2
  updateStage
  go to frame 1
end
```

Play your movie.

The flashing you see is a result of your overriding the score—at least in the exitFrame handler. When this handler finishes and the playback head loops back to frame 1, the stage is restored to the rectangle. This problem is easily solved, but let's first examine the new lines of code you added to this handler.

The set command is used to change an object's properties. All Director objects have a set of properties or characteristics that define them: the position of a sprite on the stage is a property; the text in a field is a property of the field; the foreground and background colors of a draw object are properties. Many of these properties, though not all, can be changed through Lingo.

For interactive projects, one of the most useful properties is the cast number of a sprite. When you look at the score from Lingo, the actual cast member that you placed on the stage is merely a property of that sprite. The set command here, then, changes the cast number of sprite 1 from cast 1 (the cast member you placed on the stage) to cast 2—the square becomes a circle when the pointer is on top of it.

Many sprite property changes require the updateStage command, which forces an immediate screen redraw, so that these changes can be seen on the stage. The stage is normally updated only between frames.

We'll come back to this little rollOver shortly and learn how to make the cast change permanent (at least for the duration of the rollOver). This would be a good place to save your movie so that you can reopen it later on. Let's explore some other uses of simple rollOvers.

Pointer Changes

One important human interface principle is that the users need to know where the active or hot spots are. Where **can** they click? A common way to provide this feedback is to change the pointer to a different shape when it is over a hot spot. The Macintosh and Windows operating systems do this when, for example, you move the pointer over an editable text area. The pointer changes to an I-beam so you know you can type.

> *Don't reinvent the wheel. Follow the conventions of your operating system. Design your pointers to be consistent with pointers found in your system.*

In Director version 4, any cast member can become the pointer. But there are some limitations. Pointers are 16 x 16 pixels and must be 1-bit cast members. If you make a larger painting, it will be cropped to 16 x 16. If you forget to change the painting to 1-bit, the command just won't work.

> *Yes, you can make a colored pointer, but it is a simulated "pointer." We'll get to it; be patient!*

Let's start by making a 1-bit, 16 x 16 pixel cast member. Our scripts have been entered in the score as we've entered them into the Script Window. Let's push them up in the cast to make room for our pointer. My Cast Window is shown at right after rearranging the cast members.

My Cast Window

Open the Paint Window from the Windows Menu and create a new cast member by clicking on the pink Plus Button. You should be editing cast 3.

> *Be sure you are creating cast 3. The scripts in this section depend on cast numbers. We'll learn a better way shortly, but for now we must both be working with the same cast numbers.*

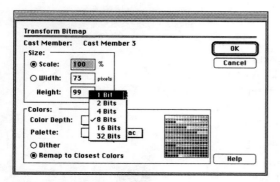

The Bit-Depth Button (right) and
dialog box (above)

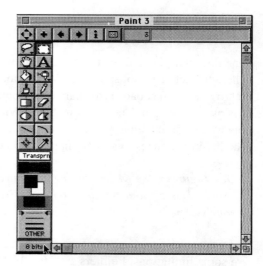

Double click on the Bit-Depth Button in the lower left-hand corner of the
window.

And make this cast member 1-bit.

Then draw your pointer. Mine is shown at left.

Note that I drew a 17 x 17 pixel box and am working in a zoomed-in mode.
Before finalizing the design, erase the box.

My pointer

Let's revise the script in the Script Channel of frame 1 to use cast 3 as
your new pointer. Double click on the Script Channel of frame 1 and edit
your handler to read:

```
on exitFrame
  if rollOver(1) then cursor [3]
  go to frame 1
end
```

Play your movie, and voilà: When you pass the mouse over the rectangle, the pointer changes from an arrow to a hand (or whatever you drew
in cast 3).

If you don't put square brackets around the "3" in the cursor command,
you'll get a very different pointer. Try it. Edit the handler to read:

```
on exitFrame
  if rollOver(1) then cursor 3
  go to frame 1
end .exitFrame
```

Director supports the built-in pointers of the operating system. Cursor 3 happens to be a large plus sign often used in spreadsheet applications. For more about pointers and a list of the other built-in pointers, see the sidebar "Cursors."

The square brackets are a sign to Director that the contents are a list, not just a plain number as in our second example. We'll work extensively with lists in Chapter 10.

Name It

Earlier, I said there was a better way to define your pointer. In Chapter 1 you named the key frames of your movie; you can also name cast members. Referring to a cast member by name means you can rearrange the cast without having to change all of your scripts.

Let's give this cast member a name. In the Cast Window, select your pointer, then click on the blue Information Button at the top of the Cast Window. Name your cast member "Hand," like so:

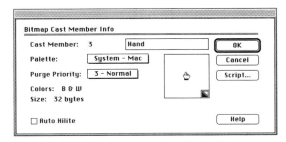

To use your newly named pointer, edit the Script Channel of frame 1 to read:

```
on exitFrame
  if rollOver(1) then cursor [cast "Hand"]
  go to frame 1
end exitFrame
```

On Cursors

Custom pointers are one of the easiest ways to provide real polish to your movies. The term "cursor" is really a misnomer as graphical user interfaces (GUIs) don't normally have cursors. Instead, they have pointers and insertion points. However, the toolbox routines of both the Mac OS and Windows that draw the pointer use the term cursor, so I guess we're stuck with it.

Director's built-in pointers are:

cursor 200 Causes the pointer to disappear.

In addition to the 16 x 16 pixel, 1-bit cursor image, cursors also have a "hot spot" and can have a mask.

The hot spot is the precise place in the image where the mouse is currently pointing. In the arrow pointer that Director normally uses, the hot spot is the tip of the arrow. It's very easy to define the hot spot in your own home-brewed cursors. Simply move the registration point (using the Registration Point Tool in the Paint Window) of the cast member. In your hand pointer, the hot spot should be the tip of the index finger.

Pointer masks are defined the same way you define other Director masks. Make a copy of your cast member (don't forget to convert it to 1-bit), and put black pixels everywhere you want the pointer to be opaque. Where both the mask and the pointer have a pixel, the pointer will be opaque.

And there you have it. Well, you sort of have it—the pointer never changes back to an arrow.

The Else Option

So now you know how to make something happen if a function (like rollOver) generates a true. What if it generates a false? Lingo provides a solution in the form of the else keyword.

Edit your script in frame 1 to read:

```
on exitFrame
  if rollOver(1) then cursor [cast "Hand"]
  else
    cursor -1
  end if
  go to frame 1
end
```

Play your movie. The pointer is a hand only when it is on top of your rectangle.

The else clause of the if statement allows you to specify what happens when the condition or test in the if statement is false. The -1 cursor happens to be the standard arrow pointer of Director. With the else clause in an if statement, you're in total control—by definition either the then command(s) or the else command(s) **must** execute, so something will always happen.

The form of the if command is a common source of confusion. Unlike some other programming languages, Director limits syntax to the forms I've already used or:

```
on exitFrame
  if rollOver(1) then
    cursor [cast "Hand"]
  else
    cursor -1
  end if
  go to frame 1
end
```

This is the form I use most often as I think it reads more clearly than the form currently in our movie. Fortunately, Director provides you with an aid to determine if you've structured the command correctly: indenting.

Director's Script Editor "pretty prints." That is, it automatically indents to make your scripts more readable and as a result shows you how it is interpreting the commands. If for some reason a script is not indenting correctly, you can force Director to pretty print by pressing the Tab key. If the script doesn't pretty print, it probably has an error.

One of the most common errors is a missing end if keyword. You must have one end if for each else statement.

You may have noticed that your hand pointer doesn't look all that great. It's semitransparent. This is because pointers usually are accompanied by a mask that defines the opaque portions of the pointer. To make a mask, open your pointer in the Paint Window.

Make a duplicate of it by choosing Duplicate from the Edit Menu. Be sure your duplicate is 1-bit.

Using the Pencil, Paintbrush, or Paintbucket Tool, fill the inside of the duplicate with black. Anything painted black in the mask will be opaque.

Close the Paint Window and name your new pointer mask "Hand Mask."

To tell Director to use this mask, edit your rollOver script to read:

```
on exitFrame
  if rollOver(1) then
    cursor [cast "Hand" , cast "Hand Mask"]
  else
    cursor -1
  end if
  go to frame 1
end exitFrame
```

The second argument to the cursor command is the mask for the pointer.

Circling the Square

Let's go back to our original rollOver in this movie. Open your original rollOver movie. Edit the script in the Script Channel, frame 1, to read:

```
on exitFrame
  if rollOver(1) then
    set the castNum of sprite 1 to 2
  else
    set the castNum of sprite 1 to 1
  end if
  updateStage
  go to frame 1
end
```

When you play this movie, you'll find no difference between it and the original version, even with the else clause. Actually, the else clause here is superfluous because Director restores the rectangle when it loops back in the last line of this handler.

The score of your movies has priority over whatever Lingo programming you might do, unless you declare that a sprite—a channel—is a puppet.

Puppets are objects under the control of Lingo rather than the score. You can't make an object mysteriously appear out of thin air—you **must** place it (or a place holder, a stand-in) on the stage and, therefore, in the score in the frame in which you want it to appear. But once you've declared the object to be a puppet, the score is ignored. Section 2 of this book is all about puppets, but to get our rollOver working, here's a sneak peek.

The command to turn a sprite—channel—into a puppet is:

```
set the puppet of sprite n to true
```

Note that the set command indicates that we are altering a property. Instead of "n," you enter the channel number of the object you want to control. Director 4 still supports an older version of this command that looks like this:

```
puppetSprite n, true
```

Because this version of the command is shorter, a lot of people use it, but I prefer the longer version because it shows clearly that you are setting a property.

So where do we put this command? Ask yourself when you want it to be executed. You want this command to execute when you play the movie; you want the square to turn into a circle and stay a circle until the pointer is no longer on top of the sprite.

In Chapter 1, you made both Frame Scripts and Cast Scripts. Here, you'll make a Movie Script. Why? Director generates a startMovie message when a movie is played. By writing a startMovie handler, you can turn sprite 1 (the rectangle you placed on the stage) into a puppet, and then your cast number change will become permanent because Director won't bother to redraw the stage to reflect the score—at least channel 1 of the score.

To make a Movie Script, double click on any script in the Cast Window. Click on the pink Plus Button at the top of the Script Editor Window. Director automatically creates a new Movie Script:

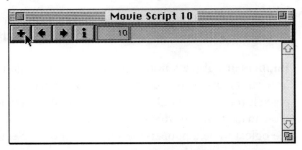

Unlike Frame and Cast Scripts, Director does not provide you with a handler "skeleton"—the on/end bookends. Movie Scripts are used for all sorts of messages. The handler you need here must respond to the startMovie message, like so:

```
on startMovie
  set the puppet of sprite 1 to true
end
```

Now try the movie. Now that sprite 1 is a puppet, Director puts you in control and does not redraw sprite 1 each time it loops back to frame 1.

Sprite 1 will remain a puppet throughout the movie. If you no longer need to manipulate the object from Lingo, be sure to set the puppet property to false:

```
set the puppet of sprite 1 to false
```

The most likely place for this command is an enterFrame handler in the section of the score where you want the score to be in control again. We'll see examples of this later on.

Pop-up Help

Apple's System 7 introduced Balloon Help, where small text objects appear to define or describe the object under the pointer. Many Windows applications have a similar feature for their toolbars. By using rollOvers, it's easy to add such a feature to your movies.

Click on frame 1, channel 5. Create a new text cast member (also called a "field") using the Tools Menu. Type "Click here to return to the Main Menu" into this field. You can use the Text Menu to change the font or style of the object and the Tools Palette to change the foreground or background color of the field.

Here's what my score looks like:

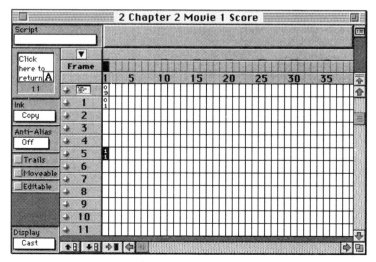

Don't worry if your cast numbers are different; this won't affect the scripts here. You must, however, be certain that your field is in channel 5.

Unfortunately, you cannot name sprites—channels. You can only name cast members and frames.

Edit your startMovie script to read:

```
on startMovie
  set the puppet of sprite 1 to true
  set the visible of sprite 5 to false
end
```

The visible sprite property is the Lingo way to make a sprite visible (if set to true) or invisible (if set to false). Setting this property from Lingo is the same as clicking on the small bump to the left of the channel number in the score. In fact, this bump changes when Director executes your Lingo command to reflect the visibility property.

Now the Help Balloon will be invisible at the start of the movie. We can use a rollOver to make it visible.

Edit your frame 1 Script Channel script to read:

```
on exitFrame
  if rollover(1) then
    set the castNum of sprite 1 to 2
    set the visible of sprite 5 to true
  else
    set the castNum of sprite 1 to 1
    set the visible of sprite 5 to false
  end if
  updateStage
  go to frame 1
end
```

Try it! With this script, sprite 1 changes shape **and** your help message appears.

You can combine all of these rollOvers into one script:

```
on exitFrame
  if rollover(1) then
    cursor [cast "Hand" , cast "Hand Mask"]
    set the castNum of sprite 1 to 2
    set the visible of sprite 5 to true
  else
    cursor -1
    set the castNum of sprite 1 to 1
    set the visible of sprite 5 to false
  end if
  updateStage
  go to frame 1
end
```

Use this handler as a "template" for your rollOvers. You may or may not need the updateStage command, depending upon what your rollOver is doing—changing castNum and the position of a sprite are two actions that require updateStage.

We'll see some more rollovers in Section 2, but for now let's turn to moveable sprites.

Command Summary

cursor *cursorNumber* | *cursorList*

Changes the pointer to the value specified. (See the sidebar "On Cursors" for cursorNumber values.) If you are using cast member cursors, use the list form where the first value is the pointer and the second is the mask.

Examples:

```
cursor -1
cursor [3]
cursor [cast "Triangle," cast 5]
```

if *test* **then** *command*
if *test* **then** *command*
    {else *command*
    end if}

Evaluates the test to either true or false. If the test is true, the command is executed. If the test is false and an else clause is present, the command following the else clause is executed. End if is required if there is an else clause or if more than one command follows the then.

Examples:

```
if i = 5 then beep

if the text of cast 5 = "Hello" then
  beep
  go to frame "Greeting"
end if

if answer = 10 then
  beep
  go to frame "Right"
else
  go to frame "Wrong"
end if
```

set *propertyName* to *value*

Changes an object's property.

Example:
```
set the text of cast 5 to "Hello"
set the locH of sprite 2 to 200
set the movieTime of cast 1 to 0
```

See Appendix A for a complete list of objects and their properties.

updateStage

Forces Director to redraw the stage. The stage is normally updated only when the exitFrame message is generated.

Example:

```
updateStage
```

3 ◆ On Target

Interactive applications, especially games, often require the user to move a sprite from one place to another. In an adventure game, for example, you might want the user to drag a key from a table to a treasure chest to open the chest.

You may have toyed with the Moveable option in the Score Window. With it, you can make Director ignore any movement you have created in the score, allowing the user to drag a sprite around the stage. That's about all you can do without Lingo. With Lingo, you can add tests and have your movie do something when the moveable sprite is touching or within a target sprite.

Let's start with a simple movie to see the basics of moveable sprites.

In a new Director movie, create a small circle (I used the Tools Palette to draw mine) and, in the Paint Window, a parallelogram. My Cast Window is shown at right.

My Cast Window

Put our usual loop script in the Script Channel of frame 1:

```
on exitFrame
  go to frame 1
end
```

Place your cast on the stage with the parallelogram in channel 1 and the circle in channel 2. The order is important because you're going to make the circle moveable, and you want it to stay on top of the parallelogram.

Finally, select sprite 2 and click on the Moveable option on the left side of the Score Window.

Here's what my completed score looks like:

Try your movie. As it plays, you can drag the circle around. So far, so good. Now let's add the programming to make something happen when the circle is inside the parallelogram.

Double click on the Script Channel of frame 1 and add the following line:

```
on exitFrame
  if sprite 2 within 1 then beep
  go to frame 1
end
```

Try it! When you drag the circle into the parallelogram, Director beeps; the condition "sprite 2 within 1" evaluates to true.

The order of arguments is important here. Sprite 1 can never be within sprite 2. It's too big!

There's another comparison operator that's slightly different. Edit your script to read:

```
on exitFrame
  if sprite 2 intersects 1 then beep
  go to frame 1
end
```

Try it again. This time, Director beeps when the circle touches the bounding rectangle of the parallelogram. Be sure you use the operator that tests for the specific condition your movie requires.

In this simple movie, it's OK to put the if statement in the Script Channel, but if your movie involves animation stretching over 10, 20, or more frames, I suggest you turn the script into a handler and put it in a Movie Script.

The bounding rectangle

Calling All Handlers

Movie Scripts, as we've already seen, are the proper place to put a start-Movie handler. (They're also the place for a stopMovie handler.) Another type of handler properly resides in the Movie Script. I like to call these "utility" handlers—handlers that you use throughout your movie. By using the Movie Script to contain most of your code, you don't ever have to wonder where a handler is.

Director automatically executes startMovie and stopMovie handlers. That is, Director sends a startMovie message when you play a movie, so you don't have to do anything special to get the handler to execute. How do you get other Movie Script handlers to execute? Just call them.

Edit your frame 1 script to read:

```
on exitFrame
  checkWithin
  go to frame 1
end
```

Run your movie. Director will complain that a checkWithin handler is not defined. Click on the Script Button on the error dialog. Director will automatically open the frame 1 script.

Click on the pink Plus Button at the top of the window, and Director will create a new Movie Script for you. Recall that unlike a Frame or Button Script, Director does not guess at what type of handler you might want to put in a Movie Script, so you must type the on/end lines too. Enter the following handler:

```
on checkWithin
  if sprite 2 within 1 then beep
end
```

Try it! Now the movie works properly. When Director encounters "check-Within" in the Frame Script, it looks for a checkWithin handler and, this time, finds it.

This technique is critical as your movies grow in complexity. By clustering your handlers in the Movie Script, you'll never have to wonder where a handler is; it's in the Movie Script.

Director supports multiple Movie Scripts. It's a matter of programming style whether you place all your utility handlers in one cast member or spread them over many.

If you're looking at a movie and can't find a handler, use the find handler command under the Text Menu to locate it.

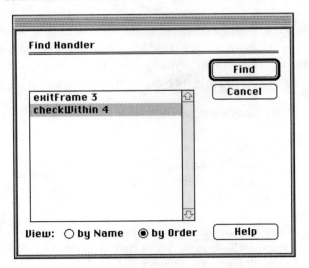

Just select the desired handler and click on Find. Director will open the handler in the Script Editor. By the way, the number that appears after the handler name is the cast number assigned to that handler.

Let's create something a little more interesting.

Alphabet Game

Matching games are common in software for young folk. We'll create a simple game in which the letters of the alphabet are on the stage and the task is to drag a small picture to the letter that corresponds to the first letter of the word it represents. Let's see how it works before tackling the programming.

Open Alpha.dir from the companion CD-ROM (Chap3 folder) and run the movie. A random picture appears at the bottom of the stage. Drag this picture to the correct letter of the alphabet at the top of the stage. When you are on top of the correct letter, Director beeps—otherwise, silence.

> *It's tempting to do something if the object is dragged to the wrong letter, but you should be careful. If the response to the wrong answer is flashier than the response to the right answer, users will intentionally make the wrong choice. Don't reward wrong choices.*

There are a zillion enhancements you could make to create a "real" game out of this, but let's get this simple version under our belts before adding bells and whistles.

Open Alpha1.dir from the Chap3 folder on the companion CD-ROM. This is the movie without the programming.

Examine the cast. I've included only the first 10 letters of the alphabet—you can easily expand this to the whole alphabet—in cast members 1 to 10. Starting at cast 27, you'll find the objects, in order, that correspond to the letters. The order is important; you'll see that I've depended upon the relationships between the cast numbers (i.e., "A" is cast 1, and the picture corresponding to it is cast 27).

In cast 60, you'll find a single pixel drawn in the Paint Window. Thereafter come the scripts.

As I was creating this movie, the cast members didn't naturally fall into these slots. I rearranged the window, as you did in Chapter 2, to achieve the proper relationships.

Look at the score. The alphabet blocks are arrayed from sprite 1 to sprite 10, and the picture of the armadillo is located at sprite 30.

I put the gap between 10 and 30 in case you wanted to encompass the entire alphabet. Just create the additional cast members (both alphabet blocks and pictures) and continue the alphabet in the score starting in frame 11 for K, 12 for L, and so on.

Let's start by making the usual loop. Open the Script Window of frame 1 and enter:

```
on exitFrame
  checkWithin
  go to frame 1
end
```

Yes, "checkWithin" again. You should name your handlers with a name that makes the most sense. Since the handler is going to check to see if the user dragged the picture onto the correct letter, "checkWithin" is a good name.

As in the simple examples earlier in this chapter, checkWithin will reside in the Movie Script. If your Frame Script is still open, just click on the pink plus sign on the upper left-hand corner of the window, or you can choose Script from the Windows Menu.

In the Movie Script, enter:

```
on checkWithin
  if sprite 30 within 1 then beep
end
```

Try your movie to see if it works. When you drag the armadillo on top of the letter A, Director will beep.

But this isn't quite the movie you looked at at the start of this section. The only picture that appears every time you run it is the armadillo. It takes a little more programming to transform this into a real game.

Randomize It

Director has a built-in randomization function: random(n) where n is a number. The function returns a random number between 1 and n. Thus, random(10) would generate a number from 1 to 10. The number could be different each time the movie is played (or it could be the same; such is the nature of random numbers). This function gives you a mechanism for picking, at random, one of the letters.

The pictures are arranged in parallel with the letters, so this number also can be used to get the proper cast member for the picture. For example, let's assume the random function generates the number 3. Cast member 3 is the letter "C." The cat is cast member 29, or 27 + 3. But wait. 27 + 3 is 30!

This is one of the most common bugs you can have in a script: an off-by-one bug. Off-by-one bugs are sometimes very hard to find. In this case, it's because random() generates a number from 1 to the number specified, **not** from 0 to the number specified. Starting with 1 works perfectly for the letters, but for the pictures, we need a number from 0 to **one less** than the specified number (e.g., number of pictures). If you use 26 as a "starting" cast member rather than 27, where the pictures actually start, the addition works correctly (26 + 1 = 27).

If you are translating programs from other computer languages like BASIC into Lingo, be careful to check how the random() function works in that language.

Where to generate this random number? You want a new letter each time the movie is played, so the startMovie handler is the logical place to generate the number.

Edit the Movie Script, adding a startMovie handler:

```
on startMovie
  set the castNum of sprite 30 to ¬
  random(10) + 26
  updateStage
end
```

The first line of this script sets the castNum property of sprite 30 to a random picture by adding 26 to the random number between 1 and 10.

By the way, random(10 + 26) would generate a number from 1 to 36! Watch your parentheses.

Recall that updateStage is required for some Lingo actions. A cast number switch is one of them.

Try it. This is a real mess. The picture appears briefly and then is replaced by the armadillo or whatever originally was placed on stage as cast 30. Further, no matter what letter you drag the picture to, Director beeps only on the letter "A."

First bug first. Even with the updateStage, Director wants to draw the cast member that you placed on stage. The stage is king here. As in the previous chapter, the solution is to make sprite 30 a puppet. By making sprite 30 a puppet, you're telling Director to ignore the score; that you're going to handle that sprite from Lingo.

Open your Movie Script and edit it to read:

```
on startMovie
  set the puppet of sprite 30 to true
  set the castNum of sprite 30 to ¬
  random(10) + 26
  updateStage
end
```

Try it! One bug fixed. I should note here that bugs are not often so easily squashed. Sometimes handlers are so intertwined that fixing one bug causes another. Fortunately, Director has some tools to help you solve these more complex problems, including the most important of these, the Message Window. See the sidebar "Using the Message Window" for more information.

Now you must get the movie to beep when the picture is dragged to the correct letter. For this you're going to need a global variable.

Why a variable? The cast number (of the picture and letter) is going to be different each time you play the movie. That's exactly the situation variables were created for—information that will vary.

Why a global? Well, you're generating the random number in the startMovie handler, but the collision check is happening in the checkWithin handler. Recall that unless you declare a global, information stored to variables is discarded when that handler ends. So if we used a simple variable in the startMovie handler, it would be forgotten once the end statement is reached.

Edit your Movie Script to read:

```
on startMovie
  global whichPic
  put random(10) into whichPic
  set the puppet of sprite 30 to true
  set the castNum of sprite 30 to whichPic + 26
  updateStage
end
```

Now you must edit your checkWithin to incorporate the global:

```
on checkWithin
  global whichPic
  if sprite 30 within whichPic then beep
end
```

Try it. It now works.

I'm still not satisfied. I don't like the armadillo appearing at the start to be quickly replaced by whatever random picture is generated. Select channel 30, frame 1 in the Score Window. Activate the Cast Window and select cast 60, the single pixel. Choose Switch Cast Member from the Score Menu, replacing the armadillo with a single pixel—much less annoying.

Of course, there's a better way through Lingo. Open your Movie Script and edit the startMovie handler to read:

```
on startMovie
  set the visible of sprite 30 to false
  global whichPic
  put random(10) into whichPic
  set the puppet of sprite 30 to true
  set the castNum of sprite 30 to whichPic + 26
  set the visible of sprite 30 to true
  updateStage
end
```

By making sprite 30 unobtrusive and quickly invisible, you don't see a switch occurring.

Using the Message Window

The Message Window is basically a command-line interpreter. If you are familiar with MS-DOS, you should have a good idea of what that means. To use the Message Window, simply type a valid Lingo command and press Return. Director will execute that command. Here's a simple Message Window session:

```
put 2 + 2
-- 4
```

Note that Director answers you with a comment ("--"). Note also that just "2 + 2" would not work here; you must type a valid Lingo command, like put.

You can use the Message Window to test algorithms, like these:

```
put random(10) + 26
```

and

```
put random(10 + 26)
```

You can also use the Message Window to trace the execution of your scripts.

Simply click on the Trace checkbox at the bottom of the Message Window, and Director will give you a complete listing of all the messages it is passing and all the commands it is executing. Here's a partial trace of the alphabet game from this chapter:

```
-- Welcome to Director --
== Movie: HD:AlphaFin.dir Frame: 1 Script: 61
Handler: startMovie
--> global theScore
--> set the visible of sprite 30 to false
--> getPic
== Script: 61 Handler: getPic
--> global whichPic
--> put random(10) into whichPic
```

```
== whichPic = 2
--> set the puppet of sprite 30 to true
--> set the castNum of sprite 30 to whichPic
+ 26
--> set the visible of sprite 30 to true
--> updateStage
--> end
== Script: 61 Handler: startMovie
--> put 0 into theScore
== theScore = 0
--> put theScore into cast "Score"
--> end
== MouseUp Script
== Script: 62 Handler: exitFrame
--> go to frame 1
--> end
--> go to frame 1
```

I've italicized the execution of getPic to differentiate it from the execution of startMovie. When Director reaches the getPic statement in the startMovie handler, it executes the getPic handler and then returns to the startMovie handler. This is a great way to see if your handlers are being executed and, if they are, if they are being executed in the correct order.

Note too that the values generated for variables are also shown in the trace. (== whichPic = 2), enabling you to be sure your algorithms are generating valid values.

You can restrict a trace to a specific part of a handler with the Lingo property "trace." Set this property to true where you want the trace to begin; set this property to false where you want the trace to stop, like so:

```
on startMovie
  set the trace = true
  set the puppet of sprite 30 to true
  set the castNum of sprite 30 to ¬
  random(10) + 26
  updateStage
  set the trace = false
end
```

Along the same lines, you can make sprite 30 moveable from Lingo, rather than in the score. Once again, we'll do it in the startMovie handler:

```
on startMovie
  set the visible of sprite 30 to false
  global whichPic
  put random(10) into whichPic
  set the puppet of sprite 30 to true
  set the castNum of sprite 30 to whichPic + 26
  set the visible of sprite 30 to true
  set the moveableSprite of sprite 30 to true
  updateStage
end
```

Cleaning Up

Although our handlers now work properly, I'm still not happy with them. The startMovie handler contains a lot of code. Well, it's not really a lot but it is sloppy to have all of these statements in startMovie. It's hard to see at a glance what is happening.

Let's pull all of the code dealing with generating the random cast member out of the startMovie handler into a handler of its own. Then just call it from startMovie.

Open the Movie Script and cut, paste, and edit so that the entire Movie Script reads as follows:

```
on startMovie
  set the visible of sprite 30 to false
  getPic
  set the moveableSprite of sprite 30 to true
end
```

```
on getPic
  global whichPic
  put random(10) into whichPic
  set the puppet of sprite 30 to true
  set the castNum of sprite 30 to whichPic + 26
  set the visible of sprite 30 to true
  updateStage
end

on checkWithin
  global whichPic
  if sprite 30 within whichPic then beep
end
```

Does this make a little more sense? You can now clearly see what's happening because you've named the code that generates the random cast member "getPic," and your startMovie handler is cleaner.

If you have a section of code in a handler devoted to a specific activity and that section grows long and cumbersome, pull it out and make it a separate handler. Just call it from the original handler.

One more modification to illustrate a slight variation on this point. Edit your new getPic handler to read:

```
on getPic
  global whichPic
  put 10 into numLetters
  put 26 into startPics
  put random(numLetters) into whichPic
  set the puppet of sprite 30 to true
  set the castNum of sprite 30 to whichPic ¬
  + startPics
  set the visible of sprite 30 to true
  updateStage
end
```

I've invented two new variables here, numLetters and numPics. These are not global variables; they're not declared in the globals statement. Instead, numLetters are used here to identify the number of letters and pictures you have drawn and the starting cast number of the pictures (minus 1). If you add a new letter of the alphabet and a companion picture, you need only change the "put 10 into numLetters" to "put 11 into numLetters."

By using well-chosen variable names, you'll find it much easier to recall what the number 10 is and why you're using it in the random() function.

Two variables are needed here because I left a hole in the score for you to complete the alphabet. This could be further simplified if your pictures **immediately** follow your letters in the cast. Don't enter this script, however, unless you complete the alphabet.

```
on getPic
  global whichPic
  put 26 into numLetters
  put random(numLetters) into whichPic
  set the puppet of sprite 30 to true
  set the castNum of sprite 30 to whichPic ¬
  + numLetters
  set the visible of sprite 30 to true
  updateStage
end
```

In this final variant, you need only change the 26 in "put 26 into num-Letters" to alter the number of letters and pictures.

A Real Game

Making this simple movie into a real game isn't that hard, but it does involve reconceptualizing our basic premise. In a real game, you'd probably want to have a score—in this alphabet game, a tally of the number of correct choices. Therefore, you must have a way for the player to indicate that he or she has to make a choice and is ready to be scored.

The game, then, falls into two phases: the game play and the scoring. I suppose you could use Lingo to invoke these two phases all on one frame, but let's use Director's score to divide our game into two phases.

Use the score when you can; don't force Lingo to do what you can more easily do in the score.

Start by duplicating frame 1 by clicking on the frame number at the top of the Score Window. Then choose Insert Frame from the Score Menu.

The most obvious way, it seems to me, to accomplish this is to check for a mouseUp. The player, then, can drag the picture around, but when the mouse is released, the game moves to an evaluation mode.

Instead of using checkWith in the Script Channel, let's put it on a sprite—specifically sprite 30, our moveable sprite. Edit the Script Channel of frame 1, removing the check within:

```
on exitFrame
  go to frame 1
end
```

and edit the Script Channel of frame 2 to read:

```
on exitFrame
  pause
end
```

Recall that pause may not be the best way to stop the playback head, depending on what you wish to accomplish. See "The Pause that Refreshes" in Chapter 1.

Finally, move the call to checkWithin to sprite 30, frame 1:

```
on mouseUp
  checkWithin
end
```

There should be no programming on sprite 30, frame 2, as this is our scoring screen.

You need a couple of additional cast members to make this a real game. Click on cast 69 in the Cast Window. Click on channel 31, frame 1 and draw a text box (or field) using the Tools Palette at the bottom of the stage, directly underneath the picture. Copy and paste the field to frame 2. This field will contain the number of correct guesses—the game score.

Let's give this cast member a name. In the Cast Window, select your new field. Click on the blue Information Button at the top of the Cast Window and enter "Score" for the field name, like so:

Text Cast Member Info

Cast Member:	69	Score	OK

☐ **Editable Text**
☐ **Auto Tab**
☐ **Don't Wrap**

1

Cancel

Script...

Size: 169 bytes

A

Style: Limit to Field Size

Purge Priority: 3 - Normal

Help

Move the playback head to frame 2 and let's add the additional elements to make our game.

You'll need two buttons on frame 2: one to stop the game and one to loop back to frame 1 and allow the player to match another picture. Draw these buttons on the far left and far right sides of the stage. I've labeled mine "Again" and "Stop" and placed them in Score Channels 33 and 34. My stage for frame 2 looks like this:

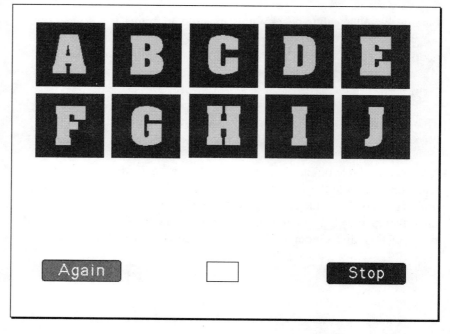

These buttons must be programmed to do anything. In this case, I've chosen to put the programming on the cast member. There's no compelling reason to do this; it would be equally valid to put the programming on the score.

In the Cast Window, select your Stop Button and click on the purple Script Button at the top of the window. Enter the following script:

```
on mouseUp
  halt
end
```

The halt command stops the movie.

Open the Script Editor for your Again Button and enter the following script:

```
on mouseUp
  set the visible of sprite 30 to false
  set the locH of sprite 30 to 319
  set the locV of sprite 30 to 324
  set the puppet of sprite 30 to false
  updateStage
  getPic
  go to frame 1
end
```

This script has to do a lot of work. Because the player has dragged the picture to a new location on the stage, you first must reset the sprite location to where it started. So first, make it invisible (so your player does not see it move); then set the locH and locV to the original locations; and, finally, make it not a puppet. You need an updateStage to cause Director to make the stage picture reflect the current state of sprite 30.

That accomplished, you need to generate a new random image—just a call to getPic does this—and then return to the game screen, frame 1.

This is getting perilously close to the point where I might take all of this script except for "go to frame 1" and put it in its own handler, perhaps named "resetGame" or somesuch.

Now let's change the Movie Scripts to accommodate the revised game design.

Open the Movie Script.

The fastest way to get to the Movie Script is Shift-Command-U or, on the PC, Shift-Alt-U.

Because you are going to keep score and you must know the score in a couple of scripts, the score must be a global variable.

Recall that it is a good idea to give variables initial values, especially global ones, so edit the startMovie script to read:

```
on startMovie
  global theScore
  set the visible of sprite 30 to false
  getPic
  put 0 into theScore
  put theScore into cast "Score"
  set the moveableSprite of sprite 30 to true
end
```

With these new lines, the game will always start with a 0 score and this score will be placed into cast 31—cast "Score."

You must also change checkWithin because you now want something special to happen when the player puts the picture on top of the correct letter (and something different to happen if the picture and letter do not match). This is a clue that you'll need to add an else clause to the if statement, like so:

```
on checkWithin
  global whichPic
  if sprite 30 within whichPic then
    win
  else
    beep
  end if
end
```

Note that Director will now beep when the picture does not match the letter; when it does match, win will be called. So we'd better write a win handler.

On a Win

Think about what you want this game to do when the player drags the correct picture over the correct letter.

First, you want the score to be increased by 1. So you need to:

Declare that you require access to the global variable "theScore."

Add 1 to whatever value Director has assigned to this variable.

Put this new value into cast "Score."

Go to frame 2, where the movie pauses until the player clicks on either the Again or the Stop Button.

Enter the following new handler in your Movie Script:

```
on win
  global theScore
  put theScore + 1 into theScore
  put theScore into cast "Score"
  go to frame 2
end
```

That's it. Your movie should work now.

Unfortunately, it's not very rewarding. The player's only reward is seeing the score increment. Let's make the game a little more gratifying.

Import a sound to play as a reward when the correct choice has been made. (In my game, I used "Horn Fanfare" from Director's ClipMedia folder.) The logical place to play this sound is in your new win handler.

You could put this sound into one of the Sound Channels of frame 2 as the player only gets to frame 2 when he or she "wins." However, you'll find the sound quickly squelched—the pause command stops all sounds. If you replace the pause with "go to the frame" or "go to frame 2," it will work.

But let's find another way to play a sound from Lingo, a way that can be triggered to a specific event and is more flexible than using the Sound Channel.

Revise your win handler to read:

```
on win
  global theScore
  put theScore + 1 into theScore
  put theScore into cast "Score"
  puppetSound "Horn Fanfare"
  updateStage
  repeat while soundBusy(1) = true
  end repeat
  puppetSound 0
  go to frame 2
end
```

Try your movie. You've got a full-fledged game, albeit not a terribly challenging one. The movie keeps score and plays a nice reward sound when the player is correct.

The puppetSound command is a great way to trigger a sound. You can use it to make your buttons click or, as in this movie, play a sound when something happens.

We'll be covering the puppetSound command in detail in Chapter 5, but let's look at the commands we added to the win handler now.

The puppetSound command itself plays the specified sound (here a named cast member) when the stage is updated. So immediately following the puppetSound command, you must update the stage. (Otherwise, the sound plays when the exitFrame message is generated.)

Sounds take time to play, although this one is relatively brief. The repeat loop assures that the sound is finished before continuing. The soundBusy(n) function generates a true if the sound in channel n is still playing and a false if not.

PuppetSounds always play in Sound Channel 1, overriding what you may have placed there in the score.

This repeat loop keeps going (doing nothing) until the Horn Fanfare is finished playing. There's a liability here—the player is "locked out" until the sound stops. Director is executing the repeat loop and isn't looking at anything else.

Finally, you must tell Director to revert to the normal sound state, to what is located in the Sound Channel. The command "puppetSound 0" does this. Try removing this statement and listen to what happens. The Horn Fanfare is played twice—once for the updateState and once when the exit-Frame handler is called when the Again Button is pressed.

If you use puppet sounds, attend to their behavior. Sometimes you must use puppetSound 0 to make sure the sound plays only once. If the sound plays twice, you need puppetSound 0.

Command Summary

halt
> Stops the movie.
>
> Example:
>
> ```
> Halt
> ```

puppetSound *sound*
> Plays the sound specified in Sound Channel 1.
>
> Examples:
>
> ```
> puppetSound "Creaky Door.AIF"
> puppetSound Cast 23
> ```

random(*n*)
> Generates a random number between 1 and n.
>
> Example:
>
> ```
> random(100)
> ```

repeat with *aVariable* = *startValue* to | down to
>   ***endValue***
>
> **end repeat**
> Creates a loop, with aVariable as the counter variable. Counts from startValue to endValue in increments of 1. If startValue is larger than endValue, use downTo instead of to. Any statements or commands between the repeat and end repeat statements are executed the specified number of times. The counter variable, aVariable, can be used within the loop where appropriate.
>
> Examples:
>
> ```
> repeat with i = 1 to 10
>   put i
> end repeat
> ```

```
repeat with number = 10 down to 1
  put number
end repeat

repeat with cel = 100 to 120
  set the castNum of sprite 5 to cel
end repeat
```

soundBusy(*channel*)

Function that returns true if a sound is playing in the specified channel.

Example:

```
if soundBusy(1) <> true then puppetSound ¬
"Audio.aif"
```

sprite *spriteNum1* intersects | within *spriteNum2*

Returns true if sprite *spriteNum1* is either touching the bounding box (intersects) or entirely within the bounding box of *spriteNum2*.

Examples:

```
repeat while sprite 1 within 2
  beep
end repeat

if sprite 1 intersects sprite 2 then beep
```

4 ◆ Project: Adventure!

Adventure games, from the text-based original Colossal Cave Adventure to MYST, have long been among the most popular of computer games. Director, it turns out, is an ideal development system for such games; indeed Director was used to create many recent commercial successes. (MYST, a notable exception, was created with a highly customized version of HyperCard).

The idea of an adventure game is simple. At the start of the game you find yourself in a forest clearing, on a dock, in a dark alleyway, in the control room of a spaceship, or in some other location. You have no idea where you are and may have little idea what to do to get out. So you just start to walk: to the left, to the right, and so on. But you can't go everywhere; you may try to go through a door only to find it is locked. Eventually, you'll find yourself learning about the environment, the inhabitants of that environment, and the rules of behavior in the environment.

On your travels, you'll find objects; money, swords, keys, potions, and other such stuff are standard objects in adventure games. You must pick each of these objects up and use them somewhere to purchase food and supplies, conquer a menacing demon, open doors, recover from a nasty wound, or whatever. MYST, the best-selling adventure game ever, does away with these objects, or inventory, in favor of a series of vexing puzzles. The puzzles serve the same function as an inventory—they are the means to open "doors" and gain access to hidden areas of the adventure.

You'll also find clues, mostly rather opaque ones: "You can't open that door," "You are in the ballroom," and "You can't pick up that item." By trial and error you'll learn that if you don't release the bird, the gate won't open or that if you play a specific sequence of notes, the spaceship will take off. These are the challenges that make adventure games fun for me.

Most modern adventure games include elements from other types of computer games. Many include arcade game "rooms," and others have elements from strategy games. The foundation, however, for many of today's best-selling games is a good old-fashioned adventure as pioneered back in the late '60s and early '70s with the Colossal Cave.

Open Advent.dir from the Chap4 folder of the companion CD-ROM. Play the game. It's not very challenging, but by studying the code, you'll be familiar enough with the foundation programming to create a basic game. Not interested in making an adventure game? I think it might be an interesting concept for a résumé—it certainly beats a simple slide show.

Starting Your Adventure

The first step in creating an adventure game is mapping the environment. You may not want the player to know where he or she is going, but you must know the layout or you cannot program it.

Here's the layout of my game:

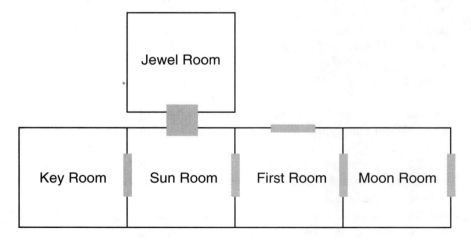

Notice that all the rooms are connected by doors (the gray bars). In this game, you cannot turn 360° and see the wall (and maybe door) behind you. I chose not to implement full rotation as there are relatively complicated interface issues involved in making such turns, not to mention a vastly expanded number of views to create. (You must provide four views for every room instead of just one.)

The usual way to provide a 360° view is to put buttons on the far left or far right of the screen. Clicking on them turns you 90°. Apple's QuickTimeVR (which runs on both Macs and PCs) makes this mechanism archaic as it allows full 360° real-time scrolling, opening up whole new possibilities for adventure games, not to mention a consistent interface.

So you are always facing the back wall of a room. Imagine looking at a doll house or stage set: You are the fourth wall.

All adventure games can be mapped this way, even complex ones such as MYST or Seventh Guest.

Most adventure games also feature corridors that connect two widely separate rooms. You normally must have an object in your inventory to traverse this corridor—although sometimes "clicking in the dark" does it. In this game, there is one corridor, between the Sun Room and the Jewel Room. The route between these two rooms does not involve a door but a secret hidden passage, **and** you have to have a key in your inventory to enter the passage. This corridor is marked on the map by a gray square. A new player would find the Jewel Room only by accident.

Examining the Score

Interestingly enough, programming the doors in an adventure game is no harder than making a simple menuing system as you did in Chapter 1. But, "You gotta know the territory!" Make your map **first**, before ever trying to link rooms.

The score of my game is shown on page 74.

I put the opening sequence at the very end of the score because I created it last and didn't want to insert a bunch of frames. Further, it's peripheral to the working of the game; once it's working, it's done.

Ditto for the closing sequence.

Note that each "room" is marked and labeled. Note also that, although there's no animation in most rooms, I've left enough space in the score for you to add a modest animation loop in each room.

Adventure Score

Script
18 on exitFrame

on exitFrame
    pause

▼Start   ▼First Room   ▼Sun Room   ▼Moon Room   ▼Key Room   ▼Jewel Room

Frame

1   5   10   15   20   25   30   35   40   45   50   55   60   65   70   75   80   85

Ink
Copy

Anti-Alias
Off

Trails
Moveable
Editable

Display
Cast

I've tried to use specific channels for specific items, and I've used Director 4's color score capabilities to mark off these dedicated channels. (If your Score Window is not colored, choose Score Window Options ... from the Score Menu and activate Colored Cells.)

Channels 1 and 2 are the background objects; channel 3 contains the objects on the back wall of each room; channels 4 and 5 are the left and right doors, respectively; channel 6 is the message area at the bottom of the screen; and channel 7 is a small blue sprite that serves as a "placeholder" for your inventory. Not all rooms have both left and right doors, so some frames are missing sprites on channel 4 or channel 5. Some rooms require additional sprites, which are located in channel 8.

Examine the Script Channel. You'll see that each room has a "go to the frame" or pause script in its last frame to hold the playback head there until the player clicks on an object or a door.

You may want to print out all of the scripts in this movie. Simply choose Print from the File Menu and in the Print dialog box choose Scripts and All.

Anatomy of a Room

Each room consists of two frames, except for the Key and Jewel Rooms, where there is some "action." This was an arbitrary choice; most rooms could have been only one frame, but I wasn't sure how far I wanted to take this little game.

The first frame of each room has an enterFrame handler:

```
on enterFrame
  put empty into cast 10
end
```

Why the "put empty" statement? Cast 10 is on stage as sprite 6 ... this text object, drawn with the Tools Menu, holds the game's messages. In the First Room, for example, if you do not have the key, the game tells you "You can't open that door." The enterFrame handler clears the message area by emptying cast 10 so that out-of-date messages don't hang around—you want to clear the message area **before** the room is drawn.

Cast 10 is also set to empty as part of the initialization in the Start Movie handler.

The playback head is stopped on the second (or last) frame of each room by the exitFrame handler:

```
on exitFrame
  pause
end
```

I chose pause here because I wasn't planning on any background sounds or animation on these frames, but it's easy enough to change this to "go to the frame" if you want to add these features. (See the sidebar "The Pause that Refreshes" in Chapter 1 for more information.)

Each room is linked to the adjacent rooms (see the map) by Score Scripts on the Sprite Channel. Thus, in the First Room, the left-door sprite (channel 4) holds the following script:

```
on mouseUp
  go to frame "Sun Room"
end
```

and the right-door sprite (channel 5) holds the following script:

```
on mouseUp
  go to frame "Moon Room"
end
```

These scripts are placed on the channels because only one left door and one right door is used throughout the game. In each room the door goes to a different place. Still, the door cast members have scripts:

```
on mouseUp
  put "Under Construction" into cast 10
end
```

Therefore, if a door has not been linked with another room by programming the **sprite**, this message from the **cast** script will be placed into the Message Window. Recall that scripts on the sprite channels override those on a cast member.

Special Effects

Two rooms have special programming to respond to the presence or absence of the key. These scripts all start:

```
on mouseUp
  global hasKey
  if hasKey then ....
end
```

The global variable hasKey is initialized to false in the startMovie script then set to true in the Key Room when the player clicks on the key. Specifically:

In the Sun Room, clicking on the sun leads to the Jewel Room; clicking without the key does nothing. Here's the script:

```
on mouseUp
  global hasKey
  if hasKey then go to frame "Jewel Room"
end
```

In the First Room, clicking on the middle door causes you to exit the game; clicking on the door without the key puts the message "You can't open that door" into the message area. Here's the script:

```
on mouseUp
  global hasKey
  if hasKey then
    put "Ta! Ta! You're out!" into cast 10
    set the puppet of sprite 7 to false
    go to frame "The End"
  else
    put "You can't open that door." into ¬
    cast 10
  end if
end
```

If you have the key, an appropriate message is put into the message area, sprite 7 is "unpuppetted," and there's a jump to the end sequence. The key disappears because once the puppet of sprite 7 is set to false, Director obeys the score—there is no sprite 7 in the First Room.

The most important special effect is grabbing the key in the Key Room. The Key Room is a "double room"—four frames. The pause on frame 61 is just like the pause on frame 2 of the other rooms. If you click on the door, the movie jumps back to the Sun Room. If you click on the key, however, the following script on channel 8, frame 61 is executed:

```
on mouseUp
  takeKey
  put "You now have the key" into cast 10
  continue
end
```

The continue command causes the playback head to move on to frame 62. Frames 62 and 63 are virtually the same as those in all the other rooms.

There's the takeKey handler (located in the Movie Script):

```
on takeKey
  global hasKey
  put true into hasKey
  set the puppet of sprite 7 to true
  set the locH of sprite 7 to 559
  set the locV of sprite 7 to 432
  set the castNum of sprite 7 to 11
```

```
      set the visible of sprite 8 to false
      updateStage
   end
```

This is the only place in the movie's scripts where the value of hasKey becomes true. The other lines turn sprite 7 into a puppet so that we can set its position and cast number from Lingo. It's no longer a little blue square; after these statements, it is the key. Next, hide the key in the room by making it invisible. (This is a property you can set without making the sprite a puppet.) Finally, the updateStage command causes Director to refresh the screen and make all of these changes on the stage.

The puppet status of sprite 7 continues until the end sequence. This way the key stays on stage wherever else you travel. Many adventure games allow you to hide your inventory or show only particular items of your inventory when they are appropriate to use. Since this game has only one inventory item, I thought it would be OK to leave it on screen.

Other Necessities

Several elements require initialization. As usual, it takes place in the Movie Script's startMovie handler:

```
on startMovie
  global hasKey
  put empty into cast 10
  put false into hasKey
  set the visible of sprite 8 to true
end
```

This handler empties the message area, assigns message area, assigns false to hasKey, and makes sprite 8 visible. (Sprite 8 is the key.)

The opening sequence was created with Director's Auto Animate feature and simply ends (frame 289) with:

```
on exitFrame
  go to frame "First Room"
end
```

The end sequence at frame 400 uses Sound Channel 1 and the Tempo Channel to reward the player with some music....

And that's it.

Enhancing the Adventure

There are a lot of things you could do to enhance this simple adventure game.

Add more rooms! This is the best way to test your basic understanding of the movie. Both the Moon Room and the Jewel Room have "Under Construction" doors.

Add more objects! Why not have some jewels in the Jewel Room? Jewels that make the moon in the Moon room do something ... how about go through its phases? Implementing this kind of animation requires a deeper understanding of the movie as you must add a new global variable and be sure to check for the contents of this variable in the proper places.

Add animation in the rooms! Bats, ghosts, spiders ... if it is a dungeon, it should be full of creepy, crawly things.

Background sounds can add a lot to the feel of this simple game. You can use the Sound Channel in each room; just be sure to change the pause commands to go to the frame commands. In the next section, you'll learn other ways to trigger sounds.

Finally, the biggest challenge ... create your own adventure! The "rooms" don't have to be rooms—outside scenes work just as well. (Much of MYST is set in the outdoors.) Instead of doors, use buttons to provide navigation.

Happy adventuring!

Section 2 ◆ Puppet on a String

Puppets, sprites under control of Lingo, are the key to creating interactive games with Director. Any cast member that's been placed on the score can be moved and manipulated in a variety of ways with Lingo. This section details some of the possibilities of this technique, ending with a simple arcade game.

5 ◆ Look, Ma: No Score!

*Fundamental to many games, especially arcade games, is the ability of
on-stage sprites to follow the player's input, be it from the mouse, the keyboard, a joystick, or any other device. This chapter reveals how to move
sprites from Lingo, both through algorithms and through user input.*

If you find a book on graphics programming from the late '70s or early
'80s, the programs will probably be written in BASIC—a then ... and
still popular programming language—and be filled with algorithms or
formulas to achieve animated effects with your graphics. There were
few, if any, user-oriented animation programs like Director back then.
Because a sprite's location is a property of that sprite, a property that can
be set, you can use Lingo to resurrect the time-honored algorithms used
in these books and pretty much abandon the score.

Let's start with a relatively simple, linear animation, just a box moving
across the stage.

Fire up Director. For the movies in this chapter, set the stage size to 640
x 480 pixels. This is the standard size for 13-inch color monitors on both
the Macintosh and the PC.

Open the Tools Palette and draw a box on the left side of the stage. Be
sure the box is in channel 1 of the score.

Let's start by creating a Movie Script to make the box into a puppet. Open
the Script Editor for a Movie Script. Enter the following script:

```
on startMovie
  puppetSprite 1, true
end
```

Coordinate Systems

In computer graphics, a pixel's location is determined by two numbers. The first number specifies the horizontal position; the second, the vertical position. Both horizontal and vertical numbers increase from the upper left-hand corner of the screen or window.

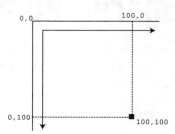

In GUI (Graphical User Interface) terminology, the x,y or h,v values are called a point. In Director, you specify (or request) a sprite's horizontal location separately from its vertical location—the locH and locV.

Pixel locations are specified or requested in relation to the **stage,** with the upper left-hand corner as the 0,0 point. In GUI terminology, these coordinates are called "local coordinates." The operating system, either MacOS or Windows, maintains the window converting the local coordinates you specify to global coordinates ... where the upper left-hand corner of the **screen** is 0,0.

This conversion that the operating system must do between local and global coordinates slows things down and is one reason many arcade-style games are not "operating system friendly." That is, they're written not for Windows but for DOS and, on the Mac side, the game takes over the entire screen, preventing you from switching back to the Finder. The programmers of such games are writing directly to the screen in global coordinates to achieve the maximum speed possible.

For sprites, Director maintains the locH and locV as properties of a sprite. The registration point of the sprite is located at the position specified by these two numbers. By default, bitmap cast members (created in the Paint Window or imported) have registration points at their centers; Object cast members (drawn using the Tools Palette) have registration points at their upper left-hand corners.

Open the Script Editor for the Script Channel, frame 1, and create the usual loop:

```
on exitFrame
  go frame 1
end
```

Nothing will happen if you play the movie now—you haven't made the puppet do anything yet.

Edit the frame 1 script to read:

```
on exitFrame
  set the locH of sprite 1 to 300
  updateStage
  go frame 1
end
```

Try your movie. Not very exciting, is it? The box simply jumps approximately to the middle of the stage and then stops.

The 300 in the set command above is the horizontal location, in pixels, from the upper left-hand corner of the stage.

Note that all pixel coordinates are relative to the stage; the size of the monitor your movie is playing on is irrelevant. See the sidebar "Coordinate Systems" for more information.

Let's use a repeat command, introduced in Chapter 3, to generate movement. Add the following lines to your exitFrame handler:

```
on exitFrame
  repeat with h = 1 to 640
    set the locH of sprite 1 to h
    updateStage
  end repeat
  go frame 1
end
```

Try it!

In this handler, "h" is just a simple, local variable, created by the repeat instruction to count. You're using its ever increasing value to specify the horizontal location of the registration point of the sprite.

This sprite moves very smoothly as it is moving in 1-pixel increments. Let's incorporate an additional variable to enable the sprite to move in different increments.

Edit your exitFrame handler to read:

```
on exitFrame
  put 10 into hInc
  repeat with h = 1 to 640
    set the locH of sprite 1 to the ¬
    locH of sprite 1 + hInc
    updateStage
  end repeat
  go frame 1
end
```

Try it!

Now the sprite moves faster; it's jumping across the screen in units of 10 pixels (the value of hInc, another local variable).

The change in the set command is an important computer animation concept. In our first animation, you were setting the horizontal location of the sprite (the locH) to an absolute value, one that happened to be identical to the loop counter.

In this revised animation, you don't know an absolute location for the sprite; the location is wherever the sprite happens to be. To move the sprite, you must start with its current position. So instead of just setting the sprite position to some value, you inquire of Director where the sprite is by using the sprite property the locH, then add the animation increment to that value.

Notice also that although the box moves off stage, the movie is still playing. Now that the box is jumping in 10-pixel increments, it needs only 64 moves to cross the stage. (The algorithm for this is simply the stage size divided by the increment size—in this case, 640 / 10.) So you don't need to make the loop go 640 times ... only 64 times. You can incorporate this algorithm into your animation loop simply enough.

Edit your exitFrame handler to read:

```
on exitFrame
  put 10 into hInc
  put 640 into stageWidth
  put stageWidth / hInc into numLoops
  repeat with h = 1 to numLoops
    set the locH of sprite 1 to the ¬
    locH of sprite 1 + hInc
    updateStage
  end repeat
  go frame 1
end
```

This revised handler takes better advantage of the computer—you can easily make this handler work for different size stages simply by changing the value in the "put 640 into stageWidth" statement. Similarly, you can make the box move slower or faster by altering the "put 10 into hInc" statement, automatically calculating the number of loops required to put the box on the far side of the stage. For more information about Director's mathematical prowess, see the sidebar "Doing Math."

The statement "put 640 into stageWidth" might best be placed in the startMovie handler. After all, this is a constant that probably won't change while your movie is running. If you put it in the startMovie handler, you'll have to declare it a global variable.

The placement of the animation loop is a little bothersome to me. Although there are many times when you want something like this to occur when the exitFrame message is called, in this simple example I'd rather make it a button script, so the animation occurs only when the user clicks on the box.

Open your exitFrame handlers, select everything from the "put 10 into hInc" to "end repeat," and cut it out of the handler. From the Cast Window, select the box, click on the purple Script Button at the top of the window, and paste the lines into the Cast Script Window. Your revised handler should read like this:

```
on mouseUp
  put 10 into hInc
  put 640 into stageWidth
  put stageWidth / hInc into numLoops
  repeat with h = 1 to numLoops
    set the locH of sprite 1 to the ¬
    locH of sprite 1 + hInc
    updateStage
  end repeat
end
```

Now when you play this movie, you must click on the box for it to animate. Notice, however, that the sprite remains on the left of the stage. You're not quite done with this handler yet.

To return the box to where it started, you must store the starting place in a variable and then restore the starting place at the end of the animation loop. Edit your Cast Script to read:

```
on mouseUp
  put the locH of sprite 1 into startingLoc
  put 10 into hInc
  put 640 into stageWidth
  put stageWidth / hInc into numLoops
  repeat with h = 1 to numLoops
    set the locH of sprite 1 to the locH of ¬
    sprite 1 + hInc
    updateStage
  end repeat
  set the locH of sprite 1 to startingLoc
  updateStage
end
```

Notice that as this Button Script is executing, you are "locked out," that is, Director is executing the lines of this script and ignores all other messages. If you make a typing error in a script and you can no longer stop the movie by clicking the control panel, press Command and . (period) or Alt and . (period) on the Mac and PC, respectively.

We'll see a couple of ways to overcome this problem, but animating and trapping other events is somewhat of a challenge.

Doing Math

Director supports two types of numbers: integers (whole numbers) and reals (decimals or floating-point numbers). If you ask for a mathematical computation between integers, the result is an integer. If one number in a computation is a real, the result is a real. For example, try these in the Message Window:

```
put 2 + 2
-- 4
put 2. + 2
-- 4.0000
```

The mathematical operators are the same as found in most programming languages: +, add; –, subtract; *, multiply; and /, divide. Multiplication and division take precedence over addition and subtraction. For example, try these in the Message Window:

```
put 2 + 2 / 4
-- 2
put 2. + 2 / 4
-- 2.0000
put 2 + 2 / 4.
-- 2.5000
```

In the first example, Director divides first before adding. The expected answer (2.5) is truncated, as no real numbers are present. In the second example the answer is real, as "2." is a real number but the division is computed as an integer. In the third example, the answer is as expected because the division results in a real that is added to the integer.

You may have expected an answer of 1 because you added 2 and 2 **before** dividing. You can tell Director to add first by using parentheses:

```
put (2 + 2) / 4
-- 1
```

When in doubt about how a mathematical computation is going to work, experiment in the Message Window to see the results of one or more test cases.

Verticality

Let's add a second sprite and make it move down the stage. Draw another QuickDraw sprite—I made a circle—making sure it is in channel 2 of the score.

Open the Cast Script of your new sprite and enter the following script:

```
on mouseUp
  put the locV of sprite 2 into startingLoc
  put 5 into vInc
  put 480 into stageHeight
  put stageHeight / vInc into numLoops
  repeat with v = 1 to numLoops
    set the locV of sprite 2 to the ¬
    locV of sprite 2 + vInc
    updateStage
  end repeat
  set the locV of sprite 2 to startingLoc
  updateStage
end
```

And that's it. You now have a vertically moving sprite. Notice that all you did was convert the references to locH to locV and modify the other variables to reflect this (i.e., stageHeight rather than stageWidth).

This is the power of algorithms ... a couple of minor changes and the script works. For decades, computer scientists have published book upon book of algorithms. Many beginning programmers try to reinvent the wheel by torturously creating their own algorithms. Take the high road and investigate what's already been done before trying to "roll your own." Appendix C lists a few places for you to start.

It's pretty easy to combine the horizontal and vertical movements into one movie, especially since we've been careful to create separate variables for the horizontal and vertical movements.

Edit your script to read:

```
on mouseUp
  put the locH of sprite 2 into startingLoc
  put the locV of sprite 2 into startingLoc
  put 10 into hInc
  put 5 into vInc
  put 640 into stageWidth
  put 480 into stageHeight
  put stageWidth / hInc into numLoops
  put stageHeight / vInc into numLoops
  repeat with v = 1 to numLoops
    set the locV of sprite 2 to the ¬
    locV of sprite 1 + vInc
    set the locH of sprite 2 to the ¬
    locH of sprite 1 + hInc
    updateStage
  end repeat
  set the locH of sprite 2 to startingLoc
  set the locV of sprite 2 to startingLoc
  updateStage
end
```

Try it ... it works, but not correctly. This is one of those logical bugs that is really hard to track down. You are defining numLoops twice—once for the horizontal increment and once for the vertical increment. To see the effect of this double assignment, add a couple of put statements to your script, like so: (Recall that values are placed in the Message Window if you don't specify a variable or text object in the put statement.)

```
on mouseUp
  put the locH of sprite 2 into startingLoc
  put the locV of sprite 2 into startingLoc
  put 10 into hInc
  put 5 into vInc
  put 640 into stageWidth
  put 480 into stageHeight
  put stageWidth / hInc into numLoops
  put numLoops
  put stageHeight / vInc into numLoops
  put numLoops
  repeat with v = 1 to numLoops
    set the locV of sprite 2 to the ¬
    locV of sprite 1 + vInc
```

```
      set the locH of sprite 2 to the ¬
      locH of sprite 1 + hInc
      updateStage
    end repeat
    set the locH of sprite 2 to startingLoc
    set the locV of sprite 2 to startingLoc
    updateStage
  end
```

Bring out the Message Window before playing your movie. When you play the movie, Director will place two numbers into the Message Window. The first is the value calculated for numLoops by the hInc division, and the second is the value calculated for the vInc calculation (64 and 96, respectively).

So the repeat loop is executed 96 times, but you need only 64 repetitions to traverse the stage. To fix the bug, you need to determine which is smaller, the vertical calculation or the horizontal calculation. A simple if statement will suffice. Try this:

```
on mouseUp
  put the locH of sprite 2 into startingLoc
  put the locV of sprite 2 into startingLoc
  put 10 into hInc
  put 5 into vInc
  put 640 into stageWidth
  put 480 into stageHeight
  put stageWidth / hInc into numHLoops
  put numHLoops
  put stageHeight / vInc into numVLoops
  put numVLoops
  if numHLoops < numVLoops then
    put numHLoops into numLoops
  else
    put numVLoops into numLoops
  end if
  put numLoops
  repeat with v = 1 to numLoops
    set the locV of sprite 2 to the ¬
    locV of sprite 1 + vInc
    set the locH of sprite 2 to the ¬
    locH of sprite 1 + hInc
```

```
    updateStage
  end repeat
  set the locH of sprite 2 to startingLoc
  set the locV of sprite 2 to startingLoc
  updateStage
end
```

That's it. Only the smaller of the two values is used for the loop variable. If you want to test it on different settings, try changing the hInc and vInc. (For example, set the vInc to 10.)

Going in Circles

I mentioned earlier in this chapter that you can resurrect algorithms from BASIC or other programming languages and reimplement them in Lingo. The little movie that follows was first seen in *Apple Graphics: Tools and Techniques,* which Roberta Schwartz and I wrote back in the '80s. I was looking for an example of more sophisticated sprite movement than the simple linear movies we just explored, and this old Applesoft BASIC program came to mind.

Open Circle.dir in the Chap5 folder of the companion CD-ROM. Play the movie and click on the circle.

The script is located, as in our previous examples, in the Cast Script of cast 1. It looks like this:

```
on mouseUp
  puppetSprite 1, true
  put pi() / 360 into increment
  put 1 into repeatFactor
  put increment * repeatFactor into increment
  put 0 into angle
  put 320 into xCent
  put 240 into yCent
  put 200 into size
  repeat with i = 1 to 720 / repeatFactor
    set the locH of sprite 1 to xCent + ¬
    sin(angle) * size
    set the locV of sprite 1 to yCent + ¬
    cos(angle) * size
```

```
      updateStage
      put increment + angle into angle
    end repeat
    puppetSprite 1, false
  end
```

We'll get to the math in a bit, but to me, the most interesting aspect of this movie is the appearance of the stage after the movie plays. The artifacts left behind are a result of Director not properly erasing the sprite, leaving behind a trace of its previous position.

The solution to this problem is a time-honored computer animation technique, similar to what Director uses internally when you animate from the score. Simply erase the old sprite before plotting the next one, like so:

```
on mouseUp
  puppetSprite 1, true
  put pi() / 360 into increment
  put 1 into repeatFactor
  put increment * repeatFactor into increment
  put 0 into angle
  put 320 into xCent
  put 240 into yCent
  put 200 into size
  repeat with i = 1 to 720 / repeatFactor
    set the ink of sprite 1 to 0 -- copy ink
    set the locH of sprite 1 to xCent + ¬
    sin(angle) * size
    set the locV of sprite 1 to yCent + ¬
    cos(angle) * size
    updateStage
    set the ink of sprite 1 to 2 -- reverse ink
    set the locH of sprite 1 to xCent + ¬
    sin(angle) * size
    set the locV of sprite 1 to yCent + ¬
    cos(angle) * size
    updateStage
    put increment + angle into angle
  end repeat
  puppetSprite 1, false
end
```

Now the circle just travels in a circular path, but it flashes. The flashing is partially a result of the execution speed of Lingo and partly a result of the simplicity of this animation technique. This code, by erasing the circle before drawing it again, means the screen is blank—for only a brief instant, but blank nonetheless—and the animation flashes.

This is neither the time nor the place to discuss the trigonometry behind this little script, but suffice it to say that the two set commands in the repeat loop are the algorithms. I just adapted them from an old high school trigonometry textbook. By feeding these algorithms angles from 0 to 720, the computer is calculating the vertex of a triangle with a hypotenuse (long side) of 200 pixels and positioning the cast member at that point. (That's why I used a bit-mapped cast member here rather than a circle object; the registration point is located in the middle of the circle.) The illustration to the right is a rough illustration of what this script is doing.

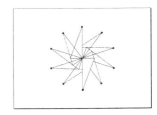

A rough representation of the algorithm of the Circle Movie

You can modify this script by altering a couple of key variables:

• repeatFactor determines how many circles get plotted; the higher this number, the fewer plots are made.

• size determines how big the triangle will be and, therefore, how far from the center the circle will be plotted.

• xCent and yCent are the coordinates of the center of the circle.

Increment is calculated from pi, so you wouldn't want to change this value, and angle is used to hold the ever increasing angle value—from 0 to 720 in "jumps" of the value of increment.

There's more math in this example than you'll probably ever run into in a Director movie, so don't panic if the math in the movie is not clear to you. But it does show that Director can be used to create math-based animations should a project require it.

Custom Pointers Revisited

In Chapter 2, you learned how to create custom pointers. However, these are limited to 16 x 16, 1-bit objects—not very exciting. Using puppets, however, you can make any cast member follow the mouse and, in effect, become a custom cursor.

Open Arrow.dir in the Chap5 folder of the companion CD-ROM. This simple little move has two cast members, a red rectangle drawn with the Tools Menu and an arrow, drawn in the Paint Window.

The idea here is to turn the pointer off—that is, make it invisible—then turn sprite 5 (the arrow) into a puppet and, finally, make the arrow follow our invisible pointer.

Some of this is best done in the Movie Script in a startMovie handler. Open the Movie Script and enter the following script:

```
on startMovie
  set the puppet of Sprite 5 to true
  cursor 200
end
```

Recall that cursor 200 is an "invisible" pointer. This handler sets up our movie.

Open the Script Channel of frame 1 and enter the following script:

```
on exitFrame
  set the locH of sprite 5 to the mouseH
  set the locV of sprite 5 to the mouseV
  updateStage
  go frame 1
end
```

The mouseH and mouseV are properties: the current horizontal and vertical position of the registration point of the mouse pointer, respectively.

Try it! You'll see, instead of the tiny arrow that is normally associated with the mouse, a large arrow that dutifully follows your mousing.

If you've read this far into the book, you probably know what I'm going to do next. The idea of all this sprite stuff in an exitFrame handler bothers me. Let's remove the cursor stuff from the exitFrame handler and make a special handler for it.

Open the Script Channel of frame 1, select the set and updateStage commands, and cut them. Open the Movie Script. (You can just click on the

green Next or Prev Button at the top of the Script Window.) In the Movie
Script, type:

```
on doArrow
```

Paste the lines you copied from the exitFrame handler. Then type:

```
end
```

Your Movie Script should look like this:

```
on startMovie
  set the puppet of sprite 5 to true
  cursor 200
end

on doArrow
  set the locH of sprite 5 to the mouseH
  set the locV of sprite 5 to the mouseV
  updateStage
end
```

Now you have to **call** doArrow from your Frame Script to make it work.
Open your exitFrame handler (frame 1, Script Channel) and add the call
to doArrow:

```
on exitFrame
  doArrow
  go to frame 1
end
```

And that's it. Isolating the pointer stuff into doArrow makes it easy, for
example, to selectively use it only in parts of your movie or even make a
rollover.

On a Roll—Revisited

Converting this movie into a rollOver is quite easy, especially now that
we've isolated our arrow code.

Edit your frame 1 exitFrame Script to read:

```
on exitFrame
  if rollover(1) then doArrow
  go to frame 1
end
```

Try it! This works but is not very satisfactory. The pointer is gone so when you are not on top of sprite 1 (the red rectangle), there's no pointer ... definitely not a good idea.

In GUI operating systems, the response of the pointer should be a major concern. If the pointer disappears, the user might assume the application has crashed.

This is a case where you know you need an else in the if statement. You want one thing to happen under one condition and another to happen under another condition ... this is the natural place for an else.

Edit your startMovie handler, removing the command that makes the pointer invisible. It should look like this:

```
on startMovie
  set the puppet of sprite 5 to true
end
```

Then edit your frame 1 exitFrame handler to read:

```
on exitFrame
  if rollover(1) then
    cursor 200
    doArrow
  else
    cursor -1
  end if
  go to frame 1
end
```

Try it! Now the arrow pointer returns when you move off the rectangle. But it's a little confusing—the arrow remains behind, stuck to the red rectangle. (Try "rolling off" the rectangle on the lower right-hand side.)

You can fix this easily enough using the visible property of sprites. Once again, edit your exitFrame handler:

```
on exitFrame
  if rollOver(1) then
    set the visible of sprite 5 to true
    cursor 200
    doArrow
  else
    set the visible of sprite 5 to false
    cursor -1
  end if
  go to frame 1
end
```

The only other change I might make to this movie is hiding the big arrow, sprite 5, in the startMovie Script so that the big arrow does not appear until the user rolls over the rectangle, like so:

```
on startMovie
  set the visible of sprite 5 to false
  set the puppet of sprite 5 to true
end
```

Using these routines, you can provide your users with colored, customized cursors to clarify their possible actions or just for fun.

6 ◆ Total Control

*Sprites are not the only things that can be controlled by Lingo. All the
special Score Window channels can be controlled—palettes, tempos,
sounds, and transitions.*

W e've seen how easy it is to move a sprite around the stage—it's
only a matter of changing the locH and locV properties of the
sprite. It's equally easy to change a palette, play a sound, or invoke
a transition from Lingo. Each of these has its own puppet command. Let's start with sounds.

In commercial Director movies, you'll often hear a clicking sound when
you click on a button.

> *This is an expression of the user-interface principle "provide feed-
> back." The click is an indication that the button was indeed clicked.*

Start up Director and make a button. It doesn't have to be a fancy button;
just use the Tools Window to make a standard button. Import the sound
click.aif from the Chap6 folder of the companion CD-ROM.

Make the usual loop to keep our movie playing, entering the following
script in the Script Channel of frame 1:

```
on exitFrame
  go to frame 1
end
```

Now let's add the click. You don't want to put this sound in the Sound
Channel; if you did that, the movie would click continuously as it plays.

There are two logical places to put a command to play the sound: on the cast member and on the button's channel in the score. For a simple example, either place is OK. But since you want the click to be built into the button, I think the best place for the script is on the cast member itself.

> *Recall that if you override the Cast Script by programming the score, this button will stop clicking.*

Select your button in the Cast Window and click on the purple Script Button at the top of the window.

Enter the following script:

```
on mouseUp
  puppetSound "click.aif"
end
```

And that's it. When you click on the button, you'll hear a click.

You can produce a different sound effect when the button is depressed by writing a mouseDown script.

 Puppet sounds override Sound Channel 1. If you want music or background sounds playing and you use this technique to make your buttons click, put the music in Sound Channel 2.

I've used the beep command extensively in the movies in earlier chapters. Anywhere you find beep, you can substitute a puppetSound command to play a more appealing sound. I tend to use beep as I'm developing a movie, and then, when I've got the logic working (that is, when the movie works correctly), I substitute more interesting sounds using puppetSound.

More on Sound

While we're discussing sound, there are four ways to play sounds or music:

The Sound Channels are the bottom line and are the best choice for looping background sounds or music.

Puppet sounds are the best choice for button clicks and other effects that must be triggered in response to something the user does while the movie is playing.

SoundPlayFile allows you to play sounds from a disk without having to bring the sound into the cast. This is a good choice for very large sound or music files. By playing from the sound file, you needn't bloat the size of your movie. (Appendix B deals specifically with such real-world considerations.)

Lastly, you can make an audio-only QuickTime or Video for Windows movie and play it using Lingo's many digital video commands. This is the best choice for synchronization as digital video, even audio-only digital video, is a time-based medium. (Chapter 13 explores Lingo's digital video commands.)

Palettes

Director's support for multiple color palettes is, from my experience, one of its least explored features. A palette or color lookup table (CLUT) is simply a collection of colors available for use. Palette manipulation is available only in 4- or 8-bit color; if your monitor is set for 16- or 24-bit color (or "true color"), the commands in this section will not work. See the sidebar "Bits and Color" for more information.

The default palette of Macintosh differs from that of Windows. Director automatically switches palettes when a movie is opened on the other platform.

Open Pal1.dir in the Chap6 folder on the companion CD-ROM. Play the movie and try the buttons. If nothing happens, be sure your monitor is set for 8-bit color.

All the buttons in this simple movie have a script that looks something like this:

```
on mouseUp
  puppetPalette "vivid"
end
```

That's all you need to do to switch palettes "on the fly."

Bits and Color

Computer graphics have come a long way from the Apple II, the Atari 800, and even the original PC CGA display. The frame buffer, that is, the part of RAM assigned to hold the screen display, of today's PCs and Macs is gigantic in comparison to the older generation of computers. This buffer may be on your video display adapter or may be part of your computer's main memory. The amount of memory required to hold this screen buffer is directly proportional to the number of pixels in the display and the number of colors each pixel represents.

In terms of numbers or pixels, 640 x 480 has become the standard display size. If you are developing a commercial movie, you should canvass your market to find the proper stage size.

In terms of color, most color Macintosh and PC VGA displays display 256 colors, requiring 8 bits per pixel ($2^8 = 256$). Graphics professionals (and many multimedia home-computer users) can display thousands (16-bit) or even millions (24-bit) of colors. ($2^{16}= 65,535$ although most 16-displays use 1 bit for an alpha channel and display 32,768 colors; $2^{24}=16,777,216$ and many 24-bit displays, additionally, have an 8-bit alpha channel—32-bit color.) Most new multimedia sold to home-computer users and to schools outclass, in power, those in the business arena. In the business arena, a fair number of PCs can still display only 4-bit color (16 available colors).

There is no question that "true color" (16- or 24-bit) is appealing; given the proper scanning or video capture, images are vivid and true in color. But they are also memory intensive. An 8-bit, 640 x 480 image requires 300K of memory, whereas a 640 x 480 24-bit image requires 900K. So Director must set aside at least this much memory for your stage. Then add the cast members (each cast member occupies as much memory as its "bounding rectangle"). Add your sounds and music to this, and it's easy to see why Director movies can be memory-intensive.

Director for Windows currently does not support pixel depths greater than 8-bit.

I prefer to develop in 8-bit color for both the raw savings in RAM and for the availability of palette commands to add flair to my movies without a lot of memory penalty. See Appendix B for more details.

The real power of switching palettes comes with building your own palettes. Open Pal2.dir in the Chap6 folder of the companion CD-ROM.

This movie has three custom palettes. Open the Palette Window and check them out. Under the system palette of the Mac, the three circles (sprites 2, 3, and 4) are hard to see because they are all in dark colors. Under the Windows system palette, these circles are more visible. Switch palettes and watch what happens.

Play the movie and click on the Go Button.

In the custom palettes I've made, two of the three colors used for the circles are black with the third color red, yellow, or green, respectively. The Go Button simply sets these palettes consecutively, like so:

```
on mouseUp
  puppetPalette "Red Light"
  updateStage
  puppetPalette "Yellow Light"
  updateStage
  puppetPalette "Green Light"
  updateStage
end
```

Puppet palettes can be used anywhere. Open Pal3.dir in the Chap6 folder and play the movie. This time the palette switch is a rollOver; the hidden message appears only when the pointer is on top of sprite 1.

The rollOver handler (in the Movie Script) looks a lot like those in Chapter 2:

```
on checkRollover
  if rollOver(1) then
    puppetPalette "Vivid"
  else
    puppetPalette "Hidden Message"
  end if
end
```

The Hidden Message palette differs from Vivid in only one color, number 31. In Vivid it's a bright orange; in Hidden Message it's black. The message appears only when the pointer is on top of the designated sprite.

Time and Again

You can also control a movie's tempo from Lingo. One of my students wanted to make a roulette-type movie that goes slower and slower until it stops at a random point, just like the ball on a roulette wheel. Tempo1.dir is a solution using the score with only a modicum of Lingo.

Play this movie a couple of times. Note that the arrow stops in different places when the movie stops, or it should. There are 16 possible ending frames, and it's possible that Director will generate the same ending frame repetitively—such is the nature of random numbers.

Examine the Tempo Channel and note that there is a series of increasingly lowered tempos—the movie starts out at 30 frames per second (fps), then on frame 25 decreases to 15 fps, then on frame 49 to 10 fps, and so on. That's how the arrow slows down.

The code to stop the movie is in exitFrame handler in the Script Channel of frame 96:

```
on exitFrame
  global stopFrame
  put random (16) + the Frame into stopFrame
end
```

There's a global variable here because you have to remember the value generated for stopFrame to use in subsequent exitFrame handlers. Were stopFrame not a global, Director would forget the value as soon as it reached the end statement of this handler.

The random number generated here is between 1 and 16 as there are 16 frames in the full arrow animation. Because the frame you want the movie to stop at ranges from 97 (96 + 1) to 112 (96 + 16), you must add an offset to the random number—an offset equal to the current frame. Director's function "the Frame" reports that the playback head is currently in frame 96.

Using a local variable to hold the number of "end" frames, you can make this handler totally generalized for any movie:

```
on exitFrame
  global stopFrame
  put 16 into nFrames
  put random (nFrames) + the Frame into ¬
  stopFrame
end
```

The variable nFrames does not have to be declared a global as it is used only within this handler. To reuse this handler in a movie with a different number of frames in the end cycle, just change the value assigned to nFrames.

The exitFrame handlers in frames 97 to 112 actually stop the movie:

```
on exitFrame
  global stopFrame
  if the Frame = stopFrame then go to the Frame
end
```

Here, the function "the Frame" is used both to determine that stopFrame has been reached and to make the movie appear to stop by looping to "the frame."

For a more Lingo-based movie, open Tempo2.dir from the Chap6 folder of the companion CD-ROM. Let's add the programming to make this movie work.

Consider what you must do in this movie, this time with only one frame. You must make sprite 1 a puppet, and to change to a different angled arrow, you must change the cast number of sprite 1. Since this cast number must be remembered through several handlers, it must be a global and must be given an initial value. As in many of the other movies in this book, the best place to initialize a variable is in the startMovie handler. Try this one:

```
on startMovie
  global whichCast
  put 1 into whichCast
  set the puppet of sprite 1 to true
end
```

Put in the usual loop and send the message that will move the arrow on the Script Channel of frame 1:

```
on exitFrame
  doRotate
  go to frame 1
end
```

Where did I get "doRotate"? It's not a built-in Lingo command. Well, I know that the scripting to make the arrow rotate is going to be longer than a couple of lines. Instead of burdening the exitFrame handler with lots of script, I chose to create a new handler—which, of course, will go in a Movie Script—to take care of the animation.

Reopen your Movie Script. If you are still editing the Frame Script, just click on either of the green arrows at the top of the Script Editor Windows, and type this:

```
on doRotate
  global whichCast
  set the castNum of sprite 1 to whichCast
  updateStage
  put whichCast + 1 into whichCast
  if whichCast > 8 then put 1 into whichCast
end
```

Because you need access to the value of whichCast, we must declare it in a global statement. Then set the castNum property of sprite 1 to the current value of whichCast (it starts at 1, thanks to our initialization in the startMovie handler). When changing castNums, you must update the stage. Next, you must increment the value of whichCast by 1 and, finally, you must check that this value is still "legal," that it has not gotten larger than the cast number of our final rotated arrow (in this case, cast 8).

Try it! The movie works fine ... except that the rotation does not slow. The code to make the rotation slow is going to look a lot like the code to move the sprites in Chapter 5. You'll set an initial value in the startMovie handler and set the movie to that tempo. Then you'll decrement that value in the doRotate handler so that the next time around, the movie will go slower.

Open the startMovie handler and add the following lines:

```
on startMovie
  global whichCast, speed
  put 1 into whichCast
  set the puppet of sprite 1 to true
  put 60 into speed
  puppetTempo speed
end
```

Now let's add the code to the doRotate handler to make the rotation slow down. Add the following lines to the doRotate handler:

```
on doRotate
  global whichCast, speed
  set the castNum of sprite 1 to whichCast
  updateStage
  put whichCast + 1 into whichCast
  if whichCast > 8 then put 1 into whichCast
  put speed - 1 into speed
  puppetTempo speed
end
```

Try it! Recall that when you were moving sprites in Chapter 5, you had to store the current position of the sprite in a global, increment it, and then store the new position into the global. The same thing is happening here. The global variable "speed" stores the tempo, and each time exitFrame is called, this variable is decremented by 1, slowing down the animation.

Now that you've got this piece in place, let's add the code to make the movie stop. We already have a way of knowing when to stop the movie: the tempo. When the movie slows to a certain speed, it's time to stop it. Open the Movie Script and add the following line to your handler:

```
on doRotate
  global whichCast, speed
  set the castNum of sprite 1 to whichCast
  updateStage
  put whichCast + 1 into whichCast
  if whichCast > 8 then put 1 into whichCast
  put speed - 1 into speed
  puppetTempo speed
  if speed < 5 then halt
end
```

Try it! This little movie is great for a stand-alone example, but what if you wanted to incorporate this routine into a larger movie—to maybe go on, to a new frame, after the "roulette" routine?

The place to start is obviously in the new if statement you just added to the doRotate handler, as this is the test for completion of the rotation.

Open the Movie Script Editor and try this:

```
on doRotate
  global whichCast, speed
  set the castNum of sprite 1 to whichCast
  updateStage
  put whichCast + 1 into whichCast
  if whichCast > 8 then put 1 into whichCast
  put speed - 1 into speed
  puppetTempo speed
  if speed < 5 then go to frame 10
end
```

Before you try this script, let's put a loop in frame 10 so that the playback head stays put when it jumps there. Double click on frame 10, Script Channel, to get a new Script Window. Type this:

```
on exitFrame
  go to the Frame
end
```

Now try your edited movie. It doesn't work. Why it doesn't work is really important to your understanding of Lingo programming.

If you watch the Control Panel or playback head in the Score Window carefully, you'll see that once speed reaches 4 fps, the movie does branch to frame 10, but it doesn't stay there ... the playback head jumps back to frame 1 immediately. Why?

The culprit is the Score Script on the Script Channel of frame 1:

```
on exitFrame
  doRotate
  go to frame 1
end
```

Look carefully at this little handler and "play computer" in your head, trying hard **not** to think of what you **want** to happen. When speed reaches 4 (speed < 5) Director does, indeed, jump to frame 10. But look! There's still another line of this handler to execute: "go to frame 1." So bingo, you're back to frame 1. And so on, forever. The loop stays in frame 1 because your exitFrame handler tells it to, even though you've jumped to frame 10 elsewhere.

This bug is really easy to fix, and the fix should reinforce the idea of using the most flexible code possible. Edit your frame 1 Score Script to read:

```
on exitFrame
  doRotate
  go to frame the Frame
end
```

Recall that the function "the Frame" refers to the frame the playback head is in. In this revised handler, then, after the jump to frame 10, the playback head stays in frame 10 and the exitFrame handler of frame 10 takes over from the exitFrame handler of frame 1.

A very common source of Lingo errors is failing to consider the order of execution. A go to frame command in a handler does not keep the playback head there if another command later in the handler moves it somewhere else.

You're almost there. This revised movie always stops at the same place, so you need to create randomness. Edit the Movie Script, changing both the startMovie and the doRotate handlers:

```
on startMovie
  global whichCast, speed, whenStop
  put 1 into whichCast
  set the puppet of sprite 1 to true
  put 60 into speed
  puppetTempo speed
  put random(8) into whenStop
end
```

and

```
on doRotate
  global whichCast, speed, whenStop
  set the castNum of sprite 1 to whichCast
  updateStage
  put whichCast + 1 into whichCast
  if whichCast > 8 then put 1 into whichCast
  put speed - 1 into speed
  puppetTempo speed
  if speed < whenStop then go to frame 10
end
```

Yes, another global variable. There are other ways to stop this movie without resorting to globals. You could, for example, simply make the last line of the doRotate handler read:

```
if speed < random(8) then go to frame 10
```

and omit the changes to the startMovie handler. I, however, like to use variables so that, if something is not working, I can use the Message Window to determine the current value ... or even to put a fixed value into the variable. Debugging is sometimes the hardest part of programming, especially when you are dealing with random numbers.

At this point our handlers are pretty much independent of the specifics of this movie—the only hard-coded parts are the number of cast members in the rotation. This value is fixed at 8, as is the position of the cast members in the Cast Windows ("if whichCast > 8 then whichCast = 1") and in the definition of whenStop ("put random(8) into whenStop"). These could easily, and perhaps appropriately, be replaced by a variable—a global variable, naturally, as it must be used both in startMovie and in doRotate.

In a Transition

The Transition Channel is the final Score Channel that can be controlled by Lingo. Transitions, used from Lingo, are simply numbers. The puppetTransition command looks like this:

```
puppetTransition 2
```

The most common mistake made with transitions is to include the transition **in the loop**. Open trans1.dir from the companion CD-ROM and play it.

Note how the pointer disappears or flickers. Stop the movie and look at the Script Channel, frame 2. Here's the script:

```
on exitFrame
  puppetTransition 23
  go to the frame
end
```

Transition 23 is the "dissolve pixels fast" transition and one of the most popular transitions. The pointer disappears because it is dissolving the screen **in the loop.**

To fix this problem, the Frame Script, frame 1 remains the same:

```
on exitFrame
  puppetTransition 23
end
```

But edit the Frame Script of frame 2 to read:

```
on exitFrame
  go to the frame
end
```

Try it! The pointer "comes back" after the transition. In this revised movie, the transition happens only once—when frame 1 is exited and the loop, on the Script Channel of frame 2, keeps the playback head stationary on frame 2.

This problem is not only seen with Lingo; you can fall into this trap simply by using the Transition Channel of the score improperly. If your pointer is disappearing, this is one of the most common reasons.

Aside from this little snag, using puppet transitions is a snap. You could even use the random() function to make random transitions to add a little zing to a simple slide show.

The puppetTransition command has a couple of parameters to allow you to customize the transition. See the Command Summary for more info.

Command Summary

puppetPalette *paletteNumberorCastName {,speed} ¬*
{,nFrames}

where paletteNumberorCastName represents the name or number of a palette and the optional parameters specify the speed (in fps) of the transition and the number of frames over which the transition will occur.

Example:

```
puppetPalette "Grayscale"
```

Note: Puppet palettes only "work" at a bit depth of 8 or 4 bits.

puppetSound *soundNameorCastNumber*

where soundNameorCastNumber represents the name or number of an imported sound.

Examples:

```
puppetSound "click.aif"
puppetSound Cast 23
```

Note: The puppetSound will play when you updateStage (or when Director automatically updates the stage upon exitFrame). Use puppetSound 0 to "turn off" the puppetSound.

puppetTempo *framesPerSecond*

where framesPerSecond represents the frame speed of the movie (60 maximum).

Example:

```
puppetTempo 20
```

```
puppetTransition number {,time} {,chunksize} ¬
                {,changingarea}
```

where number represents the number of the desired transition from
the table below and the optional parameters are identical to those you
can set in the Transitions dialog box.

Examples:

```
puppetTransition 2
puppetTransition 1, 4, 20, true
```

01	Wipe right	02	Wipe left
03	Wipe down	04	Wipe up
05	Center out, horizontal	06	Edges in, horizontal
07	Center out, vertical	08	Edges in, vertical
09	Center out, square	10	Edges in, square
11	Push left	12	Push right
13	Push down	14	Push up
15	Reveal up	16	Reveal up, right
17	Reveal right	18	Reveal down, right
19	Reveal down	20	Reveal down, left
21	Reveal left	22	Reveal up, left
23	Dissolve, pixels fast *	24	Dissolve, boxy rectangles
25	Dissolve, boxy squares	26	Dissolve, patterns†
27	Random rows	28	Random columns
29	Cover down	30	Cover down, left
31	Cover down, right	32	Cover left
33	Cover right	34	Cover up
35	Cover up, left	36	Cover up, right
37	Venetian blinds	38	Checkerboard
39	Strips on bottom, build left	40	Strips on bottom, build right
41	Strips on left, build down	42	Strips on left, build up
43	Strips on right, build down	44	Strips on right, build up
45	Strips on top, build left	46	Strips on top, build right
47	Zoom open	48	Zoom close
49	Vertical blinds	50	Dissolve, bits fast *†
51	Dissolve, pixels *†	52	Dissolve, bits *

* does not work on 24-bit displays

† Windows and Macintosh effects different

7 ◆ Brickout

Commercial arcade games began with Pong and have developed into photo-realistic, virtual reality–tinged experiences. Director is probably not the development system of choice for the latter, but it's more than capable of handling the former. Here you'll create a simple version of one of the original games—Brickout.

The idea of Brickout is simple. You control a moveable paddle at the bottom of the screen. A ball appears and moves toward the bottom of the screen. You must slide the paddle under the ball so that it bounces upward off the paddle. If you miss the ball, you lose that ball and are given another (until you run out of balls). If you hit the ball, it bounces upward and may hit a brick and remove it from the playing screen. The idea is to remove all of the bricks by hitting them with the ball.

Open Bricks.dir from Chap7 folder of the companion CD-ROM and try a game or two. I've left out a few bells and whistles, but this is the core of the game. Of course, in a real Brickout game you'd have more than one row of bricks but with only 48 sprite channels, there's only "room" for 46 bricks as the ball and paddle must occupy channels. If you want to provide scoring and other such features, you'll need a couple more channels. So a full implementation of this game in Director may be impossible without resorting to some pretty fancy tricks. Nonetheless, this is a good example of how to approach programming an arcade game. (And this section's project—Chapter 8—will show you another.)

Open Bricks1.dir from Chap7 folder of the companion CD-ROM. This movie contains the needed cast members without the programming to make the game work. (Save for our typical Frame Script loop in cast 11 and placed on the Script Channel of frame 1.) The paddle is already in position as sprite 1 and the ball as sprite 2.

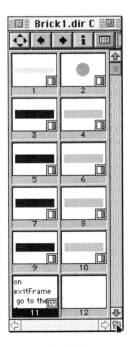

The Brickout cast

The first step in approaching such a project is to break it into logical pieces. Which elements (and actions) can be isolated from others? Get each piece working and then combine the elements to make a fully working game. In large commercial products, these pieces may be worked on by separate teams of programmers.

> *In* Voyage of the Mimi, *a project I worked on in the '80s, we hired a math specialist to do all the trigonometric programming for four separate programs/games. We just plugged her programming into each individual game and avoided a lot of duplicate work and a debugging nightmare. But first we had to analyze each game, discovering that they shared a trigonometric base.*

Let's look at the pieces you'll need to make Brickout work:

You must make a paddle move horizontally across the bottom of the stage.

You must make a ball move diagonally from the middle of the stage.

You must make this ball bounce off the edges of the stage and the paddle.

You must make this ball bounce off a brick in the middle of the stage.

When a brick is hit, you must make it disappear.

Those are the basics. The other elements include the scoring and the ball count.

Let's start by making the paddle move. Obviously, it must be a puppet as you cannot anticipate, in the score, how the user will move the mouse. As this will be the puppet throughout the movie, the startMovie handler is the logical place to put this command.

Open the Movie Script and enter the following:

```
on startMovie
  set the puppet of sprite 1 to true
end
```

Now let's make it move in sync with the mouse. I have the advantage here of knowing where this is going to end. (You do, too, if you looked at the scripts in the finished game.) I know there's going to be a fair amount of code here because a lot must be done. So instead of putting a burgeoning amount of code in the Frame Script of channel 1, I'm going to invent a new handler called "doBricks" to handle my anticipated code, and only send this message in the exitFrame handler of frame 1.

Reopen the Movie Script and, after the startMovie handler, add:

```
on doBricks
  set the locH of sprite 1 to the mouseH
end
```

Then open the Frame Script of channel 1 and add:

```
on exitFrame
  doBricks
  go to the frame
end
```

Try it! That's all there is to making the paddle work. Note that the paddle does move off the stage when you move the pointer off the stage, if your display is larger than 640 x 480 pixels. This is fine; in fact, it adds an interesting level of difficulty, as you must consciously stop the paddle at the edge instead of relying on the program to do it for you.

By the way, we don't need an updateStage command here, even though we're moving a sprite as the movie is a tight loop and the exitFrame handler executes Director's normal stage updating.

Now let's get the ball moving.

Moving the Ball

Sprite 2 must also be a sprite, and it must have a starting position. You want the sprite to appear at random horizontally but at a fixed vertical position.

Further, you don't know how much to move the ball horizontally or vertically to make for a good game. Let's make these values into variables so that it's easy to fine-tune them. (I have to admit that, when I was a beginning programmer years ago, I would not have thought of doing this.

I hope you will. Use a variable for any parameter that you think might change or that is clearer if referred to by name.)

All of this is initialization, so it should be in the startMovie handler. Open your Movie Script and add the following lines to the startMovie handler:

```
on startMovie
  global incH, incV
  set the puppet of sprite 1 to true
  set the puppet of sprite 2 to true
  set the locH of sprite 2 to random(620) + 10
  set the locV of sprite 2 to 200
  put 10 into incH
  put 20 into incV
end
```

Note that I'm using a 10-pixel offset for the horizontal location. This means the range of horizontal values will be from 11 to 631, meaning the ball will always appear **on** the stage. If you used random(640), the first appearance of the ball could be at 640, and it would be off the screen.

For the horizontal and vertical increment (incH and incV), 10 and 20 pixels seem to work ... this makes for a nice angular movement. I got these values by trial and error; you may prefer other values.

You may be feeling a bit uncomfortable with this handler, as it is beginning to bloat with statements that do a specific thing and that look, more and more, as if they should have their own handler. But let's get the ball bouncing first.

Our clever prescience to invent a doBricks handler provides the natural place to put the code to move the ball. That is, after all, why I called it "doBricks." Edit this handler as follows:

```
on doBricks
  global incH, incV
  set the locH of sprite 1 to the mouseH
  set the locH of sprite 2 to the locH ¬
  of sprite 2 + incH
  set the locV of sprite 2 to the locV ¬
  of sprite 2 + incV
end
```

Try your movie now. The ball appears randomly and moves downward, to the right, and off the screen, not unlike the linear sprite movie in Chapter 5.

Bouncing the Ball

You have three basic conditions to deal with to bounce the ball.

The ball can go off the bottom of the stage, in which case the ball is lost.

The ball can bounce off the paddle, in which case it must ricochet upward.

The ball can bounce off the side or top walls, in which case it must ricochet back into the playing field.

Each of these conditions demands an if statement in the doBricks handler.

The first condition is the simplest. Add the following statements to your doBricks handler:

```
on doBricks
  global incH, incV
  set the locH of sprite 1 to the mouseH
  if the locV of sprite 2 > 460 then
    set the locH of sprite 2 to random(620) + 10
    set the locV of sprite 2 to 200
  else
    set the locH of sprite 2 to the locH ¬
    of sprite 2 + incH
    set the locV of sprite 2 to the locV ¬
    of sprite 2 + incV
  end if
end
```

Try it!

Now I'm not only uncomfortable with all that extra code in the startMovie handler, I'm annoyed. The same code is now duplicated in the doBricks handler when the locV of the ball is bigger than 460. Time for a new handler. Let's call it newBall, because that's what it will do: generate a new ball.

Edit both your Movie Scripts to read as follows:

```
on startMovie
  global incH, incV
  set the puppet of sprite 1 to true
  set the puppet of sprite 2 to true
  put 10 into incH
  put 20 into incV
  newBall
end

on doBricks
  global incH, incV
  set the locH of sprite 1 to the mouseH
  if the locV of sprite 2 > 460 then
    newBall
  else
    set the locH of sprite 2 to the locH ¬
    of sprite 2 + incH
    set the locV of sprite 2 to the locV ¬
    of sprite 2 + incV
  end if
end

on newBall
  set the locH of sprite 2 to random(620) + 10
  set the locV of sprite 2 to 200
end
```

That's better. Try it! This movie runs just as it did before, even though you've eliminated two lines of code.

So much for making the ball disappear off the bottom of the screen. Now let's make it bounce off the paddle.

It's easy to tell if the ball hit the paddle; just use the intersect operator you used back in Chapter 3. Making it ricochet is a little trickier.

For this, I'm resorting to a time-honored programmer's trick. To make the ball move down the stage, the value of incV must be positive; to make the ball move up the stage, the value of incV must be negative.

To turn a positive number into a negative one, multiply it by –1; to turn a negative number into a positive one, multiply it by –1.

Read the previous paragraph over as many times as you need—it's tricky: A number multiplied by –1 becomes positive; multiplied again, it becomes a negative, and so on.

The place to check for this condition is in your doBricks handler. Add the following lines to this handler:

```
on doBricks
  global incH, incV
  set the locH of sprite 1 to the mouseH
  if the locV of sprite 2 > 460 then
    newBall
  else
    set the locH of sprite 2 to the locH ¬
    of sprite 2 + incH
    set the locV of sprite 2 to the locV ¬
    of sprite 2 + incV
  end if
  if sprite 2 intersects 1 then
    put incV * -1 into incV
    beep
  end if
end
```

This statement makes the ball bounce upward when it hits the paddle.

Try it! It works, but you must be fast enough to hit the ball, or it will go off the bottom of the stage and be lost.

Now for the final condition. When the ball hits the sides or the top of the stage, it must bounce back into the playing field instead of going off the stage as it does now. This means a few more if statements in your doBricks handler:

```
on doBricks
  global incH, incV
  set the locH of sprite 1 to the mouseH
  if the locV of sprite 2 > 460 then
    newBall
  else
    set the locH of sprite 2 to the locH ¬
    of sprite 2 + incH
    set the locV of sprite 2 to the locV ¬
    of sprite 2 + incV
  end if
    if sprite 2 intersects 1 then
    put incV * -1 into incV
    beep
  end if
  if the locV of sprite 2 < 0 then ¬
  put incV * -1 into incV
  if the locH of sprite 2 < 10 then ¬
  put incH * -1 into incH
  if the locH of sprite 2 > 620 then ¬
  put incH * -1 into incH
end
```

Try it! I chose the values for the maximum (0 for the top, 10 for the left, and 620 for the right) arbitrarily. I chose numbers and decided that these worked best for this game and this "ball." A smaller, or larger, ball might need different values.

There's still a small problem. The ball can get "trapped" beneath the paddle for a bit, only to eventually work its way free. This is a function of where the test for intersection with the paddle occurs. Try cutting this test and pasting it earlier in the handler, like so:

```
on doBricks
  global incH, incV
  set the locH of sprite 1 to the mouseH
  if sprite 2 intersects 1 then
    put incV * -1 into incV
    beep
  end if
  if the locV of sprite 2 > 460 then
    newBall
```

```
else
  set the locH of sprite 2 to the locH ¬
  of sprite 2 + incH
  set the locV of sprite 2 to the locV ¬
  of sprite 2 + incV
end if
if the locV of sprite 2 < 0 then ¬
put incV * -1 into incV
if the locH of sprite 2 < 10 then ¬
put incH * -1 into incH
if the locH of sprite 2 > 620 then ¬
put incH * -1 into incH
end
```

Better. This way the test for the intersection occurs **before** the ball is moved so incV is set properly for the next bounce.

I don't know if this problem could have been foreseen. These types of bugs seem to appear all the time. Luck occasionally prevents them from happening, but more often, hard-nosed debugging ferrets them out. In this case, doing a trace in the Message Window clearly shows where the problem is.

Now you've accounted for all four possible ball positions, and the movie works pretty much as expected—except that it's not much of a game: There are no bricks, and you have an endless supply of balls.

Laying Bricks

There are a couple of ways to get the bricks on the stage. You could just drag them on and then fine-tune their positions with the arrow keys. Let's try something different. Select the bricks in the Cast Window by dragging across cast members 3 to 9 or shift-clicking to select each. Drag these to the Score Window, channel 5. The cast members will be placed on top of one another, starting at cast 5. The vertical position of the bricks should be about 128. You can choose the "Extended" view from the bottom of the Score Window to verify the vertical position.

Select channel 5 and shift-drag this brick to the far right of the stage. Continue the process until all bricks are distributed across the stage.

Don't forget to press the shift key first. Director does not recognize the key to constrain a drag unless you press it first.

Your stage should resemble that of the Bricks.dir movie you viewed at the start of this chapter. Like this:

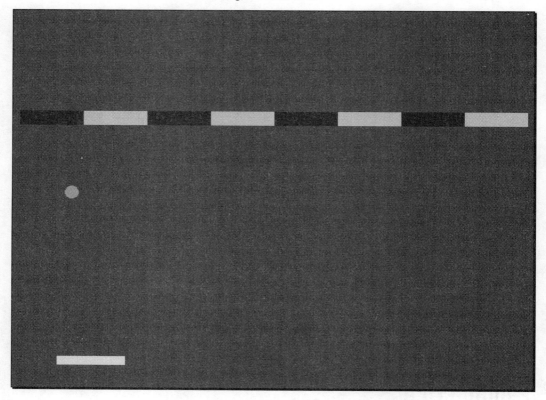

Try your movie. It works fine except that the ball blithely goes under all your bricks, although it still bounces off the side or top wall.

The script to make the ball ricochet off a brick is similar to the code for the wall bouncing, with one important difference: When a brick is hit, it must disappear.

You've already toyed a bit with the visibility property, so you should have an inkling of how to make the brick disappear. Something like this:

```
set the visible of sprite n to false
```

You just have to put this line in a workable way into the doBricks handler. Try this:

```
on doBricks
  global incH, incV
  set the locH of sprite 1 to the mouseH
  if sprite 2 intersects 1 then
    put incV * -1 into incV
    beep
  end if
  repeat with i = 5 to 12
    if sprite 2 intersects i and the visible ¬
    of sprite i = true then
    set the visible of sprite i to false
    beep
  end if
end repeat
  if the locV of sprite 2 > 460 then
    newBall
  else
    set the locH of sprite 2 to the locH ¬
    of sprite 2 + incH
    set the locV of sprite 2 to the locV ¬
    of sprite 2 + incV
  end if
  if the locV of sprite 2 < 0 then ¬
  put incV * -1 into incV
  if the locH of sprite 2 < 10 then ¬
  put incH * -1 into incH
  if the locH of sprite 2 > 620 then ¬
  put incH * -1 into incH
end
```

Try it! Not bad. The brick you hit now disappears when the ball hits it.

Since there are 8 bricks and they are placed consecutively in the score, you can use the loop counter (i) to do double duty. In this loop, the counter not only counts to 8 (from 5 to 12), it also identifies the bricks by sprite number for use in the intersection comparison operator and in the set command.

This loop reveals one of the barriers traditional programmers have when working with Director. The arrangement of the Cast Window and Score Window is not immediately apparent as a sort of array.

Careful placement of cast members and sprites can save tremendous amounts of coding.

But there's something both grossly and subtly wrong. Grossly in that, once you've hit all the bricks, they're gone, and they don't return when you replay the movie. On a more subtle level, the ball should bounce back when it hits a brick, not continue toward the top. Just a couple of little tweaks fixes both of these problems. Edit your Movie Script like so:

```
on startMovie
  global incH, incV
  set the puppet of sprite 1 to true
  set the puppet of sprite 2 to true
  set the locH of sprite 2 to random(620) + 10
  set the locV of sprite 2 to 200
  put 10 into incH
  put 20 into incV
  repeat with i = 5 to 12
    set the visible of sprite i to true
  end repeat
end

on doBricks
  global incH, incV
  set the locH of sprite 1 to the mouseH
  if sprite 2 intersects 1 then
    put incV * -1 into incV
    beep
  end if
  repeat with i = 5 to 12
    if sprite 2 intersects i and the visible ¬
    of sprite i = true then
    set the visible of sprite i to false
    put incV * -1 into incV
    beep
  end if
end repeat
  if the locV of sprite 2 > 460 then
    newBall
  else
    set the locH of sprite 2 to the locH ¬
    of sprite 2 + incH
```

```
    set the locV of sprite 2 to the locV ¬
    of sprite 2 + incV
  end if
  if the locV of sprite 2 < 0 then ¬
  put incV * -1 into incV
  if the locH of sprite 2 < 10 then ¬
  put incH * -1 into incH
  if the locH of sprite 2 > 620 then ¬
  put incH * -1 into incH
end
```

A simple repeat loop in the startMovie handler restores the bricks to visibility. In this loop you're once again using the loop counter (i) to identify the specific sprite.

One single command in the brick intersection loop—basically the same command you've used to make the ball bounce off the top wall—suffices to make the ball bounce back to the bottom of the screen.

Final Enhancements

This is a pretty good start to a game, but I'd like to make one big and two little enhancements before moving on. First the big enhancement: When you "clear the board," another row of bricks should appear. As for the minor enhancements, there should be some kind of scoring and a limit to the number of balls the player is given. First things first.

Careful readers might have a sense of what I am going to do here. You've put all of your initialization code in the startMovie handler, yet much of it is the same code you need to restore the screen after the player eradicates all of the bricks.

So let's pull out—cut and paste—the relevant code into its own handler. Here's what your startMovie and your new drawScreen handlers should look like:

```
on startMovie
  global incH, incV
  set the puppet of sprite 1 to true
  set the puppet of sprite 2 to true
  put 10 into incH
```

```
   put 20 into incV
   drawScreen
end

on drawScreen
  newBall
  repeat with i = 5 to 12
    set the visible of sprite i to true
  end repeat
end
```

Now you have a handler that restores the bricks to the screen, one that can be called at the beginning of the game to set up the board or whenever you need to restore the screen.

I'm a little uneasy about this handler as it also creates a newBall. But in this game, you always get a new ball with a new screen, so it's OK for here. Be careful "nesting" handlers like this.

How do you know when the board is clear? Well, there are 8 bricks, and when a brick is hit, its visible property is set to false, so the board is cleared if all 8 bricks (sprites 5 through 12) are **invisible.** You must place this check in doBricks as that's where all the action is. Further, since you need only check for this condition when a brick is hit (is it the last one?), the logical place to put the code is in the brick intersection repeat loop.

I've isolated the relevant code here by placing blank lines in the handler. Because the check for a win is a thing unto itself, let's make a new handler for it:

```
on doBricks
  global incH, incV
  set the locH of sprite 1 to the mouseH
  if sprite 2 intersects 1 then
    put incV * -1 into incV
    beep
  end if

  repeat with i = 5 to 12
    if sprite 2 intersects i and the visible ¬
    of sprite i = true then
    set the visible of sprite i to false
```

```
    put incV * -1 into incV
    beep
    if checkWin() = true then drawScreen
  end if
end repeat

  if the locV of sprite 2 > 460 then
    newBall
  else
    set the locH of sprite 2 to the locH ¬
    of sprite 2 + incH
    set the locV of sprite 2 to the locV ¬
    of sprite 2 + incV
  end if
  if the locV of sprite 2 < 0 then ¬
  put incV * -1 into incV
  if the locH of sprite 2 < 10 then ¬
  put incH * -1 into incH
  if the locH of sprite 2 > 620 then ¬
  put incH * -1 into incH
end

on checkWin
  repeat with i = 5 to 12
    if the visible of sprite i = true then ¬
    return false
  end repeat
  return true
end
```

Most programming languages have constructs called "user-defined functions." Lingo, per se, doesn't have user-defined functions, but any handler can return a value. Because functions are **defined** as subroutines or code segments that return values, Lingo, de facto, **has** functions. The only difference between a regular handler and a handler that behaves as a function is the keyword "return."

Since winning is a true or false situation and since you have a very clear idea of when a win has occurred—the board has been cleared and all bricks are invisible—this is a perfect place for a handler that returns a value.

Like the built-in functions of Lingo, handlers that return values must include parentheses. (Like pi() you used in Chapter 5.) That's why the if statement in doBricks is "checkWin()," not just "checkWin." If you must feed the function—I'm tired of typing "handlers that return values"—one or more values, these go inside the parentheses. You've already done this with the sin() and cos() functions in the Circle Movie in Chapter 5, and we'll see it again later on.

By returning a value, I mean that checkWin() acts something like a variable; that is, wherever it is used Director **substitutes** a value (in this case, "true" or "false"). This is very different from a simple handler that does something but doesn't compute to a value. You couldn't use simple handlers in an if statement; they don't have a value.

The checkWin() statement itself is simple, just a loop through the brick sprites. If any are visible, checkWin() returns false; otherwise, it returns true. Note here that the keyword return also halts the execution of the handler. In the case of checkWin(), once a visible sprite is found, checkWin() becomes false and is over with.

It's not easy to know when a function is a better choice than a simple handler that uses global variables to pass information. This skill falls into the realm of the expert programmer. Where you have a clearly defined process and that process generates a value, try making it a function.

Now you have a game that plays and plays forever. It would test even the patience of a 4-year-old. Let's restrict the number of balls you have and add scoring. Then at least you'll know when your 4-year-old beats you!

Limiting the number of balls is easy. You could hard-code a value into the game or use a variable. I think a variable is a better choice, for although we're giving it a definite value in this version of the game, the player can ultimately choose the number of balls he or she has. Of course, the number of balls has to be a global variable because you want this value to "hold" throughout the movie. The logical place to put the initialization of this variable is, as usual, in the startMovie handler.

You must also initialize the ball counter that will increase each time a ball is lost until it reaches the value of maxBall. Open your Movie Script and add or edit the following lines of your Movie Script:

```
on startMovie
  global incH, incV, numBalls, maxBalls
  set the puppet of sprite 1 to true
  set the puppet of sprite 2 to true
  put 10 into incH
  put 20 into incV
  put 0 into numBalls
  put 10 into maxBalls
  drawScreen
end
```

Ten balls is generous for Brickout, but what the hey ... it's your game! As to why we're starting with 0 balls, this is an artifact (some would say a side effect) of the decision to make a new ball when we redraw the screen.

In the Movie Script, scroll to the newBall handler and add the following:

```
on newBall
  global numBalls
  set the locH of sprite 2 to random(620) + 10
  set the locV of sprite 2 to 200
  put numBalls + 1 into numBalls
end
```

You see? By starting numBalls at 0, the first ball made becomes #1. If you started with 1, as is common sense, your first ball would be ball 2—drawScreen adds one to the value of numBalls and startMovie calls numBalls. This type of thing is very tricky. Be careful when you "cascade" handlers as you did in the drawScreen handler.

Now where do you put the check to determine if the maximum number of balls (maxBalls) has been reached? Once again, in the Movie Script, add or edit the following lines, this time to doBricks:

```
on doBricks
  global incH, incV, numBalls, maxBalls
  set the locH of sprite 1 to the mouseH
  if sprite 2 intersects 1 then
    put incV * -1 into incV
    beep
  end if
```

```
if numBalls > maxBalls then halt
  repeat with i = 5 to 12
    qif sprite 2 intersects i and the visible ¬
    of sprite i = true then
    set the visible of sprite i to false
    put incV * -1 into incV
    beep
    if checkWin() = true then
      drawScreen
    end if
  end if
end repeat
  if the locV of sprite 2 > 460 then
    newBall
  else
    set the locH of sprite 2 to the locH ¬
    of sprite 2 + incH
    set the locV of sprite 2 to the locV ¬
    of sprite 2 + incV
  end if
  if the locV of sprite 2 < 0 then ¬
  put incV * -1 into incV
  if the locH of sprite 2 < 10 then ¬
  put incH * -1 into incH
  if the locH of sprite 2 > 620 then ¬
  put incH * -1 into incH
end
```

With this new line, the movie halts when the numBalls exceeds maxBalls.

And that's about it. This game is by no means complete. If you are anything like me, you'll want to add a lot of bells and whistles to make this more than just a programming challange. I've included a "bounce" sound in the Chap7 folder of the companion CD-ROM that you can incorporate as puppet sounds instead of the simple beep. And you might want to include on-screen scoring and a speed-up (using puppet tempo) each time a screen is cleared. And ... well, this could go on and on.

Command Summary

halt

    Stops the movie. Exits the current handler and any handler calling it.

    Example:

```
halt
```

return *expressionOrValue*

    Returns the expression (2 + 2) or the value (true) to the calling statement.

    Examples:

```
return n + 2
return myVar
```

    Note: Return halts the execution of a handler.

8 ◆ Project: Shooting Gallery

Arcade games are probably the most popular of all computer games. They date back nearly to the first CRT display. From Space Invaders to Star Wars: Rebel Assault, computer shoot-'em-up games have proven very successful. I've chosen a kinder, gentler game to create here: an old-fashioned carnival shooting gallery.

Arcade games differ from adventure games—such as we created in Chapter 8—in that they take place in "real time," that is, the player must interact with the game elements rapidly; there is no time for reflection. Reflexes are what this kind of game is about.

In planning this book, I had not intended to introduce major new commands in the project chapters. For this game to work well, however, a new command is necessary: when.

The Lingo command when sets up an "event trap." The basic syntax of this command is:

```
when message then command
```

The *message* can be either one of the built-in messages of Director, like mouseUp and keyDown, or one of your own message handlers.

The magic of the when command is that it sets up a response to a condition so that Director will interrupt anything it is doing to execute the action (well, almost anything; an already executing handler will not stop, but as soon as it does, your when command gets executed immediately).

Open Arcade.dir from Chap8 folder of the the companion CD-ROM. Play the movie. Move the mouse horizontally to move the gun at the bottom of the stage. Click to fire a "bullet." If the bullet hits the duck, the score will increase incrementally and the duck will explode. Unlike a real shooting gallery (or arcade game), you have an unlimited number of bullets.

Examining the Cast and Score

Open the Cast Window.

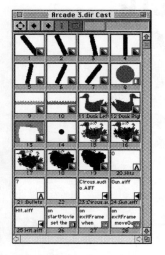

The Arcade.dir cast

The first seven cast members are the gun barrel in various stages of rotation. Cast members 8–10 are a Tool Palette circle (that serves to cover up the bottom of the gun barrel) and the two waves. The two ducks come next, one facing left and one facing right, then the stage "frame" and bullet. Cast members 15–19 are a five-cast sequence for the exploding duck, followed by two fields to hold the scoring. Finally, the sounds and scripts.

Yes, if you watch carefully as you play the game, no matter which direction the duck is moving, it always blows up facing left. I'll leave it to you to create a right-facing explosion.

Open the Score Window. The score is simplicity itself: two frames and nine sprites.

The Arcade.dir score

I placed the background music in Sound Channel 2, because I'm using puppet sounds for the sound effects, and puppet sounds always play in Sound Channel 1. To keep the sound level constant, a null sound sits in Sound Channel 1. This way, the music stays at a constant volume when the sound effects play. Puppet sounds override the sounds placed in the Sound Channels.

The Frame Script on frame 1 sets up the when condition. The script on frame 2 does most of the work in this movie, as well as providing the usual "go to the frame" loop.

Channel 1 is the gun barrel; channel 3, the background wave; channel 4, the duck; channel 5, the foreground wave. The order of wave, duck, wave sandwiches the duck between the two waves.

Next come the bullet and circle cover-up. The bullet is going to become a puppet; recall that you cannot **create** a sprite from Lingo ... you must place something on the stage. The circle covers up the bottom of the gun barrel and makes for a better-looking animation.

Finally, in channels 10 through 12, the foreground "curtain" serves to cover up the edges of the waves and frames the screen and the text areas for scoring.

Examining the Scripts

As in most non-trivial Lingo-based movies, a startMovie handler provides initialization of variables and other elements. Here's the startMovie handler:

```
on startMovie
  set the puppet of sprite 1 to true
  set the puppet of sprite 4 to true
  set the puppet of sprite 5 to true
  put 0 into cast "Hits"
  put 0 into cast "Bullets"
  initDuck
end
```

Recall that sprite 1 is the gun barrel, sprite 4 is the duck, and sprite 5 is the foreground wave. So the first three lines of this handler simply set these sprites to puppets. Next, the text areas are initialized to 0. Cast "Hits" is the number of times the bullet hits the duck, and cast "Bullets" is the number of bullets fired. And, finally, the first duck is initialized.

The code was getting so long, I decided to pull it out into its own handler rather than clutter up startMovie. Here's initDuck:

```
on initDuck
  global duckDirection
  if random(2) = 1 then
    put "L" into duckDirection
    set the locH of sprite 4 to 580
    set the castNum of sprite 4 to 11
  else
    put "R" into duckDirection
    set the locH of sprite 4 to 20
    set the castNum of sprite 4 to 12
  end if
end
```

I wanted the duck to appear either on the left or the right side of the screen, at random. Since this information must be known in other handlers, it must be a global variable.

Random (2) generates either a 1 or a 2, so the if statement here decides whether the first duck is moving left or right. (If random(2) returns a 1, the duck will move to the left; otherwise, it moves to the right.) The three statements for each condition set up the first duck: an "L" or "R" is assigned to the global duckDirection, the horizontal location is set to 580 or 20, and the castNum is set so the duck is facing the correct direction.

That's the initialization sequence.

Open the Script Channel, frame 1:

```
on exitFrame
  when mouseUp then doBullet
end
```

This handler sets up the event trap. Whenever the mouse button is released, the doBullet handler is called.

If this movie had another section where the doBullet handler was not appropriate, the following handler, placed on the first frame of that section, would stop the event trap:

```
on enterFrame
  when mouseUp then nothing
end
```

Open the Script Channel, frame 2:

```
on exitFrame
  moveGun
  moveDuck
  moveWave
  go to the frame
end
```

As you've seen over and over again, I like to keep my Script Channel scripts as simple as possible—the code to handle these activities is stashed in a Movie Script. Let's look at each of these, one by one.

Moving the Gun

Director contains no inherent commands to rotate a cast member on the stage—you must provide pre-rotated bitmaps. I used the Paint Window's Auto Transform command to create the seven rotated gun barrels. Then I rearranged them in the Cast Window so that they were arrayed properly from most rotated to the left to most rotated to the right.

The programming problem here, stated simply, is to relate the position of the pointer on the stage to the castNum on stage as sprite 1, the gun barrel. When the pointer is located at the far left of the stage, the cast member most rotated to the left should be on stage; when the pointer is located at the middle of the stage, the non-rotated barrel should be on stage; and when the pointer is at the far right of the stage, the cast member most rotated to the right should be on stage.

Since there are seven cast members, you must divide the stage into seven zones. Then relate each of those zones to the cast member representing the correct rotation based upon the position of the pointer. This process is easier to do than it is to describe.

The stage of this movie is 640 horizontal pixels, the size of a standard 13-inch monitor. Dividing 640 by 7, you'll find that each "barrel zone" is 91 pixels wide. (Actually, 640 / 7 is 91.41, but remember that Director does integer—whole number —math, unless one of the values is a decimal. So you can ignore the decimal.)

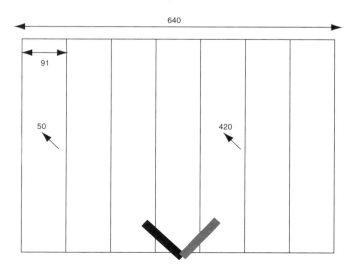

So when the pointer is in any horizontal location from 0 to 91, the cast number of the barrel sprite should be 1; when the pointer is between 92 and 184, the cast number of the barrel sprite should be 2; and so on.

It's easy to determine where the pointer is on the stage: The mouseH function reports this information back to you.

Here's the algorithm expressed in Lingo code:

```
on moveGun
  set the castNum of sprite 1 to 1 + ¬
  (the mouseH/91)
  updateStage
end
```

The parentheses aren't necessary here (Director will divide before it adds), but I think they clarify the operations. Simply dividing the mouse location by the "zone factor" yields the cast number we need. Well, almost; it's off by one. That is, when the pointer is at a locH of, say, 41, the division yields a 0 ... remember that Director is using integer math. So you must add an "offset" to this operation to generate the proper cast number ... an offset of 1. If the barrel cast members started at cast number 10, you could use a 10 here—that's the idea of an offset.

That's almost it. If you look in the arcade movie, the number I've used in this handler is 92:

```
set the castNum of sprite 1 to 1 + ¬
(the mouseH/92)
```

I used 92 to correct a specific situation: When the pointer is at the far right of the stage, from pixels 638 to 640, the mathematically correct algorithm yields a 7 (638 / 91 = 7). With the offset, the gun barrel would be set to cast number 8—not one of the gun barrels. By using 92 in the denominator, this problem is avoided. Although the "zones" are slightly off by this correction, it doesn't make any difference to the play of the game.

The final step in moving the gun is updating the stage to show the current status of the barrel.

Remember this little algorithm. It can come in handy in a surprising number of situations.

Moving the Duck

It's obvious that you'll need two routines to move the duck—the values used to move the duck to the right must be positive, and those to move the duck to the left must be negative.

```
on moveDuck
  global duckDirection
  if duckDirection = "L" then
    put -20 into hMove
  else
    put 20 into hMove
  end if
  set the locH of sprite 4 to ¬
  (the locH of sprite 4) + hMove
  if the locH of sprite 4 > 580 then
    put "L" into duckDirection
    set the castNum of sprite 4 to 11
  end if
  if the locH of sprite 4 < 20 then
    put "R" into duckDirection
    set the castNum of sprite 4 to 12
  end if
end
```

This handler must know whether the duck is moving left or right, so a global declaration allows access to this value that has been assigned in the initDuck handler.

A simple if/then/else statement assigns a value to the local variable hMove, either -20 or 20. This means the duck moves in jumps of 20 pixels, either to the left (-20) or to the right (+20). You can make the duck move faster or slower by altering these values.

Next, the duck's locH is set to the current value plus the locH. Once again, the parentheses are not necessary, but I've used them to clarify the algorithm. You've used this same mechanism to move puppets in other movies in this book.

That would be all that's needed, except that if the duck were moving to the right, it would keep moving to the right ... off the stage. So I added two if statements to check to see if the duck has moved too far. I chose the values of 580 and 20 arbitrarily; they seemed to work well visually. If either of these extremes is exceeded, duckDirection is assigned the *other* direction, and the cast numbers are switched.

It's possible to be very clever here and simplify these if statements. For instance, you could use 1 and -1 for the direction and use that little multiplication by -1 trick you learned in this section. But then your code would become difficult to understand. With all of the other things going on in this movie, I don't think it's a good idea to be too *clever.*

Moving the Wave

MoveWave is the simplest of these three basic handlers:

```
on moveWave
  if the locH of sprite 5 = 351 then
    set the locH of sprite 5 to 322
  else
    set the locH of sprite 5 to 351
  end if
end
```

This handler simply checks to see if the wave is located horizontally at 351 pixels and, if it is, moves it to 322. The wave, then, "flip-flops" between locH of 322 and 351.

To get these numbers, I registered the front wave with the back wave and noted this position in the extended display of the Score Window. I then moved the wave until I liked its position and noted the new position in the Score Window.

The wave in the back could also be moved, but I didn't think it was necessary.

These are all the scripts that are normally executed as this movie is playing, except for one condition: When the player releases the mouse button. Because the event trap is located in the Script Channel of frame 1, when the mouse button is released, Director executes doBullet.

Moving the Bullet

Moving the bullet is the most complicated handler in this movie, but what it must do is not that complicated. Let's list what doBullet must do before looking at the actual script.

To move the bullet, the script must:

Play the bullet sound.

Increment the cast member, storing the number of bullets used.

Be sure the puppet and visible properties of the bullet are right for the bullet to animate.

Animate the bullet, based upon the angle of the gun.

Check to see if there has been a collision between the bullet and the duck (and if a collision has occurred, animate the collision).

"Unpuppet" the bullet and sound. Make the bullet invisible.

That's it. Now, here's the code. Because it is so long, I'm going to split it into segments and discuss each segment individually.

```
on doBullet

puppetSound "Gun.aiff"
```

plays the sound.

```
put value (the text of cast "Bullets") + 1 ¬
into cast "Bullets"
```

increments cast "Bullets" by 1. Note the use of the function value here to convert the text cast member "Bullets" to a number before trying to add. The parentheses *are* necessary here as value is a function.

```
set the puppet of sprite 7 to true
set the visible of sprite 7 to true
```

Be sure the bullet is ready to be animated. That is, make sure it is a puppet and that it is visible.

Diagonal Moves Made Simple

Here's a picture of the stage from the arcade movie with most of the sprites turned off and with trails activated for the bullet sprite:

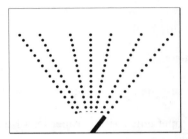

Notice that vertically, each bullet is in the same position as its neighbor. That is, bullet 4 from the left-most gun barrel position is at the same vertical coordinate as bullet 4 from all other gun angles. What differs is the horizontal position.

The bullet from the middle gun position is the simplest to understand. Here, the bullet moves only vertically (xinc = 0), so there is no horizontal movement.

The bullet from the right-most gun angle is moving across the stage in increments of -14 pixels, whereas the bullet from the second gun angle is moving in increments of only -10 pixels. At the fourth animation loop, the fourth bullet, the bullet from the left-most gun angle has traversed -56 pixels, whereas the bullet from the second gun angle has moved only -40 pixels. A diagonal move!

The actual numbers I used for xinc in the doBullet handler were determined empirically. I tried different values until it looked as though the bullet was actually coming out of the barrel.

Actual bullets, fired from guns (or thrown balls or anything that is projected through the air) are subject to a variety of forces, especially gravity, that are not included in this simple game. It's not hard to add such calculations to doBullet if you know the algorithm to use. For such realistic moves, xinc would not be a constant, nor would the vertical increment; instead, they would be computed each time through the animation loop to reflect the effects of whatever force you were simulating.

```
put the castNum of sprite 1 into gunAngle
if gunAngle = 1 then put -14 into xinc
if gunAngle = 2 then put -10 into xinc
if gunAngle = 3 then put -4 into xinc
if gunAngle = 4 then put 0 into xinc
if gunAngle = 5 then put 4 into xinc
if gunAngle = 6 then put 10 into xinc
if gunAngle = 7 then put 16 into xinc
```

This is the core of the bullet-move routine. By looking at the cast number currently in place for the barrel of the gun, you can assign a horizontal increment to the bullet. See the sidebar "Diagonal Moves Made Simple" for more information on how the bullet manages to move at different angles.

```
set the locV of sprite 7 to the locV of ¬
sprite 1
set the locH of sprite 7 to the locH of ¬
sprite 1
updateStage
```

Draw the bullet on stage at the registration point of sprite 1. Check out the Paint Window. I've set the registration point of the barrel to the middle of its base, just where the bullet should begin its trek.

```
repeat with i = 1 to 20

  if i mod 2 then
    moveDuck
    moveWave
  end if

  set the locV of sprite 7 to the locV ¬
  of sprite 7 - 20
  set the locH of sprite 7 to the locH ¬
  of sprite 7 + xinc
  updateStage
  if sprite 7 within 4 then
    set the visible of sprite 7 to false
    put value (the text of cast "Hits") ¬
    + 1 into cast "Hits"
    doExplode
```

```
      wait 300
      initDuck
      exit repeat
   end if

 end repeat
```

This is the animation loop. Twenty bullets are drawn if no collision occurs (repeat with i = 1 to 20).

In developing the game, I realized that the duck and wave had to move when the bullet was fired; otherwise, it looked really dumb. But if I called moveDuck and moveWave with every move of the bullet, the animation slowed to a snail's pace.

The mod operator is a variant of division, except that it reports a 0 if there is no remainder and a 1 if there is a remainder. Thus, 1 mod 2 = 1 (because there is a remainder), whereas 2 mod 2 = 0 (because there is no remainder). The result? The duck and wave move only every other time. There are all sorts of ways to modify this algorithm to make the bullet, duck, and wave move differentially. This simple mod operator, however, works pretty well.

Next, the bullet is drawn on the stage with the vertical location (locV) fixed at 20 pixels and the horizontal position (locH) based on its current position + the value of xinc (which was predetermined by the gun angle).

The next section of doBullet checks for a collision between the duck (sprite 4) and the bullet (sprite 7). If this condition evaluates to true:

The bullet is hidden.

The value of Hits is incremented.

The handler doExplode is called.

The handler wait is called with a parameter of 200.

A new duck is made.

The repeat loop is exited. There's no reason to move the bullet if it has hit the duck.

```
set the puppet of sprite 7 to false
set the visible of sprite 7 to false
puppetSound 0
```

Unpuppet the bullet, make it invisible, and turn off the puppetSound.

```
end
```

End the doBullet handler.

I realize that this routine is a lot to take in, but we've seen almost all of these keywords and commands in simpler settings. They function the same here. Take things step by step and explore alternate values:

Try changing the numbers assigned to xinc and see what happens.

Try changing the vertical increment from 20 to some other value.

Try moving the wave and duck more or less frequently.

Try **not** moving the wave.

Making the Explosion

Compared to doBullet, doExplode is simple:

```
on doExplode
  puppetSound "Hit.aiff"
    repeat with i = 15 to 19
      set the castNum of sprite 4 to i
      updateStage
  end repeat
end
```

First, play the collision sound. Then, in a repeat loop, set the cast number of the duck sprite to the exploding ducks (cast numbers 15 to 19), updating the stage with each cast switch. I'm using the loop counter, i, here to hold the changing duck cast numbers.

Waiting

Director has a delay command that serves to slow the playback head by waiting a defined number of ticks (ticks are 1/60th of a second) between frames. Delay works wonderfully for lots of purposes, but like pause, it has a drawback when working with Lingo. The playback head must be moving. In the doBullet handler, the playback head is not moving—not until it finishes the doBullet handler, returns to the moveGun handler (which is called doBullet), then does moveDuck and moveWave, and finally ends the exitFrame handler that started the whole thing off. So delay won't work here.

The problem is that if you don't stop for a bit, the play goes too fast. The duck starts moving immediately, and there's no time to appreciate the fact that you hit the target. So I concocted "wait" to stop for a second and let the player catch his or her breath.

Here's wait:

```
on wait n
  startTimer
  repeat while the timer < n
  end repeat
end
```

The parameter n means that you must call wait by specifying the number of ticks to make the pause—something like wait 300. This value is plugged into n and used in the handler.

The startTimer keyword resets Director's internal clock to 0, whereas the property "the timer" reports the number of ticks the clock has counted. Thus, the repeat loop continues until the internal clock is equal to or greater less than the number of ticks specified (in this case, 300). You must reset the timer for this handler to work.

This handler is not a panacea. While wait is executing, Director is doing nothing else but counting; you're virtually locked out. Rollovers won't happen, for example. So if you must keep interactivity in a movie while there is a pause, you must find a way to use delay or puppetTempo, both of which require a moving playback head.

And that's how you might write a simple arcade game in Lingo!

Enhancing the Game

The hardest part of creating arcade games in development systems like Director is the overhead imposed by Director itself. Director is doing a lot of stuff over which you have no control, so making an arcade game move fast and be responsive is a major problem.

In toying with this game to improve performance, I discovered that the largest performance penalty is from the front-most wave. If you "comment out" all references to moveWave, the game moves much faster. By "comment out," I mean place the comment mark ("--") in front of the lines that call doWave—in frame 2 of the Script Channel and in doBullet (the if mod statement).

There's not much you can do about this type of performance hit except redesign your game. The wave is a large bit map, and drawing it on stage with Matte or Background Transparent Ink (as it must be drawn) takes some computing time.

But there are several things you can do to improve this game:

Provide a duck exploding in a different direction so that the duck explodes in the direction it is traveling.

Make different targets that are randomly chosen. In a real shooting gallery there are lots of types of targets.

Provide a "Start" and "End" sequence so that the player is not immediately thrown into the game, has a limited number of bullets, and is offered his or her reward at the end. Maybe a teddy bear? And, of course, a chance to play again.

Add a second target.

Command Summary

exit
> Returns control to the calling handler, stopping execution of the current handler.

> Example:

> `exit`

delay *nTicks*
> Stops the playback head for nTicks. Ticks are 1/60th of a second.

> Example:

> `delay 60`

> *Note: Delay will not work if the playback head is paused or if a handler is executing.*

nothing
> Does nothing.

> Example:

> `when keyDown then nothing`

> *Note: This command is used most often in conjunction with the when keyword.*

startTimer
> Resets Director's internal clock to 0. Usually used in conjunction with the timer property.

> Example:

> `startTimer`

the timer

Returns number of ticks since the timer was reset.

Example:

```
if the timer > 300 then go to frame "Time
Out"
```

value (*string*)

Returns a numeric value for the string. If the string contains non-numeric characters, a 0 is returned.

Example:

```
put value ("123") into countDown
```

when *message* then *commandOrHandler*

Sets up an event trap such that when the message is sent, the specified command or handler is executed.

Examples:

```
when timeOut then go to frame "Time Out"
when mouseInMe then beep
```

Where mouseInMe is a message sent by another handler you've created.

Note: A common error is to forget to discontinue the event trap when you jump to a part of your movie that no longer requires it. To "turn off" the event trap, use:

```
when timeOut then nothing
```

Section 3 ◆ Getting Hyper

Many applications, especially those with educational goals, require you to work with text data—strings. This section concentrates on Lingo's data-manipulation capabilities, especially for strings, lists, and files, and ends with a hypertext application.

9 ◆ Strings and Things

A string is simply a programmer's nickname for "string of characters." In other words, text. Lingo offers a full set of string-manipulation commands that we'll explore in this chapter in a simple animal game and a poetry generator.

A string is defined as a set of characters, but Lingo commands and variables are also sets of characters. To distinguish strings from other programming elements, strings are delimited with quotation marks. Thus, "abc" is a string, whereas abc could be either a Lingo command, a keyword, a handler, or a variable.

Let's start with a little game.

Animal Game

I'm stretching a bit to call this little movie a game, but it could be the *start* of an educational game for young folk.

Open Animal.dir from the Chap9 folder of the companion CD-ROM and play the movie. Type "kangaroo" and press Return. You're rewarded with a little animation. Click to go back to the first screen. Type another animal name (or misspell kangaroo) and you're given a "wrong" message.

Bring out the Score Window and let's look it. The score is divided into three segments—the starting screen, the section containing the animation for a correct answer, and the section for the wrong answer. The Start segment and the Wrong segment could have been one frame long, but I thought that eventually I might want some type of animation in these segments, so I made them several frames long.

To be frank, I don't know why I left channel 1 open. Perhaps when I made this movie—a while ago—I intended to put in a backdrop.

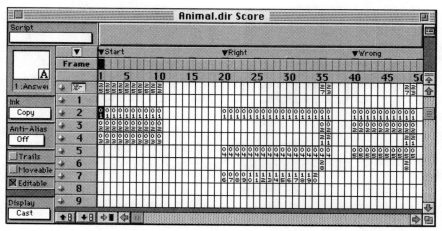

Channel 2, you'll note, contains a text cast member—a field—that has been checked as editable on the left side of the Score Window. This is the typing area.

Select the field in the Cast Window; it's cast 1. Click on the blue Information Button at the top of the screen. Note that this is a fixed-sized field—the best choice for user-input fields (otherwise, your field would resize itself).

Open Animal1.dir. This is the same movie, without the scripts.

First, you need to make the initial loop, keeping the playback head in frames 1 through 10 until the user presses Return. So open the Script Channel of frame 10 and enter this:

```
on exitFrame
  go to frame "Start"
end
```

While you are looping, add the loops to send the playback head back to the Start segment after the Right and Wrong segments. Click on the Script Channel of frame 36 and select your new exitFrame script from the script pop-up at the upper left-hand corner of the Score Window. Repeat the process for the Script Channel of frame 49.

You'll also need a go to frame command at the ends of the Right and Wrong segments of the movie to return the player to the Start segment.

There are a couple of ways you could do this. Initially I used the Tempo Channel, but, as this is a book on Lingo programming, I wanted a Lingo solution. It happens that one of my favorite interactive tricks is perfect here.

Select the Script Channel of frame 35 and enter the following:

```
on exitFrame
  pause
end
```

Pause will stop the playback head on frame 35. This command may not be the best choice here, but for this movie it works. See the sidebar "The Pause that Refreshes" in Chapter 1 for more information.

Now you have to get the playback head moving again—when the player clicks the mouse. Select frame 35, channel 6. You'll see this is a hollow rectangle drawn with the Tools Menu. It overlays the entire frame, meaning it is in the highest-numbered channel. Recall how messages are passed through stage elements—if this rectangle is scripted to "trap" the mouse-Up message, the message will end there.

Double click on frame 35, channel 6 in the Score Window; this opens the Cast Info dialog box. Click on the Script Button and enter the following:

```
on mouseUp
  continue
end
```

All our looping and go to Frame Scripts are now in place.

Try it! The movie already sort of works ... you can type in the field. But pressing Return does not evaluate your answer; you'll have to write code to do that. If you manually move the playback head into the Right and Wrong segments, though, the movie does pause on frame 35 ... and jumps back to the Start segment on a mouse click.

Easy for him to say, I hear some of you thinking! How did I know to make it loop this way? When I am developing the concept for an interactive movie, I construct diagrams that are somewhere in-between the storyboards used by film and video folk and the flowcharts used by computer programmers. So the answer to the question is planning. See the sidebar "Planning for Interactivity" for more information.

Working the Text

The editable property brings most of the text editing conventions of the Mac or Windows toolboxes into play. You don't have to write code to make the Delete or Backspace key work or to make a double click select a word, and so on.

You can make a field editable a couple of ways. You can select the sprite, across the desired frames, and use the checkbox at the left of the Score Window, as I did here. You can open the Cast Info dialog box and click on the editable checkbox. Finally, you can do it from Lingo with a statement like this:

```
set the editableText of cast 1 to true
```

For this movie, the Score Window checkbox seemed the simplest as it avoids a couple of lines of code. The field is **not** editable in the Right and Wrong segments of the score, so you'd have to set the editableText property to false when the playback head moves either to Right or Wrong Marker and then set it back to true before the loop back to the Start Marker.

We also have a little initialization to do here. If you save your movie now, the text you typed in the field will be saved with the movie and will be there the next time you open it. This wouldn't be a problem with projectors, as projectors don't save back to themselves. Still, it's a good idea to clear out the field at the start of the movie, just as it is a good idea to initialize all variables.

This initialization code naturally resides in the Movie Script. Open the Movie Script and enter the following:

```
on startMovie
  put " " into cast 1
end
```

Yes, there's a space between the two quotation marks. Director occasionally "loses" text formatting in a cast member. Putting a space into cast 1 instead of nothing maintains the formatting.

By the way, to put nothing into a text cast member, use a null string (""), two quotation marks with no space between them, or, better, use the Lingo constant empty, like this:

```
put empty into cast 1
```

Evaluating the Answer

Now let's enter the code to check the answer. Consider the kind of statement you must use to check the answer. Of the keywords and commands you've worked with to date, only the if/then statement offers the capabilities you need. Its whole reason for being is to make a decision, and you have a decision to make here.

Your statement has to be more than one line of code (if statements often are), and you know here that you are going to check for a couple of things: that the Return key was pressed and that the field contains the word "kangaroo." So let's put our key check handler in the Movie Script and simply call it from the necessary frames. Open your Movie Script. After your startMovie handler, type:

```
on checkKey
  if the key = return then
    if the text of cast 1 contains ¬
    "kangaroo" then
      go to frame "Right"
    else
      go to frame "Wrong"
    end if
  end if
end
```

Planning for Interactivity

Producers of film, video, and slide presentations traditionally create a storyboard of their project. These are thumbnail sketches of what a scene or frame will look like, accompanied, perhaps, by a brief description or maybe even dialog. Since these media are linear, there is little or no need to indicate branching or looping, although if these actions are required (in a slide presentation, for example), they can be shown by a couple of annotated arrows.

Director's score can be viewed as a kind of storyboard in that you build a presentation screen by screen—there is no "notation" for the logic your interactive needs might superimpose on the set of screens. Director has been used, for many years now, to storyboard or prototype everything from TV commercials to Hollywood movies.

Programmers, on the other hand, especially those who have been traditionally trained, often create flowcharts. Each element of the flowchart represents a specific process. A diamond, for example, represents a decision, an if statement in most languages. Over the years, several different types of flowcharts have been in vogue, but they all follow the same basic template.

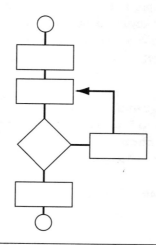

MacroMedia's other multimedia product, Authorware, in fact, uses a modified flowchart approach to the development process. To actually see your presentation, you switch into an entirely different mode.

For interactive multimedia design, both types of planning charts have their use. A storyboard can help you conceptualize the overall look of a piece and even indicate much of the interactivity by using lots of annotations. A flowchart, on the other hand, helps you solidify the logic behind your design and identify the programming elements you require.

When it comes to actually writing the code, you may find flowcharts useful for identifying specific handlers you need, maybe to the extent of flowcharting the actual lines of code a handler requires. Director, however, is message-based, so traditional line-by-line flowcharts don't work very well. A well-written handler can be used over and over again from all parts of your movie (even from other movies if you take advantage of the Shared.dir movie). Variable and handler names can be long and self-explanatory.

Newer flowcharting methods designed specifically for object-oriented programming may work better, but, again, a well-written handler should be small and compact, breaking out stand-alone code into a handler of its own. With a little experience, you'll find that 10- or 20-line handlers can be coded "on the fly" rather than developing extensive line-by-line flowcharts.

Flowcharts for code and hybrid storyboard–flowcharts for the overall flow of the project, however, are invaluable to document your work. Time and again, I've had to return to a project a year or more later to add features or to take advantage of newer technology. The flowcharts and storyboards I'd made were invaluable to me for documenting the work I and the other people on the team did.

So make that storyboard and annotate it well. Make a rough logic flowchart, detailing the flow and interactive elements. For any particularly non-obvious programming tricks you invent, make a line-by-line flowchart or comment your code extensively.

Let's get this working before looking at it closely. This handler must operate somewhat like your rollOver checks in Chapter 2. You must check for the Return key on every frame of the Start segment of the movie.

Highlight frames 1 through 9 in the Script Channel. From the script pop-up at the top of the Score Window, choose New.... In the Script Editor Window, type:

```
on exitFrame
  checkKey
end
```

You must also put this check on frame 10 so that the keyboard gets checked when frame 10 is exited. Open the Script Window for the Script Channel of frame 10 and add checkKey:

```
on exitFrame
  checkKey
  go to frame "Start"
end
```

Try it! It doesn't work beyond the first time. The problem must be with checkKey because that handler is responsible for the jump to the Right or Wrong segment. Let's examine checkKey and find the bug.

This form of an if statement is called a "nested if" because the inner if statement ("if the text of cast 1 ...") is executed **only** if the condition specified in the outer condition is true. Director's pretty printing makes this clear by indenting the inner if statement further than the outer one.

The inner loop is fairly straightforward. If the field contains the string "kangaroo," go to the Right segment; if it contains anything else, go to the Wrong segment. The comparison operator "contains" is similar to the within and intersects operators you used for sprites.

The keyword return in the outer loop is a Lingo character constant. Other character constants include backspace, tab, enter, and quote—using these keywords is the same as typing or, in this case, testing for the character.

 Don't confuse the constant "return" with the command "return value" we used in Chapter 7. Director can tell the difference by the way in which these keywords are used in your scripts.

Simply checking for the Return key is not enough. The problem is in "the key," a Lingo function that returns the last key press. This function is continually reporting back that the Return key was the last key pressed. You can't "clear out" this function by setting it to empty, so you'll have to make your test a little more sophisticated.

What *other* condition is true when it is time to jump to the Right or Wrong segments? How about a word in the field? Edit checkKey to read:

```
on checkKey
  if the key = return and the text of ¬
  cast 1 <> " " then
    if the text of cast 1 contains ¬
    "kangaroo" then
      go to frame "Right"
    else
      go to frame "Wrong"
    end if
  end if
end
```

Try it! It's still not quite working. The answer is still in the field when it jumps back to the Start segment. Let's clear out the field before looping back to the Start segment. This way when the player tries again, the wrong answer won't be staring him or her in the face.

Select the Script Channel, frame 36 and choose New from the script pop-up in the upper left-hand corner of the Score Window. Type the following:

```
on exitFrame
  put " " into cast 1
  go to frame "Start"
end
```

Place this script in the Script Channel of frame 49—both cells of the score can contain the same script.

Try it! Now your little game works.

Before we move on, I should explain one more thing about the checkKey handler. In your checkKey handler, you used "contains" rather than "equals" to test if the user typed "kangaroo." If you edit this handler changing "contains" to "=," your movie won't work.

The text of cast 1, after you pressed Return, actually was "kangaroo" + return. When you are getting text from text cast members or fields, the returns go along with the other characters; they are, after all, line separators. So if you had checked for an exact match with "kangaroo," it wouldn't have found one.

Actually, it's not a good idea to check for the equals condition in any if statement unless you are positive that the equals condition will occur. Instead, you should test for less than or equal to (<=) or greater than or equal to (>=) or, even, not equal to (<>), as these conditions don't require the exactness of equal to.

This little example exposes a major problem, which has nothing to do with Director. Rather, it concerns text processing by computers. Computers don't have much smarts when it comes to meaning. Suppose you type "joey" or "wallaby" or "wallaroo"—you'll be told you are wrong, even when you know you're right. If you choose to use text processing in a movie, be sure to consider all the possible responses, not just the obvious ones.

Manipulating Strings

Once you have data—either from user input, as in your animal game, or from another source—often you must pull it apart, analyze it, and generally process it before it can be used.

Let's explore some of the more important string commands in the Message Window before putting them together in a movie. Bring out the Message Window and type the following:

```
put "Mary had a little lamb" into lyric
```

Don't forget to press Return after "lyric"—the Return key signals Director to execute the line you just typed. The Message Window is really a command-line interpreter. PC users who have dabbled with DOS should be familiar with this concept.

If you typed this line correctly, nothing visible should have happened. But something did: You've just created a global variable called "lyric" and assigned this name to the string.

All variable assignments made in the Message Window are globals.

Retrieve the string by typing:

```
put lyric
```

and Director spits back the string.

Recall that if you do not specify a place in which to put the information, Director places it in the Message Window.

Try these commands in the Message Window:

```
put char 1 of lyric

put char 3 to 6 of lyric

put the number of chars in lyric

put word 1 of lyric

put word 1 to 2 of lyric

put the number of words in lyric

put the last char of lyric

put the last word of lyric
```

All of these commands should make sense to you. They read almost like English.

There are similar commands for lines:

```
put line 1 of lyric

put line 1 to 2 of lyric
```

but with a one-line variable, these don't make much sense. So let's make a new text cast member so that you can test these commands.

Now make a new movie. Open the Tools Menu, choose the "A" tool, and draw a text object on the stage. Then open the Information dialog box for your new cast member by selecting the cast member in the Cast Window and clicking on the blue Information Button at the top of the Window.

Name the cast member "Song" and make it scrolling. Like so:

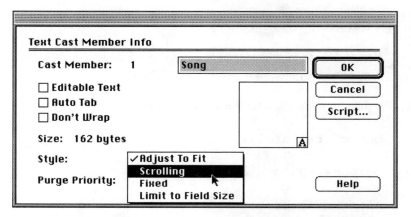

On the stage, you can now resize your new text cast member and enter more than one line of text. Open the cast member by double clicking on it in the Cast Window. Enter four lines of text:

```
Mary had a little lamb,
Her fleece was white as snow,
And everywhere that Mary went,
The lamb was sure to go.
```

And try the following commands in the Message Window:

```
put line 3 of the text of cast "Song"

put line 3 to 4 of the text of cast "Song"

put the last line of cast "Song"
```

Note here that you must use the syntax "the text of cast "Song"," otherwise Director will give you an error. Cast members are not strings, they're cast members. So you must reference the text property of the cast member. Alternately, wherever you want to access the text of a cast member, you can use the keyword field. Like so:

```
put line 3 of field "Song"
```

But there's a subtle difference between the syntax of these two commands. Try this. Make a quick button using the Tools Menu. Double click on your new button in the Cast Window and put the words "Test Button" onto the button. Click on the blue "i" button at the top of the Text Editor Window and enter "Button" as its name.

If the Message Window is visible, you may have a hard time typing the contents of a button on the stage ... your typing may appear in the Message Window rather than in the button. Either put the Message Window away, activate another window, like the Cast Window, or double click on the button in the Cast Window to open a Text Editing Window.

Try this in the Message Window:

```
put the text of cast "Button"

put field "Button"
```

The generalized version "the text of cast ..." works, whereas Director does not recognize the button as a field and gives you an error message. But

```
put field 2
```

works ... if your button is in cast 2.

Because of this inconsistent behavior, I tend to avoid using the keyword field and stick with "the text of cast ..." instead.

You've already used "contains." The other comparison operator for strings is "starts."

Try these in the Message Window:

```
put field "Song" contains "lamb"

put field "Song" contains "Snow"
```

```
put field "Song" contains "bird"

put field "Song" starts "Mary"

put field "Song" starts "mary"

put field "Song" starts "The"
```

Recall that Lingo uses a "1" for true and a "0" for false. The first two of these commands report true and the third, false. The first and third answers are no surprise. The second answer seems wrong—the field contains "snow" **not** "Snow." In the case of string operations, Director is case insensitive. That is, it does not take capitalization into consideration when comparing strings.

If you are translating programs from other programming languages, Lingo's case insensitivity may require rethinking any string processing.

There are two other basic string commands you should understand before moving on to a real movie. Try these in the Message Window:

```
put length(lyric)

put length(field "song")
```

The length function returns the number of characters—including spaces and returns—in the string. (You did recognize it as a function, didn't you? The parentheses are the giveaway.)

Finally, try these in the Message Window:

```
put chars(lyric, 1, 10)

put chars(field "Song", 36, 70)
```

This function returns a sub-string—a piece of the string specified by the two parameters following the string. In the first example here, the function returns the first character of the lyric to the 10th character and in the second example the function returns the 36th character to the 70th character.

And, finally, you can combine these functions:

```
put chars(field "song", 70, length(field
"song"))
```

This form of the function is most useful when you're working with user input as you don't often know how much your user typed.

Let's see some of these commands in action:

A Spot of Poetry

Computers have done pretty well in some areas people consider their domain—chess comes to mind. In the arts, however, especially in verbal art forms, computers have had very limited success. Still, you can have some fun with computer-created "poetry."

Open Poetry.dir from the Chap9 folder of the companion CD-ROM and play the movie. You can see why I call it "sort-of poetry."

Instead of creating this whole movie from scratch, let's study the basic scripts and then add a function to what's already there.

Open Poetry1.dir from the Chap9 folder of the companion CD-ROM. Play it. This movie constructs the basic sentence without an article. (That's the function you'll add.)

Open the Score Window and look at the score. This is a simple looping movie as you've seen elsewhere. The exitFrame handler in the frame 1 Script Channel is a simple "go to frame the frame" script.

Finally, there are cast members for the buttons and the scripts.

Open the Cast Window and look at the cast. Cast 1, "Poem," is the generated poem, so if you haven't run your movie, or cleared the poem, it's empty. Cast members 2, 3, and 4 contain the nouns, verbs, and phrases, respectively. Feel free to add or change these—just be sure to follow the conventions I've used. Simply type the nouns and verbs, one after another, with a space between each word. Separate the phrases, which may have interior spaces, by commas.

We've used the random function several times already, so you should already have an idea about how to identify which noun, verb, or phrase.

The action is in the buttons and in the Movie Script. Select the Create Button in the Cast Window (cast 7) and open its script by clicking on the purple Script Button at the top of the window. Here it is:

```
on mouseUp
  doStanza
end
```

You can be fairly certain that "doStanza" is something I've made up; it's an unlikely name for a built-in Lingo command. Take a quick look at the Clear Button before looking at doStanza. Here's the script of the Clear Button:

```
on mouseUp
  put empty into field "Poem"
end
```

So this, at least, is easy.

Open the Movie Script and let's analyze how the poem is put together.

The doStanza handler is also pretty easy:

```
on doStanza
  repeat with i = 1 to 4
    constructLine
  end repeat
  put return after field "Poem"
end
```

The repeat loop assures that each stanza has four lines. In this loop, you're not using the loop counter "i" as you have in other movies ... it's just here to count. Want random numbers of lines? Try this:

```
on doStanza
  repeat with i = 1 to random(6)
    constructLine
  end repeat
  put return after field "Poem"
end
```

In the loop, something called "constructLine" is invoked. Once again, this is an unlikely name for something built into Lingo.

Finally, the last line of doStanza assures that each stanza is separated by a new line: the return constant. Note also that the code uses the after keyword rather than into.

Play the movie and generate a few stanzas. Then type the line into the Message Window:

```
put return into field "Poem"
```

Putting information **into** a field erases any information in that field, whereas putting information **after** a field appends the information at the end.

The constructLine handler is the real workhorse in this movie:

```
on constructLine
  put randomSubject() & " " after field "Poem"
  put randomVerb() & " " after field "Poem"
  put randomPhrase() & "." & return after ¬
  field "Poem"
end
```

As you've seen, each line of the poem consists of a subject, a verb, and a phrase. So that's what constructLine does: It puts a random subject in the field, followed by a random verb, followed by a random phrase. Note that each of these constructs is built as a function (note the parentheses) ... I did this to avoid having three global variables. But what are those ampersands?

Concatenation

In text processing, it's not uncommon to "glue" separate data together. The official programmer's term for this is concatenation. Lingo's command for this is the ampersand. Try these in the Message Window:

```
put "Micro" & "Soft"

put "A kiss" && "is still a kiss"
```

One ampersand "glues" the two strings together; two does the same thing but puts a space between the strings. In constructLine, the spaces are included literally because of how I constructed the handler. To use the double ampersand, you could rewrite the handler to read:

```
on constructLine
  put randomSubject() && randomVerb() && ¬
  randomPhrase() & "." & return after ¬
  field "Poem"
end
```

I think my original version is clearer and easier to modify.

Generating the Words

The randomSubject and randomVerb handlers are basically identical, except that they operate on different cast members.

```
on randomSubject
  return word random(the number of words in ¬
  field "Subjects") of field "Subjects"
end

on randomVerb
  return word random(the number of words in ¬
  field "Verbs") of field "Verbs"
end
```

This type of complex statement is hard for a beginner to "decompose," so let's take it word by word.

The first command in this one-line handler is return. So whatever is computed in the remainder of the line is going to be sent back to the caller—in this case, constructLine.

```
return
```

What do you want to return? A word—one of the words on your list of subjects or verbs. The word keyword needs a number. (Which word?)

```
return word number of field "Verbs"
```

What kind of word?—a randomly chosen one. Random needs an argument—the highest number it's to generate.

```
return word random(number) of field "Verbs"
```

What's the highest number? The number of words in the field. How many words are in the field?

```
return word random(the number of words in
field "Verbs") of field "Verbs"
```

Phew! Fortunately, you can substitute the put command for return and try all of this out, word by word, in the Message Window. Something like this:

```
put word random(10) of field "Verbs"
```

This under your belt, the randomPhrase handler differs in only one keyword:

```
on randomPhrase
  return item random(the number of items in ¬
  field "Phrases") of field "Phrases"
end
```

Lingo knows a word is a word because it is separated from other words by spaces. Because I wanted to include spaces in the phrases, this handler uses the item keyword. By default, items are separated by commas. Try this in the Message Window:

```
put item 3 of "a horse,a cow,a pig,a donkey"
```

You get "a pig" as a response because it is the third item in the list. The character used as a separator is a property, so you can set the itemDelimiter to another character should you have to access items from strings using other separators. (You could, for example, pull a sentence from a paragraph by using a period as a delimiter.)

That's the basic poetry generator. Now for an enhancement. Let's put an article in front of the sentence.

Articulate It

Let's start simply, if grammatically incorrect. The place to put the code to add an article is in the constructLine handler; after all, this is the handler that makes the sentence. I'm guessing here that arranging this is going to take more than a line or two of code. Start by making a new handler to generate an article. (This approach has the added benefit of making constructLine look neater.) Add this to constructLine:

```
on constructLine
  put randomArticle() & " " after field "Poem"
  put randomSubject() & " " after field "Poem"
  put randomVerb() & " " after field "Poem"
  put randomPhrase() & "." & return after ¬
  field "Poem"
end
```

Now for the randomArticle handler. Type this handler anywhere in the Movie Script. I think it makes most sense to put it between constructLine and randomSubject, just as it functionally executes. However, it could be anywhere, even in another cast member.

```
on randomArticle
  if random(2) > 1 then
    return "The"
  else
    return "A"
  end if
end
```

Try it! You should now have a "The" or an "A" in front of each line. Once again, remember that the purpose of the keyword return here is to send the article back to the calling handler, **not** the constant representing the Return key.

You see what I meant when I said ungrammatical. "A ocean" and "A orchid" is a bit jarring, even in this silly poetry. Let's fix it.

By the way, this method of programming is called "stepwise refinement," meaning you're getting pieces working and then polishing them rather than jumping in and doing everything at once.

Consider when you use "a" and when you use "an." The article "an" precedes vowels. You must find some way to identify vowels so that you can return an "an" to constructLine rather than an "a." This condition should key you into thinking that you need an if statement here; there is a decision to make.

Let's make "pretend" code to see how this command "fits" into randomArticle. Don't type this; it won't work.

```
on randomArticle
  if random(2) > 1 then
    return "The"
  else
    if the first letter of subject is a vowel
      return "An"
    else
      return "A"
    end if
  end if
end
```

Does this make sense? If this handler decides to return "The," there's no decision to make, so the decision to use "a" or "an" has to be part of the else clause of the if statement. Further, it has to be another if statement.

This part's easy. There's something really wrong here, though. To decide if the first letter of the random subject is a vowel or not, randomArticle has to know what word was chosen as the random subject. This decision is made in another handler. Take another glance at your constructLine handler. It is made **after** randomArticle has done its work!

So the first thing you have to do is call randomSubject **before** randomArticle, **plus** you'll have to save the word that was chosen for use **both** in randomArticle and in the put after field statement.

So you could use a global variable. But I want to avoid globals in these handlers so that you have experience doing things another way.

We can pass the word as a parameter from constructLine to randomArticle ... and then onward to isVowel. Try these changes on these handlers:

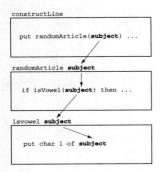

```
constructLine

  put randomArticle(subject) ...
```

```
randomArticle subject

  if isVowel(subject) then ...
```

```
isvowel subject

  put char 1 of subject
```

Flow of data through these handlers

```
on constructLine
  put randomSubject()into subject
  put randomArticle(subject) & " " after ¬
  field "Poem"
  put subject & " " after field "Poem"
  put randomVerb() & " " after field "Poem"
  put randomPhrase() & "." & return after ¬
  field "Poem"
end

on randomArticle subject
  if random(2) > 1 then
    return "The"
  else
    if isVowel(subject) then
      return "An"
    else
      return "A"
    end if
  end if
end
```

This code would be great if Lingo had an isVowel function ... but it doesn't, so you'll have to write one. Try this:

```
on isVowel subject
  put char 1 of subject into firstLetter
  if "a e i o u" contains firstLetter then
    return true
  else
    return false
  end if
end
```

The parameter listed on the first line of this handler assures that whatever appears within the parentheses of isVowel in the randomArticle handler gets passed to isVowel. All you are really interested in is the first letter of this word, so the char function assigns the first letter to the **local** variable firstLetter.

The "contains" comparison operator provides a simple way to find out if this isolated letter is a vowel. Of course, you're at a loss with this kind of test to implement the "and sometimes y" part of the rule for vowels.

And that's it! Try it!

If you are careful in your choice of words, this little movie can generate some fun stanzas. If I were developing this as a "real" movie, I'd want to add a warning to the Clear Button so that the user could cancel the clear command. I'd also want to add a print function, not to mention lots of new words. Since constructLine is isolated, you can develop other types of lines—questions or exclamations, for example.

I first wrote a program like this in a language called Logo, one of whose strengths is processing lists. Here I reworked the code to use strings. Director 4 also supports lists, and that's the subject of Chapter 10.

Command Summary

`continue`

> Restarts the playback head after a pause.
>
> Example:
>
> ```
> Continue
> ```
>
> *Note: A common place for continue is on a button, where the exit-Frame script of that frame contains the pause command.*

`char firstChar {to lastChar} of chunkExpression`

> Returns the character number of the text object (variable, expression, or field). With the optional to clause, it returns a range of characters.
>
> Example:
>
> ```
> put char 1 of cast "Answer" into firstLetter
> put char 1 to 10 of song into firstLine
> ```
>
> *Note: Many Lingo commands dealing with text processing have arguments called "chunk expressions," simply a generalized way to refer to a piece of text. The piece of text can be either contained in a field (that is, a text cast member) or in a variable that holds a string and amounts to a character, word, line, or item.*

`chars(string, firstChar, lastChar)`

> Returns a sub-string of the text object from the first character specified to the last.
>
> Example:
>
> ```
> put chars(Poem,1,30) into firstThirty
> ```

`item firstItem {to lastItem} of chunkExpression`

> Returns the item number of the text object (variable, expression, or field). With the optional to clause, it returns a range of items.
>
> Examples:

```
put item 1 of cast "Answer" into firstLetter
put item 1 to 10 of song into firstLine
```

length(*string*)
Returns the length (in characters) of the text object.

Example:

```
if length(input) <= 0 then alert ¬
"Type something!"
```

line *firstLine* {to *lastLine*} of *chunkExpression*
Returns the line number of the text object (variable, expression, or field). With the optional to clause, it returns a range of lines.

Example:

```
put word 1 of cast "Answer" into firstLetter
put word 1 to 10 of song into firstLine
```

word *firstWord* {to *lastWord*} of *chunkExpression*
Returns the word number of the text object (variable, expression, or field). With the optional to clause, it returns a range of words.

Example:

```
put word 1 of cast "Answer" into firstLetter
put word 1 to 10 of song into firstLine
```

10 ◆ List-o-Mania

In addition to supporting simple data types like strings and integers, many programming languages support some type of complex data types like arrays or records. Lingo's one complex data type is a list. Lists allow you to organize data into meaningful chunks. This chapter will uncover some of the power of lists.

Lists allow you to store related data in one object: the list. You've worked with strings in the poetry movie in much the same way that lists are used. In fact, it's a trivial exercise to rewrite that movie to use lists rather than strings. Although Lingo's powerful string commands can make strings behave as lists, why force an issue? Lingo's support of lists offers an alternative—and more intuitive—way to store related data. Not all related data, after all, is a list of nouns or verbs.

If you have worked in other programming languages, lists are very much like one-dimensional arrays—except that they have their own commands to work with them.

In this section's project, you'll see lists and strings used together with more power than either alone would provide.

A simple list in Lingo looks like this:

```
["cow","dog","cat","parrot","kangaroo"]
```

The square brackets are what makes this a list. I called lists a complex data type because this is a list of strings. You can also have lists of numbers (both integer and real) and even lists of lists.

Lingo supports a second type of list, called a property list. The items in a property list do not directly correspond to any Lingo data type.

Property lists are used in object-oriented programming and will be discussed in Chapter 16.

Information is placed in lists several ways. Like so:

```
set vowelList to ["a","e","i","o","u"]
```

or

```
set vowelList = ["a","e","i","o","u"]
```

or

```
put ["a","e","i","o","u"] into vowelList
```

I could make a coherent argument against using the set command to assign values to lists, but since the language supports both commands, I don't suppose it really matters. Just be consistent ... this is one case where I would not "mix and match." I prefer using the set command exclusively to alter properties and using put for all assignments. 'Nuf said.

List Commands

The group of commands used with lists is similar to those used with strings ... except that, by definition, all the elements of lists are items. (Recall how you constructed your list of subjects, verbs, and phrases in the poetry movie.) So there are no list equivalents to the char, word, or line commands; there's no need for them.

Bring out the Message Window and define a list:

```
put ["cow","dog","cat","parrot","kangaroo"] ¬
into animals
```

Let's retrieve the whole list:

```
put animals
```

Now let's retrieve a specific item from the list:

```
put getAt(animals, 2)
```

And let's retrieve the item number for an element of the list:

```
put getOne(animals, "parrot")
```

The 4 that was returned shows that "parrot" is the 4th item on the list. What if the item is not on the list? Try:

```
put getOne(animals, "iguana")
```

On the other hand, if you try to retrieve an item with too high an index, Director reports an error. Try:

```
put getAt(animals, 12)
```

Then there is a set of commands to construct and deconstruct a list. Try this:

```
append animals, "painted turtle"
```

Notice that there are no parentheses; this is a command, not a function. Retrieve the list with:

```
put animals
```

And there it is; "painted turtle" is the last item of the list.

Removing an animal is as simple as:

```
deleteAt animals,4
```

Retrieve your list:

```
put animals
```

And "parrot" is gone.

Note that before you can append or delete from a list, there must be a list to work on. Further, don't try these commands with strings or you'll get errors.

These are the basic list commands. A bunch of others serve in specialized areas. You can, for example, find the minimum value in a numeric list and even sort a list. But these commands have very specific uses, beyond the scope of this book.

Menuing Revisited

There are, as you learned earlier, many ways to make menus in Director. One very powerful way is using lists.

Open Menu.dir from the Chap10 folder on the companion CD-ROM and examine the Cast Window and Score Window. Here's the score:

The menu frame has each of the three objects, while each of the fruit frames has only the individual fruits and a Menu Button.

This is a very simple menu, but I hope it will give you an idea of the power of lists. Don't try to play the movie yet; only the exitFrame loops and the Menu Button are scripted!

What we're going to do here is create one mouseUp handler that can be placed on all objects on the menu screen and, when activated, will jump to any designated frame of the movie. One handler is all you need, not the many required for simpler systems.

Open the Movie Script and let's set up our list of frames:

```
on startMovie
  global frameList
  put ["Apple","Banana","Cantaloupe"] ¬
  into frameList
end
```

Note the quotation marks: This is a list of strings. This variable, frameList, must be a global, as the handler to make the jump to a frame needs to access it.

Highlight channels 1–3, frame 1 (the objects on the menu frame) and choose New... from the script pop-up at the upper-left of the Score Window. Type:

```
on mouseUp
  global frameList
  go to frame getAt(frameList, the clickOn)
end
```

The global statement allows this handler to access the values assigned to frameList in the startMovie handler. The go frame statement does the work.

GetAt retrieves a value from the list. Which value? The value stored at the number specified by the second parameter, the index. In this case, the clickOn.

The clickOn function returns the sprite number that was clicked on. So if the apple was clicked on, the clickOn returns 1; if the banana was clicked on , the clickOn returns 2; if the cantaloupe was clicked on, the clickOn returns 3.

These happen to be the perfect index values to return, from frameList, the name of the frames.

Try it!

This movie works because the sprite numbers of the menu objects correspond directly to the index value. If they don't, you could use an offset:

```
go to frame getAt(frameList, the clickOn + 10)
```

or, if your Menu Buttons are scattered, you could construct the frameList to reflect the score:

```
put ["","Apple","","","Banana","Cantaloupe"] ¬
into frameList
```

where the apple is sprite 2; the banana, sprite 5; and the cantaloupe, sprite 6.

Using this technique, you only need to keep the frameList up to date, and your buttons will work without ever changing their scripting. Let's use lists in a more sophisticated way to make a little game.

Matching Game

Open Match.dir from the Chap10 folder on the companion CD-ROM and play the movie. The idea here is to match the letters—lowercase with uppercase or vice versa. Click on a circle and a letter is revealed. Click on a second circle and you'll either make a match or, after a pause, the letters will be covered up. You can use the Peek Button to temporarily expose all of the letters.

When you have a feel for the game play, open Match1.dir from the Chap10 folder on the companion CD-ROM. This movie contains the cast members without the scripts. We're only going to construct the basic game here. I'll leave it to you to add the bells and whistles like the Peek Button.

Examine the Cast Window. The lower part of the cast contains a blue circle and the scripts. The main cast doesn't begin until cast 65. Another cluster of cast members begins at cast 97.

These cast numbers were not chosen arbitrarily; instead, they were chosen to reflect the ASCII values of the letters these cast members represent. ASCII (American Standard Code for Information Interchange) is the standard way all modern computers store characters. So the letter "A," in computer memory, is stored as the number 65; and the letter "a" is stored as the number 97. To convert uppercase to lowercase, simply add 32 to the value; to convert lowercase to uppercase, simply subtract 32 from the number (65 + 32 = 97 and 97 - 32 = 65).

A new international standard, Unicode, is rapidly replacing ASCII. Unicode allows for more characters than ASCII, as ASCII's 127 characters are woefully inadequate for today's worldwide computing.

The matching cast numbers are separated by 32. This relationship is critical for the operation of the game—the correspondence of the cast members to their ASCII value helped me as I was debugging, but isn't necessary. That said, there's no reason why these cast members have to be letters; they could just as easily be pictures.

The Cast Window

Open the Score Window. It is also carefully arranged.

Note that cast member 1 occupies all of the Sprite Channels. You'll use Lingo to substitute letters for the lower 12 sprites. The upper 12 are the "cover up" circles. Here they are hidden, as they would be at the end of the game.

Note also the "go to the frame" loop script in the Script Channel.

The Logic

Before starting to write scripts, let's look at the logic behind the game. You already know an important component of it: The cast members are carefully arranged.

But how do you represent these in Lingo? I want the letters, as well as their position on the stage, to be chosen randomly. I've chosen to use two parallel lists. One holds the cast members (or letter) for each position on the stage, and the other holds the sprite number assigned to each letter.

Here's an example:

```
put letterList
-- [89, 121, 77, 109, 87, 119, 70, 102, 78,
110, 81, 113]

put spriteList
-- [4, 11, 6, 5, 10, 12, 9, 3, 8, 2, 7, 1]
```

The first letter will be ASCII 113, or "q." Look in the sprite list. One is the last number on the list, and 113 is the last letter of letterList. The second sprite (the third from last on the sprite list or third from last on the letter list) is 110—"n." And so on.

So this movie has double randomization—the letters are randomized, as is their sprite position, their position in the score.

Now you're ready to write the routines that create the stage.

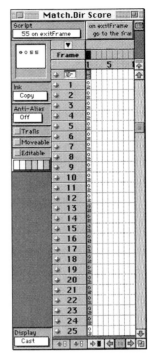

The Score Window

The Basic Handlers

To set up the stage, you'll need three basic routines and, therefore, three handlers:

> First, you'll need a sequence that sets the visible and puppet properties of the sprites. (Sprites 13–24 must be visible at the start of the game, and sprites 1–12 must be puppets.)

> Second, and most involved, you'll need the routines to generate the two random lists.

> Finally, you'll need a routine to assign the cast numbers to the sprites. You could do this when you create the lists, but remember the rule to keep utility handlers devoted to one purpose, so that when you've got the handler debugged, it's done.

All of these routines are really part of initialization, so their proper place is in the startMovie handler.

```
on startMovie
  initSprites
  putRandomLetters
  makeScreen
end
```

That part was pretty easy. Now let's write the handlers that will make this work.

```
on initSprites
  repeat with i = 1 to 12
    set the puppet of sprite i to true
    set the visible of sprite i + 12 to true
  end repeat
end
```

There's an offset again (i + 12)! This handler could just as easily been constructed with two loops, one setting the puppet and one setting the visibility of sprites 13–24 (repeat with i = 13 to 24). However, because there's a clear mathematical relationship between the letter sprites (1–12) and the cover-up dots (13–24), why not use it?

Your second handler, putRandomLetters, is not so simple. This routine will create and randomize both the letter list and the sprite list.

```
on putRandomLetters
  global letterList, spriteList
  set letterList to []
  set spriteList to []
  repeat with i = 1 to 6
    put random(26) + 64 into temp
    append letterList, temp
    append letterList, temp + 32
  end repeat
  repeat with i = 1 to 12
    put random(12) into temp
    append spriteList, temp
  end repeat
end
```

The two lists must be globals, as other handlers must access them (specifically, the makeScreen handler, not to mention the handler that will check for a correct match).

We start here by making two blank lists—one for the letters and one for the sprites. You need to generate only six random letters; the other six are the lowercase "matches."

We're storing the randomly generated number (from 1–26) with an offset of 64—yielding a number between 65 and 90—in a local variable called "temp," meaning temporary, and then using the list command append to "glue" it to the end of the letter list. Then, we'll add 32 to temp and append the result to the end of the list.

If a 1 were generated by random(), the list would start with [65, 97].

This is why you need to randomize both the letters and the sprites. Otherwise, the pattern of answers would always be the same: Sprite 1 would always match sprite 2—not a very good game idea!

Then we do the same with the sprite list, only this time, we must generate all 12 values.

Before you can try this handler, you must program the cover-up circle to respond to your mouse click. Select cast 1 (the blue circle) and open its

Script Window by clicking on the purple Script Button at the top of the Cast Window. Try this handler:

```
on mouseUp
  set the visible of sprite the clickOn to ¬
  false
  updateStage
end
```

You're using the clickOn just as you did in the simple menu movie earlier in this chapter. So this little handler makes the blue cover-up dot disappear, revealing the sprite beneath it: the letter sprite. You're making a sprite disappear, so you should update the stage so it disappears immediately.

Finally, you must write the makeScreen routine to put the letter sprites on the screen. Recall that you have two parallel lists; the sprite number is in spriteList, and the letter value is in letterList. Try this:

```
on makeScreen
  global letterList, spriteList
  repeat with i = 1 to 12
    set the castNum of sprite ¬
    getAt(spriteList,i) to getAt(letterList, i)
  end repeat
  updateStage
end
```

The global statement assures that we have access to the lists we've generated. With 12 sprites, we must loop through the list 12 times. The loop variable "i" provides access to the individual members of each list, one by one.

Recall that the getAt command retrieves the values stored in the list. So the set command here sets the castNum of each item in the spriteList to the equivalent item in letterList. For example, if the sprite list starts [6,2,...] and the letter list starts [65,97,...], sprite 6 would be set to castNum 65 and sprite 2 would be set to castNum 97, and so on.

You're now ready to try it. Play the movie, stop it, then click on the "visibility" bump to the left of the channel number in the Score Window to reveal the letters.

Something is wrong. Because you have a randomization routine here, it's really hard to figure out what might be wrong. In fact, your first run may have worked. If so, try it again. As written, this routine has a fatal flaw. Printing out the two lists might let you find it.

Bring out the Message Window and print the two lists with the put command. Here's mine (yours will be different):

```
put letterList
-- [73, 105, 74, 106, 85, 117, 69, 101, 81,
113, 67, 99]
```

```
put spriteList
-- [7, 10, 5, 7, 8, 5, 5, 9, 3, 2, 3, 6]
```

As it happens, this letterList is OK, but look at the spriteList. Sprites 7, 5, and 3 are repeated ... 5 is repeated three times! The same error could have been in letterList, and may have been in yours. Duplicates in either letterList or spriteList prevent this movie from playing properly.

The putRandomLetter handler, then, must screen for duplicates, and if there are duplicates it must replace them with unique sprite numbers or ASCII values.

```
on putRandomLetters
  global letterList, spriteList
  set spriteList to []
  set letterList to []
  repeat with i = 1 to 6
    repeat while getOne(letterList, temp) <> 0
      put random(26) + 64 into temp
    end repeat
    append letterList, temp
    append letterList, temp + 32
  end repeat
  repeat with i = 1 to 12
    repeat while getOne(spriteList, temp) <> 0
      put random(12) into temp
    end repeat
    append spriteList, temp
  end repeat
end
```

Fortunately, Lingo offers a "search list" command—getOne—that returns a 0 if the item specified is **not** on the list and returns the position of the item if it **is** on the list. In this case, you don't care **where** it is on the list; you only care that it **is** on the list. If it is already on the list, generate another number.

The two new nested repeat loops, then, keep generating new random numbers until the number generated does not match one already on the list.

If you try to close the Script Window to try your handlers now, you'll get one of Lingo's most cryptic error messages:

```
Script Error: Variable used before assigned a
value.
repeat while getPos(letterList, temp)? <> 0
```

Note the position of the question mark. The word just in front of the question mark is the one that generated the error: The problem is temp. Because the repeat loop depends on a value for temp, Lingo can't determine what value to use. Unassigned variables have values of <void>.

If you have programmed in BASIC or another programming language, this error can be very frustrating. BASIC automatically assigns variables in these situations a value of 0. This kind of error would not occur.

It turns out the fix to this error is simple:

```
putRandomLetters
  global letterList, spriteList
  set spriteList to []
  set letterList to []
  put random(26)+64 into temp
  repeat with i = 1 to 6
    repeat while getPos(letterList, temp) <> 0
      put random(26) + 64 into temp
    end repeat
    append letterList, temp
    append letterList, temp + 32
  end repeat
  put random(12) into temp
  repeat with i = 1 to 12
```

```
    repeat while getPos(spriteList, temp) <> 0
      put random(12) into temp
    end repeat
    append spriteList, temp
  end repeat
end
```

By giving temp a value before the loop starts, Director has no problem with this handler.

Try it now! You've got a go here. Now let's add the routines to check the answer and make this movie into something more like a game.

Checking the Answer

First you must decide where to put the check for a correct answer. The exitFrame handler wouldn't be a good choice as the movie is continually looping; the player may not have chosen two sprites by the time exitFrame is called.

You want to avoid a "Check Answer" Button, as this artificially divides the game into a "play mode" and a "check answer mode." On the other hand, if you wanted to give the player a chance to change his or her mind, a button might not be a bad choice. In this game, however, I think not.

> *Don't make users do things just because it is easier for you to program. Consider the flow, and adapt your programming to the flow. You should suspect you're breaking this rule when you must invent a "mode" that must be activated before something will happen.*

That pretty much leaves only one place—the script of the blue cover-up circle. After all, when the user clicks on a circle, he or she is doing one of two things: selecting the first choice or selecting the second (matching) choice.

Without even thinking much about what must be done to check the answer, you can be pretty certain that it will be longer than a simple if statement. (You must, for example, figure out if the first circle or the second circle was chosen.) So, instead of actually putting the checking code in the mouseUp script, we'll just send a message from the Cast Script to the Movie Script and put the actual handler there.

What type of information does our new check answer handler need to know? The same information used to make the blue circle disappear: the sprite that was clicked on.

Edit the Cast Script of cast 1 to read:

```
on mouseUp
  set the visible of sprite the clickOn to ¬
  false
  updateStage
  checkAns the clickOn
end
```

By putting the clickOn after checkAns, you're telling Director that check-Ans expects one parameter. So checkAns is going to look like this:

```
on checkAns n
```

The value of the clickOn will be automatically assigned to the local variable "n." Using a global variable to pass this information, in this case, is a bad choice, as every use of a global increases the possibility of side effects. Further, the parameter here is so tied to the handler that it is of no use elsewhere.

The clickOn, however, is not exactly what you need to have when processing the answer. Review the Score Window. The user clicks on sprites 13–24, but the letters are sprites 1–12. So to make the clickOn useful to index the lists, you must subtract 12 from it.

Now how to determine if the first circle was clicked, in which case nothing should happen; or the second circle, in which case the answer check should happen. There are a couple of ways to do this. Most programmers would think first of a flag—a simple true/false variable that can be used to trigger if statements. Set a flag to indicate that something has happened. But you need to know more than if a circle was clicked on; you need to know **which** circle was clicked on the first time so you can compare it with the circle clicked on the second time. The best place to put this information is in a variable, which you will make work something like a flag.

We'll save the clickOn from the first click to compare it to the clickOn from the second click. This means the variable will have to be a global; it has to hang around from one execution of checkAns to another.

That's the most important logic to this handler. The rest is finding the correct Lingo commands to generate the data we need:

```
on checkAns n
  global firstAns
  put n-12 into n
  if firstAns = 0 then
    put n into firstAns
  else
    put getAt(letterList,getOne(spriteList, ¬
    firstAns)) into temp1
    put getAt(letterList, getOne(spriteList, ¬
    n)) into temp2
    if temp1 = temp2 + 32 or temp1 = ¬
    temp2 - 32 then
      beep
    else
      wait 100
      set the visible of sprite n+12 to true
      set the visible of sprite firstAns+12 to ¬
      true
      updateStage
    end if
    put 0 into firstAns
  end if
end
```

Before this will work, you must type in the wait handler.

```
on wait n
  startTimer
  repeat while the timer < n
  end repeat
end
```

Try it! The game should now be fully functional. Let's see how this handler works.

Look at the indentation of checkAns very carefully:

> If firstAns is 0 (on the first click), assign n to firstAns. That's it; all other statements are executed only on the else condition.

If firstAns is not 0 (on the second click), check the answer.

To check the answer, you have to pull data from the letter list. Which data? Recall that letterList is indexed by spriteList. You need data from letterList, so that's the getAt command. The getAt command requires an index value (which item to get?). So you getOne (which returns an index value) from spriteList as indexed by firstAns or by n.

I normally avoid such double indexing, but in the case of this game it's a slightly tricky, but still elegant solution.

Let's decompose one of these lines command by command, starting from the inside:

```
put getAt(letterList,getOne(spriteList,
firstAns)) into temp1
```

Here's a sample spriteList:

```
[2, 8, 7, 4, 5, 6, 11, 1, 10, 3, 9, 12]
```

If the player clicked on sprite 13, the 13 would turn to a 1 (set n = n - 12), and the getOne command would be executed as:

```
getOne(spriteList,1)
```

and the value returned would be 8 (1 is the 8th item on the list). GetOne() takes a list and a data value and returns the index to that value.

This value is now fed to the getAt command:

```
put getAt(letterList,8) into temp1
```

Here's the corresponding letterList:

```
[88, 120, 84, 116, 74, 106, 81, 113, 90, 122,
73, 105]
```

The 8th item on the list is 113, or the letter "q." GetAt() takes a list and a data value (an index) and returns the data at that position on the list.

Finally,

```
put 113 into temp1
```

The temporary variable temp1 is assigned a value of 113.

This same command is executed twice—once for the previous click (saved as a global in the previous execution as firstAns) and once for the current click (in n). Temp1 is the result of the first click, and temp2 is the result of the current click.

If these values match, they will be 32 apart. Thus:

```
if temp1 = temp2 + 32 or temp1 = temp2 - 32
then
  beep
else
  do stuff when there's no match
end if
  put 0 into firstAns
```

Note the or in the if statement here: You don't know if the player has clicked first on a lowercase letter or on an uppercase letter. You must, therefore, check each condition, and if **either** is true, they match. If they do match, Director beeps and jumps over all the rest to end if.

If they don't match, you want to wait a bit (100 ticks). Remember wait? See Chapter 8 for a discussion of this handler.

You may have noticed here that I'm using "n" in both checkAns and in wait. This is not a problem, as n is a local *variable and the parameter 100 is not assigned to n until Director starts executing wait. The value of n in checkAns is maintained separately. If n were a global, that'd be another story.*

Next, make the cover-up sprites (sprites n + 12) visible again and update the stage.

This movie is more sophisticated than most beginners would probably attempt as an original movie. However, I hope you grasp the organization of the handlers and the logic of the game, even if you could not invent such a game on your own.

You can adapt these handlers to other matching-type projects involving pictures or words—maybe synonyms or a bilingual game with French and English words. Just keep the objects that match 32 cast members apart ... and you've got a game!

Command Summary

append *list, value*
Places the designated value at the end of the specified list.

Example:

```
append bookList, "Interview with the Vampire"
```

Note: The list must exist before you can append to it.

the clickOn
Returns the sprite number that was clicked on.

Example:

```
if the clickOn = 1 then go frame "Menu"
```

deleteAt *list, index*
Removes the designated value from the specified list.

Example:

```
deleteAt bookList, 2
```

Note: The list must exist before you can delete from it, and the index value must be no larger than the number of items on the list.

getAt(*list, index*)
Returns the value stored at item index on the list.

Example:

```
put getAt(booklist, 1)
```

Note: The index value must be no larger than the number of items on the list.

getOne(*list, value*)

Returns the index value where the specified value is on the list.

Example:

```
put getOne(booklist, "Interview with the
Vampire")
```

Note: Returns a 0 if the value is not on the list.

11 ◆ File It

Many movies must save information to a file. An educational movie might store a student's name and his or her score in that movie, a marketing movie might contain a questionnaire that is saved to disk for later scrutiny, and almost every commercial game allows you to save your place so that you don't have to start from scratch should you want to stop playing for awhile.

Lingo, itself, has no built-in file capabilities. Instead, these are implemented as an external command. External commands (XOBJs) are written in C or another programming language to specifications provided by MacroMedia. "Hooks" inside Director allow these external commands to be called, to receive data from Director, and to pass data back to Director. If you have used Photoshop plug-ins or Quark-XPress extensions, you should be familiar with the concept.

As shipped, Director for the Macintosh contains, internally, three external command libraries: FileIO, XCMDGlue, and SerialPort. Director for Windows contains only the FileIO library. The concept of an internal, external library is kind of weird, but that's how MacroMedia chose to include these functions.

Chapter 16 deals specifically with working external commands. Here we'll cover the basics of creating, writing to, and reading a text file.

Finding Your Way

The first thing you have to be concerned about when working with files is where the files are located on the disk. I'm sure you've saved something quickly, without looking at the Save dialog box, only to discover later that you can't find it. It's inside some folder, somewhere.

By default, Director looks for files only in the folder containing the current movie. This includes linked pictures, digital video, and sounds as well as external commands—in fact, all external data.

The location of a file on a disk is called its "path." On the Macintosh, the path elements are separated by colons; on the PC, by backslashes. A full path name always includes the volume (hard disk, floppy disk, CD-ROM, whatever) name or, on the PC, letter (a:). To retrieve the path name Director is currently using, use the pathName function. Bring out the Message Window and try this:

```
put the pathName
```

Director's response, in the Message Window, is the full path name of the current movie.

> If you make a new movie and don't save it, the path name will be the path name of the previous movie.

> If you have just started Director and have not saved your movie, the path name will be the path name of the Director application. (Unless you've set your operating system to save to a default folder.)

You can retrieve and manipulate this path name as a string. Try this in the Message Window:

```
put the pathName into where
```

then, on the Macintosh:

```
set the itemDelimiter to ":"
```

or on the PC:

```
set the itemDelimiter to "\"
```

then:

```
put item 1 of where
```

The itemDelimiter property tells Lingo which character to use to separate items in a string. By default, Lingo uses a comma (as we used in the strings in Chapter 10). Be careful with this; typing the command in the Message Window changes the itemDelimiter for your entire Director session—it won't revert to a comma until you quit and restart Director or until you reset the value with:

```
set the itemDelimiter to ","
```

If you change the itemDelimiter, you should restore it to a comma in your movie's stopMovie handler.

Notice that the pathName function does not include the name of the movie; instead, it ends with the delimiter. You can retrieve the current movie's name with:

```
put the movie
```

You cannot set the pathName to a suitable value; it's a function, not a property (even if the "the" makes it look like a property). But in all file commands, you can include a full path name so you can write or read anywhere on a mounted volume.

XOBJs Basics

Director interfaces with XOBJs as if they were a hybrid between a user-defined function and a variable. That is, you first access the XOBJ using the put or set command, something like this:

```
set name = XOBJ(nNew,parameters)
```

You then use *name* to access the XOBJ as if it were a function, something like this:

```
put name(command, parameters) into theData
```

If an error occurs in either statement, the *name* or *theData* is set to the error message (often a negative number).

I discuss what's happening here in greater detail in Chapter 15. For now, these "boilerplate" commands are enough to allow you to work with text files.

File Basics

The process of working with data files in a traditional programming language usually involves at least three steps:

Opening the file.

Writing to, appending to, or reading from the file.

Closing the file.

You don't normally want to keep the file open very long, as a lot of things can go wrong that might damage the information in the file.

In Director, as in many high-level languages, you open a file for writing, appending, or for reading. You close the file by disposing of the XOBJ. The steps look something like this:

```
set readFile = fileIO(mNew,"read", ¬
the pathName  & "file")
```

which opens the file "file" for reading. "mNew" is a fileIO command. Reading from this file looks like:

```
put readFile(mReadFile) into theData
```

Once again, "mReadFile" is a fileIO command that spits the entire contents of the file into a specified text container ... in this case, a variable.

Finally, you close the file with:

```
readFile(mDispose)
```

The fileIO command mDispose closes the file and removes the XOBJ from memory.

Once you get used to the rather strange syntax used to access these XOBJs, using them is no harder than using built-in Lingo commands.

The movie you'll develop in this chapter is a piece of a kiosk or the end piece of a self-running promotional piece. The viewer has looked through the offerings of "Sylvia's Pet Supplies" and is now asked for a name, address, and phone number. I've also included an extra frame to allow you to easily see the contents of the file (and to demonstrate how to read from a file).

By the way, don't try to run this example from the CD-ROM; it won't work. (You cannot write to a CD-ROM, so you'll get an error.)

Copy the Chap11 folder of the companion CD-ROM to your hard disk. Open File.dir in this folder; this is the final movie. Play it and get a feel for how it works. On the first screen, type some information into the name, address, and phone fields—you must enter information in each field. Then click on the OK Button. There's a slight pause as Director creates a data file (or opens an existing one). The second frame, in a kiosk movie, would probably thank the viewer and then loop back to the beginning of the movie ... the teaser screen. Here, though, I've provided a button—Check File—to take you to another screen to allow you to see the data saved to the file. Just click on the Read File Button.

And now for something a little different: a digression into database territory.

Information in databases is generally organized into records. Records are chunks of data that relate to one individual, item, or whatever. In our little data file, then, a record comprises a person's name, address, and phone number. Records, then, are divided into fields. So in our database, a person's name is a field, as is his or her address and phone. In a real database, you'd probably break the name down into first name and last name; the address into street address, city, state, and ZIP; and the phone into area code and number. This way you can easily sort by area code to find, for example, all individuals living in area code 203.

If you have a kiosk or promotional movie to which users must add information, consider carefully how you might want to use this information after *it is collected. Better to err on the side of too many fields than to plop all the information into one field and then have to pay someone to divide your file into meaningful chunks after the fact.*

The fileIO commands offer no method of organizing the information into records or fields. You must impose order by how you write the file. Database XOBJs are among the most popular XOBJs for Director. Using one of these instead of the built-in fileIO will provide you with far superior database capabilities. That said, the fileIO library provides enough power for the vast majority of Director movies.

Analyzing the Movie

Open File1.dir from the Chap11 folder of the companion CD-ROM. This is the movie with no Movie Script. I've left the button and the Frame Scripts intact; you should already have a good handle on how these work.

Let's start by looking at the Score Window:

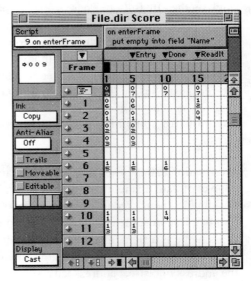

I think it's a good idea to erase information left by previous viewers in movies such as this. Of course, in a projector, this would not be a problem (projectors don't save to themselves), but I like to see the screens that the user will see as I am developing them.

The first frame, which looked like only one frame, is actually two. Since the data entry screen (frame 5) uses the usual "go to the frame" handler to keep the frame on screen, you cannot use the enterFrame handler to empty out the fields. If you did, they would empty constantly as the movie loops, and you wouldn't be able to type anything. As this is a movie fragment, I decided to solve this problem by using an initialization frame (frame 1) that empties out the fields and then jumps to the frame "Entry." You've seen this technique elsewhere in this book. A startMovie script would also have been an OK place to empty the fields.

Here is the frame 1 handler:

```
on exitFrame
  put empty into field "Name"
  put empty into field "Address"
  put empty into field "Phone"
  go to frame "Entry"
end
```

I initially separated this into an enterFrame handler (to empty the fields) and an exitFrame handler to jump to the data entry frame. However, the enterFrame handler didn't always work.

Be careful with enterFrame handlers. They may not work as you expect.

All the other Frame Scripts are simply loops.

The Button Scripts are also fairly simple.

For the No Thanks Button:

```
on mouseUp
  go to frame "Done"
end
```

The viewer must be given a way out, in case he or she decides not to enter the information.

Don't back users into corners that they can't cancel out of gracefully.

For the OK Button:

```
on mouseUp
  if field "Name" = empty then
    alert "Please enter your name."
    exit
  end if
  if field "Address" = empty then
    alert "Please enter your address."
    exit
  end if
```

```
   if field "Phone" = empty then
     alert "Please enter your phone number."
     exit
   end if
   saveData
   go to frame "Done"
end
```

Before going on, you must check to see if the user has entered the information you've requested. The Lingo command alert puts up a simple dialog box containing the message you specify.

Checking for empty is kind of a wimpy way to do this. Phone numbers, for example, have a distinctive pattern. You could check for this pattern before accepting it. For our purposes, though, this simple check is enough.

Note that the error messages are specific so that the user will know which *information is incorrect. Make your error messages as specific as possible.*

At the end of each of the three if statements is exit. Exit, you recall, leaves the handler immediately, so if the name field is empty, this handler never checks for the address or phone number field.

Assuming the fields have been filled in, this handler then calls saveData and jumps to frame Done. The saveData handler will be in the Movie Script, and you must create it before this button will work.

For the Check File Button:

```
on mouseUp
  put empty into field "The Data"
  go next
end
```

The first line of this handler is akin to the first frame of this movie, only this is for you, not for the user of Sylvia's movie. I didn't want whatever you had done earlier to be left in the field. The first line empties the field I'm using to display the file for you, and then jumps to the next marker. I used next because it's been a while since we've used this command, and I wanted to remind you that it's available.

For the Read File Button (on the final screen):

```
on mouseUp
  readIt
end
```

That's simple enough. The readIt handler will be defined in your Movie Script.

Building the Movie Script

The Movie Script, as you can see, contains all of the "action" in this movie. From the previous handlers, you can see you'll need at least two handlers in the Movie Script: saveData and readIt. You'll also need a couple of other handlers to deal with errors.

Here's the logic for the saveData handler:

```
on saveData
  open file for append
  append file field "Name" & return
  append file field "Address" & return
  append file field "Telephone" & return
  close file
end
```

Don't type this! It won't work; this is just the logic you need.

Why append not write? If you open a file for writing, whatever is in the file gets erased. (It's very much like the difference between putting data **into** a field as opposed to putting data **after** a field as you did in Chapter 9.) Using append preserves the information in the file.

Why the & return? By separating each line of data with a return, the separate data items won't mush together. The append command does not automatically add a return; you must do it.

There is a problem with this logic, however: There is no easy way to separate the records—the address field, for example, may contain 1, 2, 3, or even more returns. So I'm adding to my logic a "record separator," like so:

```
on saveData
  open file for append
  append file field "Name" & return
  append file field "Address" & return
  append file field "Telephone" & return
  append file "---" & return
  close file
end
```

If you are working on a PC, you might want to modify this script. For some reason, Apple defined line endings differently from IBM/Microsoft. On the Mac, a carriage return alone marks the end of a line (ASCII 13); on the PC, a line feed and a carriage return marks the end of a line (ASCII 10 + ASCII 13). Director for Windows has no problem reading Mac files, but if you must export your data to another PC program, you'll probably want to add the line feed character, like so:

```
on saveData
  open file for append
  append file field "Name" & numToChar(10) ¬
  &return
  append file field "Address" & numToChar(10) ¬
  & return
  append file field "Telephone" & ¬
  numToChar(10) & return
  append file "---" & numToChar(10) & return
  close file
end
```

The numToChar function converts a number into the equivalent ASCII character and allows you to specify characters such as a line feed in a script.

Many database programs accept "tab delimited" files. To make this handler create such a file, do this:

```
on saveData
  open file for append
  append file field "Name" & tab
  append file field "Address" & tab
  append file field "Telephone" & return
  close file
end
```

With this logic, the **fields** are separated by the Tab character and the **records** by the Return character. (This would be a good structure to use to create a data file to be imported into Microsoft Excel.)

We've been pretty casual about errors so far, and we could afford to be. The scripts in this book have been carefully debugged so that they should not produce "run-time" errors—errors that occur when the user is interacting with your movie. When dealing with files, however, you can't be so sure that a volume might not be taken off-line or that some other error might occur. In commercial projects I've done, error-handling code has been a major priority.

Where in our logic can we anticipate possible errors? Every line!!! The user can eject the disk at any point, so each line needs to contain error checking.

Recall that these XOBJs work like a user-defined function. So if you put the results of the file commands into a variable, that variable will contain the error code, if any. Error codes are always negative numbers, so it's easy to check to see if an error occurs. (Unless, of course, the file you're reading contains a bunch of negative numbers!)

As you might imagine, the error check must be more than one simple line of code, so we'll put it in its own handler.

You're ready to create the saveData handler. Open the Movie Script and enter:

```
on saveData
  if objectp(appendFile) then ¬
  appendFile(mdispose)
  set appendFile = fileIO(mNew,"Append",¬
  the pathName & "DataFile.txt")
  if appendFile < 0 then checkError appendFile
  put appendFile(mWriteString,field "Name" & ¬
  return) into error
  checkError error
  put appendFile(mWriteString,field "Address" ¬
  & return) into error
  checkError error
  put appendFile(mWriteString,field "Phone" & ¬
  return) into error
```

```
checkError error
put appendFile(mWriteString,"---" & return) ¬
into error
checkError error
appendFile(mDispose)
end
```

What sounded clear now looks like gibberish, I know. But as I said earlier, once you get used to the bizarre syntax required by XOBJs, it's not that hard to understand.

The bulk of this script is simple put commands that you've used over and over again. This command is putting the result of the fileIO library's action into a variable "error." Then this error is sent to checkError, where it is dismissed (no error occurred) or a dialog box is put up. We'll get to check-Error in a sec.

The first line is required for all XOBJs. Each time you tap into either an internal XOBJs or load an external, memory is used. You don't want to make a new reference to this XOBJ each time you need the command; memory would fill up, fast if you called it a lot. So this command removes any reference that exists before making a new one in line 2.

The second line, which opens the file, is the required syntax for the fileIO's mNew command—the specific mNew action, in this case, "Append," and the full file name, path included. The same syntax is used to open a file for writing or for reading. (You'll see this in action in the readIt handler.) The bottom line here is that the variable appendFile is used to trigger the fileIO XOBJs to append to the specified file. See Chapter 16 for more information about what's happening in this command.

The next line checks for an error. If appendFile is less than 0, an error occurred, so send this value to the errorCheck handler; otherwise, keep going.

The next eight lines—four sets of two lines—each accomplish exactly the same thing. They send the specific information to the file, appending a string of the specified fields or "---" to the end of the file. These lines are all written as put commands. If there's an error, the error will be returned in the local variable "error." So you send this variable "error," as a parameter, to checkError for processing.

Finally, the fileIO command "mDispose" releases the instance of fileIO in memory, disguised as the variable appendFile, and closes the file.

Now for the error checking. Enter the following in the Movie Script:

```
on checkError error
  if error >= 0 then exit
  alert "Error:" & error & "."
  halt
end
```

The local variable (in saveData) "error" is sent as a parameter to this handler. If the error is greater than 0, no error occurred, so exit the error handler. If the error is less than 0, put up an alert dialog box and halt the movie.

These two handlers make most of the movie functional, but you still need to provide a readIt handler so you can see what the movie actually wrote to the file. (You can, of course, open the data file in any word processing program, but that's a pain ... better to stay in Director.)

Enter the following in the Movie Script:

```
on readIt
  if objectp(readFile) then readFile(mdispose)
  set readFile = fileIO(mNew,"read", ¬
  the pathName & "DataFile.txt")
  if readFile < 0 then checkError readFile
  put readFile(mReadFile) into field "The Data"
  if readFile(mStatus) < 0 then checkError ¬
  readFile(mStatus)
  readFile(mdispose)
end
```

Compare the first three lines of this handler with the first two lines of appendFile. They are virtually the same but for the substitution of the variable name and of the second parameter to fileIO.

The next line actually reads the file and places it into the field "The Data."

But what if there was an error? The user should be informed. So in this handler, you're checking the error after the fact, using the fileIO command "mStatus." This command returns the error number associated with the last activity. I've used a slightly different way to call the error message to show you the versatility Lingo offers. Here, checkError is called only if mStatus reports a number less than 0. Using this method in append-File would eliminate the need for the first line of checkError.

> *Some programmers would argue for the first approach; others would argue for the second. Programming style is the issue. Find a style that makes sense to you, and stick with it.*

Finally, you dispose of the reference to readFile.

That's it. Your full movie should now be functional. But there's one flourish I'd like to add.

A Final Flourish

I don't know about you, but receiving an error like "Error -43" doesn't cut it for me. I said earlier in this chapter that you should make your error messages as complete as possible. "-43" is way too vague.

Open the Movie Script and let's add a handler to make these cryptic error messages into something more meaningful. Edit checkError to read:

```
on checkError error
  if error >= 0 then exit
  alert "An error occurred:" && ¬
  getMessage(error) & "."
  halt
end
```

If you've worked this far into the book, you should recognize getMessage as a user-defined function—a handler that contains, somewhere, a return command.

Here it is. Add this to your Movie Script:

```
on getMessage error
  put error into temp
  if error = -33 then put "File Directory ¬
  Full" into temp
```

```
  if error = -34 then put ¬
  "Volume Full" into  temp
  if error = -35 then put "Volume Not Found" ¬
  into temp
  if error = -36 then put "I/O Error" into temp
  if error = -37 then put "Bad File Name" ¬
  into temp
  if error = -38 then put "File Not Open" ¬
  into temp
  if error = -42 then put ¬
  "Too Many Files Open" into temp
  if error = -43 then put "File Not Found" ¬
  into temp
  if error = -56 then put "No Such Drive" ¬
  into temp
  if error = -65 then put "No Disk in Drive" ¬
  into temp
  if error = -120 then put ¬
  "Directory Not Found" into temp
  return temp
end
```

Each of these numbers is defined in the documentation for the fileIO XOBJ; other numbers, say -41, aren't defined. So these are just passed through the sequence of ifs in the temporary variable "temp." The final return command either passes the number, unchanged, back to the alert command in checkError or passes the error message substituted for the number by the appropriate if command.

Data file manipulation is the most important deficiency in Director. Perhaps Director 5 will offer native Lingo commands to handle this problem. Until then, the fileIO XOBJ provides at least rudimentary capabilities—enough, at least, for most multimedia purposes.

Command Summary

alert "*string*"

Creates a dialog box with the operating system Alert Icon, containing the message in the string and an OK Button.

Example:

```
alert "You can't move the ball to the trash."
```

numToChar(*number*)

Returns the text character represented by the ASCII value of the number.

Example:

```
put numToChar(65) into theLetter
```

halt

Stops execution of the movie.

Example:

```
if i > 100 then halt
```

12 ◆ Project: Alice in Hyperland

From interactive versions of children's books like Just Grandma 'n' Me *and* The Cat and the Hat *to serious adult works like* MAUS *and Minsky's* Society of Mind, *books are the foundation for a large segment of the multimedia market. In this section project, you'll build the beginning of an interactive* Alice in Wonderland.

The key to making multimedia books work is to use the capabilities of the computer to provide features that aren't easily available in a paper edition of the book—features like animation, video clips, audio clips, or reference materials that are available at the click of a word. The computer screen may not be the best medium for reading, but if the material is significantly enriched by the information, multimedia books do work.

The ideas and techniques presented in this project, however, go beyond just creating interactive books—they can be employed in almost any type of Director movie that uses text cast members. See the sidebar "When to Use Text" for more information.

Open Alice.dir from the Chap12 folder of the companion CD-ROM. Play the movie and see how it works. Click on the title page to start, then click on Chapter 1 on the Table of Contents. I've only implemented the first chapter of the book in this project.

Once on a page, click on the buttons at the top right to page forward or backward. If you move the mouse over the text, the pointer occasionally turns into a little lightning bolt. These are the "hot links." Click, and you'll jump to an explanatory page.

When to Use Text

Most professional multimedia titles use text—real text—sparingly, if at all. On-screen type is usually created in Adobe Photoshop or a similar program that can anti-alias or soften the type. Further, the type may be floated, semitransparently, over a background or otherwise fancied up.

You have almost none of these options when using a text object or field in Director. If you use True Type or PostScript typefaces with Adobe Type Manager (ATM) and the printer fonts installed, you are able to use any size typeface in a field. If you distribute your movie to others, however, the playback computer must have the same fonts installed, or font substitution will kick in and probably change the way the text is displayed.

For cross-platform movies, the FONTMAP.TXT file enables you to control the substitution that occurs when a movie developed on the Macintosh is played back on a PC. This capability cannot, however, provide identical font metrics.

That said, there are compelling reasons, as we've seen in this chapter, to use text objects. If you must work with data that the user will be entering, as we did in Chapter 11, or if you want to perform computations on the text, as we did in this chapter, you must use text objects or fields.

Some rules of thumb when working with fields:

Stick to simple faces, like Geneva or Ariel—faces you know most users will have.

Beware of fixed-size fields. Font substitution may "cut off" part of your text, as the substituted face may be wider than the original.

Beware of scrolling fields—scrolling gets tiresome really fast. Not to mention that the default operating system scroll bars used by Director are not the most attractive gizmos. Consider, instead, "paging" your text as was done in this chapter.

Test your text objects on other computers with different font configurations.

Making the Links

Let's look at the cast and score before examining the scripting. The cast contains lots of text cast members—no surprise in such a movie. The entire text of Chapter 1, however, is located in cast 2.

One of my major design goals for this project was to limit the processing of the text. There are, fundamentally, two ways to approach a hypertext project: Include the links directly in the text or create other data structures to hold the text.

Including the links and connections in the text requires the scripts that put the text on the screen to filter out the symbols used for the connections. This is the approach taken by HyperText Markup Language (HTML), the scripting language of the Internet's World Wide Web (WWW). The text for such an approach might look something like this:

> Alice\Alice\ was beginning to get very tired of sitting by her sister\Family\ on the bank, and of having nothing to do: once or twice she had peeped into the book her sister\Family\ was reading, but it had no pictures or conversations in it, "and what is the use of a book," thought Alice\Alice\ "without pictures or conversation?"

The words between the backslashes would not normally be seen by the reader but would be processed only if the reader clicked on the word preceding the link. (On the WWW, these links may reference other "pages," either at the same site or another site, halfway around the world.)

For this project, I chose the second approach, using other data structures to hold the links. The major advantage of storing the links elsewhere is that you need not overly process the text—any raw ASCII text can be input directly into this type of system. To provide the hot links, you then must create the data structures—strings and lists.

Of course, the main reason I chose the second approach is to give you additional experience with data, especially strings and lists.

MacroMedia is working with vendors of WWW "browsers" to incorporate support for Director movies directly in the browsers. A future version of Director, then, might directly support HTML from Lingo.

The hot links in this text are accomplished by lists of strings (implemented as global variables). The list of hot words looks like this:

```
["alice","sister","waistcoat","latitude",
 "longitude","antipathies"]
```

and the list of links, like this:

```
["Alice","Sister","Glossary","Glossary",
 "Glossary","Glossary"]
```

The links here are to frames. The lists are parallel; that is, the link to "waistcoat" is "Glossary," whereas the link to "sister" is the frame "Sister." If the word appears on the list of hot words, the index to the hot words yields the index to the link list.

I considered combining the lists, something like this:

```
[["alice","Alice"],["sister","Sister"],
 ["waistcoat","Glossary"] ...
```

But there was too much overhead in the processing of this list of lists ... it worked too slowly—not in the processing of the link to jump to the page, but in the more time-critical area of changing the cursor to the lightning bolt when it is on top of a link.

Perception of speed is one of the most important user-interface principles. If something takes a long time, you should inform the user somehow—turn the pointer into a watch, put up a Progress dialog box, and so on.

So why change the cursor? The links embedded in the text should not be a mystery to the user. He or she needs to know where there is more information. WWW browsers change the color of or underline the words that are linked to more information. Unfortunately, the way this movie puts text into the page precludes this technique: All text is changed to the style assigned to the "Page" cast member (cast 4). So even if you take the time to color or underline the links in the source (cast 2), when it is moved to cast 4 for display, the formatting disappears.

Another approach to the problem of showing users the links is to place a special character in the text to indicate a link. Something like this:

Alice ■ was beginning to get very tired of sitting by her sister ■ on the bank, and of having nothing to do: once or twice she had peeped into the book her sister ■ was reading, but it had no pictures or conversations in it, "and what is the use of a book," thought Alice ■ "without pictures or conversation?"

But I find this approach intrusive; the text is broken up by symbols that are not really part of the text. Not to mention indirect—you click on the symbol rather than the word in question to activate the link.

So, in this movie, the links are maintained by parallel lists: a list of hot words and a list of links. One word, one link.

Preparing the Text

The source text came from Project Gutenberg, an Internet-based project whose goal is to:

Give Away One Trillion Etext Files by the December 31, 2001. [10,000x100,000,000 = Trillion]

This is ten thousand titles each to one hundred million readers.

The source text is included in the Chap12 folder on the companion CD-ROM. The text is provided in pure ASCII and includes carriage returns at the end of each line of text. I removed these, leaving carriage returns only at the end of a paragraph, allowing me to use the chunk expression "line" to refer to a paragraph of text.

Initially I decided to display two paragraphs of text for each "page" of the book. This didn't work because several pages have illustrations and there wasn't room to put both the text and the illustration on screen. I could have made viewing the illustrations an option, then placed the illustrations in a floating window. (We'll do this in Chapter 15.) But these illustrations are part of the book, so I chose to place them on the page.

Therefore, I decided to make a list of "pages." This list would have the starting line and the ending line of each "page" of the chapter. To navigate through the chapter, then, you need only maintain a pointer to the particular page currently displayed. Here's part of the list of pages:

```
[[1,2],[3,3],[4,6],[7,8],...]
```

So the first "page" displayed is lines 1 and 2, the second is line 3, the third is lines 4 to 6, and so on. The first item of the sublist is the starting line, and the second item is the last line.

Like the list of hot words, the illustrations are also stored in a parallel list:

```
[[],["White Rabbit"],[],[],...]
```

Where the sublist is empty, there's no illustration. Where the sublist contains a string, it is the illustration. Combining this list, then, with the list of "pages," you can see that the illustration "White Rabbit" is shown on the second "page" of the text.

If the project required audio or video clips, they could be handled in the same manner. My gut feeling is that each additional medium each should be allotted its own list.

Making the Book

You might be asking yourself, did he really think about all of that stuff before considering how to actually formulate the movie to present the book? Yes. The way I chose to implement the linking and the paging determined the way the movie had to be constructed.

The Score Window for this movie looks like this:

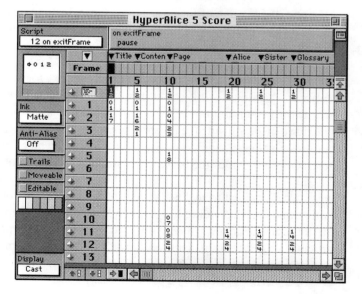

The marked frames make up the major pages: the title page, the contents page, the book page, and pages for the links. Since several of the links "connect" to the glossary page rather than having a dedicated page, there are only three link pages.

Channels 10 to 12 contain the buttons. Other programming is located directly on the channel and, of course, on the Script Channel.

The Script Channel scripts to halt the playback head are identical:

```
on exitFrame
  pause
end
```

The large white rectangle in channel 1 of frame "Title" contains the following handler:

```
on mouseUp
  go to frame "Contents"
end
```

Which "starts" the movie by jumping to the Table of Contents frame.

The field (cast 16) containing the Table of Contents (TOC) in channel 2 of frame "Contents" contains the following handler:

```
on mouseUp
  if the mouseLine <> 1 then
    alert "Sorry," && line the mouseLine of ¬
    field "TOC" && "is not available."
  else
    put line the mouseLine of field "TOC" ¬
    into field "Chap Title"
    pageFore
    go to frame "Page"
  end if
end
```

The function "the mouseLine" returns the line number that was clicked on. Since each line of the TOC is a chapter, this function, essentially, returns the chapter number. Because this project has only the first chapter implemented, I first check to see if the first line was clicked on. If it was not, an alert dialog box is put up and the handler ends. Otherwise, the chapter title (line the mouseLine of field "TOC") is placed into the Chapter Title Field, pageFore is called (more about this in a minute), and we jump to frame "Page."

To modify this procedure to work with other chapters, the call to pageFore requires modification.

Those are the basic score scripts. The rest of the action takes place in the buttons and in the Movie Script.

Paging

As I described earlier, I divided the text into pages using a list. At the start of the movie, the pointer (thePage) that keeps track of which page is on screen must be initialized. We must also initialize the lists containing the major data structures used by the movie, empty out the cast member used to hold the page, and make any illustration still present (from an earlier playing) invisible. Thus, the startMovie handler looks like this:

```
on startMovie
  global thePage, nPages
  setUpLists
  put 1 into thePage
  put count(pageList) into nPages
  put empty into field "Page"
  set the visible of sprite 5 to false
end
```

This handler takes care of everything. Because there were so many lists to initialize, I pulled them out into a handler of their own:

```
on setUpLists
  global hotWords, pageList, picList, linkList
  put ["alice","sister","waistcoat","latitude",¬
  "longitude","antipathies"] into hotWords
  put [[1,2],[3,3],[4,6],[7,8],[9,9],[10,10],¬
  [11,12],[13,13],[14,15],[16,16],[17,20],¬
  [21,22],[23,24],[25,30]] into pageList
  put [[],["White Rabbit"],[],[],[],[],[],¬
  ["Alice & Door"],[],["Drink Me"],[],[],¬
  [],[],[],[]] into picList
```

```
    put ["Alice","Sister","Glossary","Glossary",¬
    "Glossary","Glossary"] into linkList
  end
```

The lists in both the startMovie and the setUpLists handler must be globals, as we will be using them in other handlers in the movie.

With the pointer initialized to 1 by startMovie, then, the buttons to move through the text need only to increment and decrement this pointer to reflect the "page" being displayed. Here's the Right Button (cast 8), which moves forward one page in the text.

```
on mouseDown
  set the castNum of sprite 11 to cast ¬
  "Right Down"
  updateStage
end

on mouseUp
  set the castNum of sprite 11 to cast ¬
  "Right Up"
  updateStage
  pageFore
end
```

Wow! Both a mouseUp and a mouseDown handler! Actually, only the mouseUp handler is required for functionality; the pair, however, provides aesthetics. See the sidebar "Hilighting Buttons" for more information.

The handler "pageFore," in the Movie Script, does all the work here:

```
on pageFore
  global thePage, pageList, nPages
  put getAt(pagelist,thePage) into temp
  put getAt(temp,1) into startLine
  put getAt(temp,2) into endLine
  doPage startline, endLine
  put thePage + 1 into thePage
  if thePage >= nPages then put nPages into ¬
  thePage
end
```

Highlighting Buttons

Director automatically highlights buttons (or any paint cast members used as buttons), so why reinvent the wheel and write your own highlighting routines?

Because Director does it badly.

Director simply inverts the colors of your buttons. Thus, white (always color 0) becomes black (always color 255), but color 10 (an orange in the Mac palette) becomes color 246 (a light gray in the Mac palette). Light gray is probably not the color you want a button to turn to when a button is clicked—dark orange is a better choice.

There are two simple solutions to this problem.

First, create a new palette to represent your highlighted button. Then use a puppet palette, on the mouseDown script of the button, to change the palette temporarily to this palette. If only a couple of colors change, those used in your buttons, this is a good choice, as it takes virtually no memory—palettes occupy next to no memory—and is efficient.

If you are displaying photorealistic images and the movie is set for "true" (16- or 24-bit) color, this approach won't work. So the approach I took in this chapter's movie may work better.

Design two buttons, one representing the "up" state and one representing the "down" state. Then, use the castNum property to set the proper cast number to display the button as "pressed" or "not pressed."

Don't forget to update the stage after switching the cast numbers.

I prefer the palette solution; if you have a lot of different buttons, it provides the most memory-efficient solution to this problem. However, the alternate cast solution works just as well—if you can spare the RAM and if you must work in "true color."

Further, the alternate cast solution allows you to use totally different graphics. For example, a light switch in the down position and one in the up position.

Using thePage (our pointer to the page currently to be displayed), the first getAt command stashes the item on the list of pages (pageList) in the temporary variable "temp." (Recall that getAt retrieves the **values** stored on a list.) Then, once again, using getAt, we pull out the starting line and the ending line. A diagram of the process is at the right.

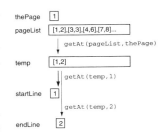

Pulling startLine and endLine
from the pageList

Having retrieved the starting line number and the ending line number, feed these values, as parameters, to the doPage handler. Here's doPage with the lines dealing with pictures removed:

```
on doPage startLine, endLine
  put empty into field "Page"
  repeat with i = startLine to endLine
    put line i of field "Chapter 1" after ¬
    field "Page"
    put return & return after field "Page"
  end repeat
end
```

We start by emptying the field, making a blank page. Then we put, line by line, from startLine to endLine, the lines we designated as a page in the pageList. Two return characters double space the paragraphs. What if there is a picture, designated on picList, for this page? Here's the full doPage handler:

```
on doPage startLine, endLine
  global thePage, picList
  set the visible of sprite 5 to false
  updateStage
  put empty into field "Page"
  repeat with i = startLine to endLine
    put line i of field "Chapter 1" after ¬
    field "Page"
    put return & return after field "Page"
  end repeat
  if getAt(picList, thePage) <> [] then
    put getAt(getAt(picList, thePage),1) into ¬
    picName
    set the castNum of sprite 5 to cast picName
    updateStage
    set the visible of sprite 5 to true
  end if
end
```

Start by making any picture (sprite 5) invisible—you don't want an old picture hanging around while you are drawing the lines of text. Then do the text stuff. Finally, if the picList is an empty list ("[]"), end the handler; otherwise, get the name of the picture "(put getAt(getAt...))," set the castNum of the "picture placeholder" to that cast member, update the stage, and make the picture visible.

That's the logic ... it makes sense. From a programming perspective, however, you may be wondering: Why two getAts?

Let's look at the picList before trying to understand the double command:

```
put [[],["White Rabbit"],[],[]…] into picList
```

This is a list of lists. The first use of getAt retrieves a **list.** (If you've played the movie, you can try this in the Message Window.)

```
getAt (picList,2)
--["White Rabbit"]
```

You cannot

```
set the castNum of sprite 5 to cast ["White
Rabbit"]
```

You must refer to a cast member by a string—its name. So the second getAt command is required to pull the **string** out of the list.

```
getAt (getAt (picList,2), 1)
--"White Rabbit"
```

You can

```
set the castNum of sprite 5 to cast ¬
"White Rabbit"
```

Returning to pageFore, we then add one to the page, check to see if it is out of bounds (thePage > nPages), and end the handler.

Paging backward is substantially the same, yet it's different. Here's the pageBack handler (also in the Movie Script):

```
on pageBack
  global thePage, pageList, nPages
  put thePage -2 into thePage
  if thePage <= 1 then put 1 into thePage
  put getAt(pageList,thePage) into temp
  put getAt(temp,1) into startLine
  put getAt(temp,2) into endLine
  doPage startline, endLine
  put thePage + 1 into thePage
  if thePage >= nPages then put nPages into ¬
  thePage
end
```

Most of this script is the same as pageFore, but note that here we decrement thePage by two before pulling the actual line numbers from the pageList (because pageFore increments thePage before it exits). So thePage variable is set, after clicking the Forward Button, to one page in advance of the page on the screen. To go one page backward, you must subtract two from this. To the right, here's what this looks like diagramed.

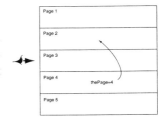

Paging back

That accomplished, pageBack is identical to pageFore.

With these scripts, you have a working book, but no hypertext. The remaining handlers provide this feature.

Getting Hyper

The setUpLists handler has already created the data we need for a hypertext function. We need to find the word the user has clicked on, then feed this word to a handler that will jump to the correct frame based on the linkList (or not jump, if the word isn't "hot").

To trigger the hypertext function, the user must click on a "hot" word. So you should immediately think "mouseUp" is the message to catch. Where to catch it? On the field containing the text. This is the script of cast 4, the "page."

```
on mouseUp
  doHyper word the mouseWord of field "Page"
end
```

The function "mouseWord" returns the number of the word that was clicked on—the first word returns a 1, the second word a 2, and so on. In conjunction with the word keyword, you can pull out, from the field, the actual text that was clicked on. This is sent, as a parameter, to the doHyper handler, which looks like this:

```
on doHyper theWord
  global hotWords, linkList
  put stripIt(theWord) into theWord
  put 0 into which
  put getPos(hotWords, theWord) into which
  if which <= 0 then exit
  put getAt(linkList,which) into whichFrame
  go frame whichFrame
end
```

Let's ignore stripIt for a second. The clicked-on word gets passed as theWord. This word is fed to the getPos command, which searches a list and returns the position of its argument on the list. If theWord isn't found, quit the handler; otherwise, use the position returned by getPos to index getAt, pulling the marker name from the linkList. Finally, go to this frame.

The stripIt handler is required because the text contains punctuation and, perhaps, other encumbrances to making a match between the list of hot words and the word clicked on by the user. That is, if the mouseWord command sends "Latitude!" to the doHyper handler, it will not match "Latitude" found on the list of hot words. Rather than enter all possible combinations of punctuation on the list of hot words, it's more efficient to strip theWord of any punctuation before attempting to compare it to the list of hot words.

While we're at it, stripIt also converts uppercase letters to lowercase. Similar handlers I've written for various projects have also removed plurals, possessives, and (my favorite) from user input, dirty words.

StripIt uses the string commands we examined in Chapter 9, and it looks like this:

```
on stripIt theWord
  put the last char of theWord into theLast
  if theLast = "." or theLast ="," or theLast ¬
  = ":" or theLast = ";" or theLast = "!" or ¬
  theLast = "-" then
    put chars(theWord, 1, length(theWord) -1) ¬
    into theWord
  end if
  repeat with i = 1 to length(theWord)
    if (charToNum(char i of theWord) >= 64) ¬
    and (charToNum(char i of theWord) <= 90) ¬
    then
    put numToChar(charToNum(char i of theWord)¬
    + 32) into char i of theWord
    end if
  end repeat
  return theWord
end
```

The first part of this handler removes any trailing punctuation. That is, if this routine is fed "Latitude," "Latitude" comes out of it. The handler does this very simply by putting the last character of the word into the local variable theLast and checking theLast against a period, comma, colon, semicolon, exclamation point, and dash. If any of these is the last character, theWord is truncated by one character, the length of theWord **minus 1.** Otherwise, nothing happens.

So if a word were connected to another by an em dash as in "that is—a fact," this routine would not work; theWord would remain "is—a."

The second part of this handler converts any uppercase characters in the word to lowercase. Recall the magic number 32—the ASCII value of all uppercase characters is 32 lower than the lowercase. So the second part of this handler loops through each letter in the word (repeat with i = 1 to length(theWord) and using the numToChar and charToNum functions determines if the character is uppercase (that is, its ASCII value is greater than 64 but less than 90). If it is, the routine replaces that character with the same character with 32 added to it, the lowercase equivalent.

The stripIt handler is one of the most useful handlers in this book. Use it often, and use it well.

That's about it. The doHyper handler jumps to the frame specified in the linkList based upon a word in the hotList—parallel lists.

The only other piece needed here is the Return Button on the linked pages. This script is simple:

```
on mouseDown
  set the castNum of sprite 10 to cast ¬
  "Return Down"
  updateStage
end

on mouseUp
  set the castNum of sprite 10 to cast ¬
  "Return Up"
  updateStage
  go frame "Page"
end
```

These are pretty much identical to your Page Forward and Page Backward Buttons: They jump unconditionally back to the "Page" frame. For an explanation of why there are both mouseDown and mouseUp scripts, see the sidebar "Hilighting Buttons."

But we're not done yet. With the handlers we've discussed so far, the movie would work. The text would be displayed, page by page, and the hot links specified in your lists would assure a jump to the correct information.

Showing the Links

Herein lies the rub: The users of your movie should know where there is a hot link.

This is "active feedback" a very important user-interface principle.

If you could color or underline the text that you wanted to hot-link, this section would not be necessary. Alternately, you could lay out each page, individually, using Go To Buttons, much as we did in the Menu Movies in the first chapter of this book. But I chose to make this as general a movie as possible: Feed it text, construct some link lists, and you've got hypermedia.

Given that you can't color or underline the hot text and that I didn't want to insert characters throughout the text, there aren't many choices left. Changing the cursor when it is over a hot link is, perhaps, the best choice.

But how? You cannot put such a handler on a mouseUp or mouseDown handler; it would work only when the button was pressed or released. ExitFrame or exitFrame, ditto. This movie uses pause a lot; these messages aren't triggered all that much. StartMovie or stopMovie are equally not useful. So what's left? Director sends a message when it isn't doing anything else: idle.

Idle is a tricky message to program; it happens a lot. Putting too much programming on idle will slow a movie to a crawl. But a little bit is possible. So the scripts to change the cursor have a home in the idle handler. Here it is:

```
on idle
  global hotWords
  put word the mouseWord of field "Page" ¬
  into theWord
  if the mouseWord < 0 or theWord = "" then
    cursor -1
    exit
  end if
  put stripIt(theWord) into theWord
  if getPos(hotWords, theWord) > 0 then
    cursor [cast "Link"]
    exit
  else
    cursor -1
  end if
end
```

This handler starts by putting the clicked-on word into the local variable theWord. Yes, we've used this in other handlers, but it's local, so it's created anew when this handler is called. If theWord is out of range (less than 0 or empty), then keep the cursor as an arrow (cursor -1) and exit this handler.

Otherwise, strip the Word of punctuation and uppercase letters. Check it against the list of hotWords. If it isn't on the list, keep the cursor as an arrow. If it is on the list (the position on the hotWords is greater than 0), then set the cursor to cast "link."

And that's it. On slower computers, there is a slight delay in the appearance of the lightning bolt cursor—not too much to be annoying, but I'd be very hesitant to add more to the idle handler.

Be careful of idle. It's very handy, but you can easily overburden this message so that your movie runs like molasses. Use idle as a last resort—exitFrame is often a better choice.

Command Summary

charToNum(*string*)

Returns the ASCII code of the first character of the string.

Example:

```
put charToNum("A") into theNumber
```

mouseWord

Returns an index to the word clicked on.

Example:

```
put the mouseWord into whichWord
```

Section 4 ◆ Advanced Topics

The commands, keywords, and data structures discussed earlier in this book are the core of all interactive Director movies. But for that professional polish, you'll probably want to incorporate digital video, custom menus, and, maybe, external commands to provide features that Director itself does not support.

13 ◆ Digital Video

Director supports digital video in two ways: You can import digital video cast members for use anywhere in your movies, and you can export a Director movie in digital video format. Exporting a movie as a digital video file removes all interactivity, so we are most interested here in using digital video in movies.

To create the movies in this chapter you must have QuickTime installed on your computer. Virtually all recent Macintosh computers come with QuickTime installed; many PC computer users have installed QuickTime as part of the installation of a game or other interactive CD-ROM title. The default installation of Director for Windows will enable you to use the movies in this chapter. If you did a minimum install, you must install the QuickTime components to explore the digital video commands.

Video Basics

Unlike Director movies, digital video is time-based. That is, a one-second video assembled at 30 frames per second (fps) will contain 30 frames and play back in 1 second. You can make a 30-frame Director movie and specify that it run at 30 frames per second, but if the playback computer cannot meet this speed, it will play slower. The digital video file, however, will play in 1 second on any computer, even if it has to drop every other frame to do so.

Standard American television video plays at 30 frames per second. Digital video, however, is not limited to this broadcast standard—you can make a video at 15 fps or at 60 fps. Similarly, you can make digital video at any frame size; you're not limited by the size and aspect ratio imposed by broadcast standards.

Due to hardware limitations of most of today's computers, 15 fps is a common frame rate, especially for larger images. Full-screen, 640 x 480, 30-fps video with sound is possible only with a hardware assist.

With the latest crop of PowerPC- and Pentium-based computers, playback speed and frame size are becoming less of a problem—as long as the video is playing from a hard disk. Playing from floppy disks is problematic—the medium is too slow.

Director has a full set of properties assigned to the digital video cast member or sprite to allow you to control how and when the video cast member plays. The most important of these properties are embedded in the Info Window of the digital video cast member.

```
Digital Video Cast Member Info

Cast Member: 1          [ ABCDEF.movie ]         [   OK   ]
Length: 0      seconds
  ☐ Loop    ☒ Paused at Start                    [ Cancel ]
  ☒ Video   ☐ Crop           ┌──────────┐
  ☒ Sound   ☐ Center         │    A     │        [ Script... ]
  ☐ Enable Preload into RAM   │          │
  ☐ Direct To Stage          └──────────┘
      ☐ Show Controller
      ☐ Play Every Frame
        ◉ Play at Normal Rate
        ○ Play as Fast as Possible
        ○ Play at Fixed Rate: [ 10 ]  fps

  Purge Priority: [  3 - Normal  ]
  Memory Size:  42.5 K
  File Name: [ Apollo:...:ABCDEF.movie ]          [  Help  ]
```

The Loop property is similar to the Loop property of sounds; that is, the movie will not stop playing, but will automatically rewind and continue to play. The Paused at Start property is very important for interactive applications, as this stops the movie from automatically playing when the playback head reaches the frame containing the movie. The Video and Sound properties determine whether those components are shown when the movie is played. Crop allows you to cut off parts of the movie by dragging handles on the stage, and Center, which is available only when you crop, centers the movie in the reduced frame size. The Enable Preload into RAM property is highly recommended, if you can afford the RAM space, as movies run most efficiently from RAM.

The Direct To Stage property alters the way Director draws the movie on the stage. You cannot animate on top of a Direct To Stage movie, but the movie may play better. Activating Direct To Stage also activates two additional options. You can choose to show a standard QuickTime movie controller and/or you can activate the Play Every Frame property, which allows you to control the playback rate. Play Every Frame may disable audio to achieve the specified frame rate.

In the Windows version of Director, all movies play Direct to Stage.

Almost all of these properties can be set from Lingo as well as from the Information dialog box, using commands similar to this:

```
set the directToStage of cast 1 to true
```

Note that this command is setting the property of a cast member. Another group of properties control the settings of the digital video sprites. The most important of these are the startTime, stopTime, and movieRate.

Using the Properties

Open QT1.dir from the Chap13 folder of companion CD-ROM. This movie contains a simple movie that contains six frames—the letters A through F—created in Adobe Premiere.

I realize this movie doesn't fall into what most people would categorize as digital video. Why not just do it in Director? Because I wanted an example that would clearly show how to control video.

Notice that Script Channel, frame 1 contains a "go to the frame" command. Digital video, like sound, is not played when the pause command is used to stop the playback head.

Start by examining the Cast Information Window for the digital video cast member. Click on cast 1 in the Cast Window, then click on the blue Information Button at the top of the window. Note that the Paused At Start property is set.

I've included a bunch of buttons for you to program. Let's start with the Play Button. Click on cast 3, then click on the purple Script Button at the top of the Cast Window. Enter:

```
on mouseUp
  set the movieRate of sprite 1 to 1
end
```

Close the window and try your button. The movieRate property is your principal means of controlling the playing of digital video. A movieRate of 1 plays the movie; a movieRate of 0 stops the movie. This is a sprite property, **not** a cast property. (Which makes sense, as the cast member only plays when it is placed on the stage; a cast member does not play.)

Program the Stop Button like so:

```
on mouseUp
  set the movieRate of sprite 1 to 0
end
```

You'll have a hard time trying out this button as this little movie plays so fast. Trust me, it works.

The scripts on the Step > and Step < (step forward and step backward) Buttons should look like this, respectively:

```
on mouseUp
  set the movieTime of sprite 1 to the ¬
  movieTime of sprite 1 + 2
end
```

and

```
on mouseUp
  set the movieTime of sprite 1 to the ¬
  movieTime of sprite 1 - 2
end
```

Try your buttons.

The movieTime property controls how you set a specific frame to show on screen. We're going to be using this property in a much more sophisticated way later on in this chapter. Here, though, these commands step through the movie, showing each frame, one by one.

Note that in these scripts you're using the same type of algorithm you used to move a sprite. You are **adding** to (or subtracting from) the current movieTime of the movie rather than jumping to a specific time.

But there is a place to jump to a specific frame. Open the Script Window for the A Button and enter:

```
on mouseUp
  set the movieTime of sprite 1 to 0
end
```

Close it and in the Script Window for the B Button enter:

```
on mouseUp
  set the movieTime of sprite 1 to 2
end
```

Close it and in the Script Window for the C Button enter:

```
on mouseUp
  set the movieTime of sprite 1 to 4
end
```

Continue for the D, E, and F Buttons using 6, 8, and 10 as the movieTime values.

Try these buttons out. You'll see that each button jumps immediately to the frame specified.

Why 0, 2, 4, 6, ... ? The movieTime property, like the timer function we used earlier in this book, works with time in measurements of ticks. Ticks are 1/60th of a second. This is a 30-fps movie, so each frame is **two** ticks in duration.

Finally, the Rewind Button looks like this:

```
on mouseUp
  set the movieRate of sprite 1 to 0
  set the movieTime of sprite 1 to 0
end
```

By setting both the movieRate and the movieTime to 0, the movie stops and then rewinds. Without the movieRate setting, the movie rewinds but keeps playing—not what you'd expect from a Rewind Button.

Video Rollovers

You can use digital video for rollovers, too. Open QT2.dir from the Chap13 folder of the companion CD-ROM. This movie is the beginning of a simple menuing system. The concept here is that when the viewer rolls over the menu item or the small video in front of each item, the video will play.

We'll use the same technique to check the rollover that we used in Chapter 2.

Open the Script Channel, frame 1, and enter the following:

```
on exitFrame
  checkRollOver
  go to the frame
end
```

Now open the Movie Script and enter the following:

```
on checkRollOver
  repeat with whichMovie = 1 to 3
    if rollover(whichMovie) then
      set the movieRate of sprite whichMovie ¬
      to 1
    else
      set the movieRate of sprite whichMovie ¬
      to 0
    end if
  end repeat
end
```

Try it!

The repeat loop checks the position of the mouse in relation to sprites 1–3 using the loop variable whichMovie. If the rollOver evaluates to true, that movie is set to play using the movieRate property. If the rollOver evaluates to false, the movieRate property is set to false.

I also want the movies to play when the pointer is on the words; these, after all, should also work in the menu to trigger a jump to another section of the movie.

Edit the Movie Script as follows:

```
on checkRollOver
  repeat with whichMovie = 1 to 3
    if rollover(whichMovie) or ¬
    rollOver(whichMovie + 3) then
      set the movieRate of sprite whichMovie ¬
      to 1
    else
      set the movieRate of sprite whichMovie ¬
      to 0
    end if
  end repeat
end
```

The addition of the or clause in the if statement assures that a rollover of sprites 3–6 (whichMovie + 3) will also occur.

These are the basic commands. With these commands, you can do almost anything with digital video, including one of the hardest things to do in Director: synchronize audio and image.

Synchronization

Beyond the seductive nature of digital video, the most compelling reason to use digital video for many multimedia projects is synchronization. If you've tried to synchronize a narrative soundtrack or even music to visuals, you've already wrestled with the problem.

You can carefully lay out the score so that the visuals change on the specific frame needed, where, for example, the narrator refers to something on stage or the music changes. But try and play this movie back on another computer. If you've developed your movie on a fast machine, you'll hear your narrator refer to an object long before it appears on stage. If you've developed on a slow machine, the visuals zip by as the narrator continues at what now seems like a snail's pace.

The latter is preferable to the former, as you can use the Tempo Channel to "lock down" a frame rate and return the audio and video to synchronization. The time-based nature of digital video allows for a creative solution to the synchronization problem.

Open QT3.dir from the Chap13 folder of the companion CD-ROM and play the movie. This is a simple slide show, but the frame advance is synched to the music.

Let's do the programming necessary to make this movie. Open QT32.dir from Chap13 folder of the companion CD-ROM. This is the same movie without the programming.

Open the Score Window (shown at left).

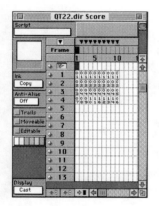

The Score Window

Notice I've marked every frame from frames 2 to 10. It's been a while since you've used the go next command. I thought this might be a good time to remind you of its usefulness.

Channel 1 contains the digital video; channel 2, the text cast member that we'll use for synchronization; channel 3, the buttons (there are three of them); and, finally, channel 4, the text and pictures that make up the slide show.

If you've looked at the digital video, you'll find that this is a mighty odd digital video. There's no video; this is an audio-only digital video movie. And that's the key to the synchronization.

We can request the movieTime of the video sprite as it plays and use this property as the "cue" to advance to the next frame.

Let's start by making a loop, so the movie plays through. Open the Script Channel, frame 1, and enter our usual loop script:

```
on exitFrame
  go to frame 1
end
```

This will hold the playback head at channel 1.

Now, let's activate the movie by programming the Play Button. In the Cast Window, select cast 3 and click on the purple Script Button at the top of the Cast Window.

Enter the following script:

```
on mouseUp
  set the movieRate of sprite 1 to 1
end
```

You have a working movie now. But it's not much to brag about ... the music just plays.

You need a "tool" to determine which movieTime values to trigger the visuals. For this, you're going to use the Director system message we used so productively in Chapter 12: idle.

Open a Movie Script, either by opening an existing script and clicking on the pink Plus Button or by typing Shift-Command-U (Mac) or Shift-Alt-U (PC). Enter:

```
on idle
  put the movieTime of sprite 1 into ¬
  cast "Time"
end
```

You're not going to want this handler in your final movie, but it's very useful here. You could also put this value into the Message Window by eliminating the "into cast "Time"" part of this instruction. But I find it more useful to place the time display on stage at this point in developing such movies.

Close the Script Window and play the movie now. As you listen to the music, the movieTime is displayed on stage. Listen for "cues," pauses or shifts in the tempo of the music, and write down the movieTime for the cue. If this were a narration, you'd note the movieTime displayed in the Time cast member on keywords or phrases.

This process is time consuming! For a demo of an interactive version of the musical "Showboat," the first scene alone contained over 100 cues to scene and lyric changes!

Equipped with the cues, you can now program the frame advances, synched with the music. You'll need to change the Play Button so that it moves the playback head to the next frame.

Like so:

```
on mouseUp
  set the movieRate of sprite 1 to 1
  go next
end
```

And on the Script Channel of each frame, you'll put the "Cue Trigger" scripts. All of them look like this:

```
on exitFrame
  if the movieTime of sprite 1 > n then go next
  else go loop
end
```

In the script, notice that I've used greater than (">") instead of equals. As we've seen with other movies in this book, testing for equals is dangerous; because of execution speed, the movieTime may never **exactly** equal 600. Testing for "greater than 600" solves that problem. Yes, the synchronization of your movie may be off by one, two, or even three ticks. Just keep this perspective—a tick is 1/60th of a second!

The value of "n" changes to reflect the cues. The cues I used in the fully programmed version of this movie were:

Frame	Cue	Frame	Cue
2	600	7	2400
3	1120	8	2900
4	1450	9	3550
5	1910	10	3800
6	2000		

Enter these Frame Scripts. On the Script Channel of frame 2, for example, you should type:

```
on exitFrame
  if the movieTime of sprite 1 > 600 then ¬
  go next
  else go loop
end
```

The script on the last frame of this movie works in this little slide show, but if you insert these routines into a larger movie, you should include the instruction to tell Director where it should go next ... after the audio has played.

That's the core of this technique. To finish the movie, however, I wanted to include a Stop and a Pause Button. These are cast members 4 and 5, respectively. The Pause Button will serve double duty and become a Go Button. Open the Script Window for the Stop Button and enter the following:

```
on mouseUp
  set the movieRate of sprite 1 to 0
  set the movieTime of sprite 1 to 0
  go to frame 1
end
```

Setting the movieRate to 0 stops the movie, setting the movie time to 0 rewinds the movie, and then it jumps back to frame 1. The Again Button is similarly programmed:

```
on mouseUp
  set the movieTime of sprite 1 to 0
  go to frame 2
  set the movieRate of sprite 1 to 1
end
```

Setting the movieTime to 0 rewinds the movie, then jumps back to the beginning of the slide show sequence and, finally, starts the movie playing again.

The final button in this movie is the Pause Button. Open the Script Window for this cast member (cast 6) and enter:

```
on mouseUp
  if the text of cast 6 = "Pause" then
    set the movieRate of sprite 1 to 0
    set the text of cast 6 to "Go"
  else
    set the movieRate of sprite 1 to 1
    set the text of cast 6 to "Pause"
  end if
end
```

Close the window, and try it.

This script contains one of my favorite programming tricks. I've saved it for here because I hope by this time you are comfortable with if commands. The activity of this button is determined by the text of cast 6. The programming of the button assures that this text will only be "Pause" or "Go." When it is "Pause," the movieRate is set to 0, stopping the movie, and the text of the button is set to "Go." Next time around, then, the else statement kicks in. After all, the text of cast 6 is no longer "Pause!" This starts the movie playing **and** resets the name of the button back to "Pause."

This simple little algorithm is useful in many circumstances, as it enables one button to do the work of two. Using bit-mapped buttons? No problem; you can use the castNum property rather than the text property to determine the state of the button.

14 ◆ Polishing Your Movie

The only interface feature we've implemented so far has been Alert Dialog Boxes. Director, however, supports other interface features, including menus and windows. Incorporating these features into your movies can make the difference between a good project and a superb one.

When designing a project, you must consider how today's applications work. GUI operating systems have set a high priority on assuring that the user is in control, giving active feedback and making the computer generally easy to use. If you design a multimedia project without considering these elements, you're in big trouble.

Fortunately, there are several terrific references on user interface issues (see Appendix C) to tell you how your movie should work, and Lingo provides considerable support to aid in the implementation of a good interface.

Menus

We tackled full-screen, graphic menus way back in Chapter 1. Here you'll develop real menus—those that appear at the top of the screen (Mac) or window (Windows).

Creating a menu is as simple as typing the required commands into a text cast member. The installMenu command, then, erases the normal menus, installing your menus in their place. When you are working in Director, the normal menus reappear when you stop the movie; when you are playing a projector, the installed menus remain until you change them or quit.

The menu text cast member must, of course, be entered in with a specific syntax. Something like this:

```
Menu:@
About This Movie ...≈ doAbout
Menu:File
Quit/Q ≈ doExit
Menu:Palette
Standard ≈ doPalette 0
(-
Vivid ≈ doPalette "Vivid"
Metallic ≈ doPalette "Metallic"
Pastels ≈ doPalette "Pastels"
Rainbow ≈ doPalette "Rainbow"
```

The keyword "Menu:" delimits each menu. So this cast member will produce three menus: an @ Menu, a File Menu, and a Palette Menu. The "at the rate of" sign (@) is used for the first menu. On the Macintosh, this will be the Apple Menu; on the PC it's just the first menu.

The slash allows for keyboard shortcuts. The only shortcut defined in these menus is for Quit.

On the Macintosh it is common for menu commands not *to have keyboard shortcuts; in Windows every menu command normally has a shortcut. Director for Windows, in fact, may invent keyboard commands for you, even if you don't specify them.*

The "≈" symbol is typed by pressing option (Mac) "x." On the PC press Alt (PC) and 0197 on the numeric keypad, the character generated by this key sequence will vary with the typeface, but it should be "Å."

The commands on the menu, one to a line, have the following syntax:

```
text ≈ instruction
```

The text is what appears as the menu command, and the instruction can be any valid Lingo command. In the example above, all of the menu items reference other handlers. This would be equally valid:

```
Menu:Go
Next  ≈ go next
Prev  ≈ go loop
Menu  ≈ go frame "Menu"
```

More often than not, however, you cannot squeeze all that you might want to do in a menu command into one line of Lingo. So most menu items call a handler that is placed in the Movie Script.

The symbol "(-" on the Palette Menu defined above produces a delimiter ... a line that is not activated by the mouse. Delimiters are used to separate distinct groups of commands from one another. For example, on the Edit Menu of most applications, the undo command at the top of the menu is separated from the cut, copy, and paste commands by a delimiter.

Open Menu1.dir from the Chap14 folder of the companion CD-ROM. Cast 2 already defines the menu, the same as used above, and the Frame Script loop. But the programming to make the menu work is not included here. Let's do it.

Because I've already listed a bunch of handlers in the menu definition, you know you must provide the handlers: doAbout, doExit, and doPalette. Otherwise your new menus will not work.

Open the Movie Script and enter the following handlers:

```
on doAbout
  alert ¬
  "This movie copyright © 1995 by Frank Smith"
end

on doPalette palName
  puppetPalette palName
end

on doExit
  puppetPalette 0
  go to frame "Quit"
end
```

These handlers take care of the commands your menus will invoke.

Notice here that the doPalette handler takes one parameter, the palette name. That's why the menu command is defined, in cast 2, as

```
Vivid ≈ doPalette "Vivid"
```

"Vivid" is the parameter, the palette name, to be "fed" to the doPalette handler.

All that's left is to actually install the menu when the movie plays. This is the type of thing a startMovie handler does:

```
on startMovie
  installMenu cast "theMenus"
end
```

Try it! You should have customized menus that work. That's all there is to it.

Don't "invent" menus. In this movie, you've created a File Menu with Quit, which is where you'd expect to find a quit command. Some user interface pundits would argue that you should also include an Edit Menu with disabled undo, cut, copy, and paste commands. About this, I'm not sure. However, if commands you implement do the same thing as commands in other widely used programs, use the same menu titles.

I'm still not happy with these menus. In most applications, features such as the current palette would be checked in the menu. Look, for example, at the Font Menu of Director—the current typeface is indicated with a check mark.

Let's add the instructions necessary to put check marks on the Palette Menu to reflect the current palette. Open the Movie Script and edit the doPalette handler to read:

```
on doPalette palName
  puppetPalette palName
  repeat with i = 1 to the number of ¬
  menuItems of menu "Palette"
    set the checkMark of menuItem i of menu ¬
    "Palette" to false
```

```
      end repeat
      if palName = 0 then put "Standard" into ¬
      palName
      set the checkMark of menuItem palName of ¬
      menu "Palette" to true
   end
```

This looks like a lot of code, but it's really quite simple. The repeat loop removes any check marks on the Palette Menu, then a simple "set the checkMark" command sets the menuItem property to true. The only difficulty here is the System Palette. You're using Palette 0 to set this palette ... and "0" is not on the menu. One simple if statement "corrects" the palName variable.

If you try your movie now, you'll find it works but for one detail. If you do not choose a palette, nothing on the menu is checked. But the system palette is being used at the start of the movie. Open the Movie Script, and let's make sure this is the case:

```
on startMovie
  installMenu cast "theMenus"
  puppetPalette 0
  set the checkMark of menuItem 1 of menu ¬
  "Palette" to true
end
```

I suppose it would be better to use the name of the menu item in this handler, but you're in control here, and you know that the first menu item will be the system palette. So it's probably OK to hard code it here. This might be better from a theoretical perspective:

```
on startMovie
  installMenu cast "theMenus"
  puppetPalette 0
  set the checkMark of menuItem "System" of ¬
  menu "Palette" to true
end
```

Windows are as easy to work with as menus.

Windows

Any Director movie can open another movie in what MacroMedia calls a "Movie in a Window" (MIAW). The secondary movie is fully functional, including any interactivity you've programmed. Further, the two movies can communicate with each other in a couple of ways.

We've used the alert command several times. This is a very handy command for a quick error message, but the dialogs created by the alert command have only one button. What if you needed two—perhaps a Cancel Button in addition to the standard OK Button? MIAW to the rescue.

Open MIAW.dir from the Chap14 folder of the companion CD-ROM and play the movie. Click on the OK Button and you'll be greeted with what looks like an animated dialog box. This is actually a second movie. Notice that underneath the dialog box, the main movie continues to play.

The dialog box movie is called "AAlert.dir," and you can open it, just like any other Director movie. Aside from the unusual size of the stage, this is pretty much a plain-vanilla movie: a text cast member, a couple of buttons, and the bit-mapped rotating exclamation point. If you play this movie now, the buttons won't seem to do anything. They only work when the movie is played as an MIAW.

Before programming the main movie, look at the programming on the Yes and No Buttons. They both look something like this:

```
on mouseUp
  global theAnswer
  put "No" into theAnswer
  close window "AAlert.dir"
end
```

On the Yes Button, the variable is set to "Yes."

The close window command does just what you'd expect: closes the window.

In these movies, a global variable provides communication between the movies. Recall that globals, once declared, are maintained until you quit Director or the projector. We'll explore another way to pass information between movies in the second window example.

Open MIAW1.dir from the Chap14 folder of the companion CD-ROM. This is the main movie without any programming.

Let's start with the Movie Script. Since you're going to be using a global variable, you should start by declaring it and giving it an initial value. Open a Movie Script and enter:

```
on startMovie
  global theAnswer
  put empty into theAnswer
end
```

Now let's make the OK Button work. Select cast 1, the OK Button, in the Cast Window and click on the purple Script Button at the top of the Cast Window. Type:

```
on mouseUp
  open window "AAlert.dir"
end
```

Try it! That's all there is to creating MIAWs!

Stop the movie by clicking on the Stop Button on the Control Panel. Notice that the MIAW continues to animate, even though you've stopped the main movie.

Notice also that, upon closer inspection, this MIAW is not exactly correct. The idea was to make this look like a dialog box. Here it looks something like a standard document window, rather than like a dialog box window. (See right.)

Director is capable of making several kinds of windows. The type of window is controlled by the windowType property. Bring out the Message Window and type:

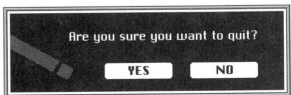

```
set the windowType of window
"AAlert.dir" to 1
```

See Appendix A for a list of windowType property values. Notice that the window type inherits many of the expected window behaviors. That is, if

The windowType property in action

there is a title bar, you can drag the window around the screen; if there is a close box, you can close the window by clicking it; and so on. This is because the open window command calls on the standard operating system window routines. So Macintosh windows look like Macintosh windows and Windows windows look like Windows windows.

Let's incorporate this command into the OK Button script so the window opens with the correct type. Edit the button script like so:

```
on mouseUp
  set the windowType of window "AAlert.dir" ¬
  to 1
  open window "AAlert.dir"
end
```

I find this a little weird—setting a property of an object that does not yet exist. But it works.

Your movie now looks right, but the buttons don't work. There are a couple of ways to make the buttons on the MIAW work, but as you are using a global variable, let's make a handler to check for the status of that variable and call it from every frame (something like a roll over). Open the Movie Script and add the following handler:

```
on checkAnswer
  global theAnswer
  if theAnswer = "Yes" then halt
end
```

Now add a call to this handler to the exitFrame handlers of frames 1–19. Like so:

```
on exitFrame
  checkAnswer
end
```

And to frame 20, like so:

```
on exitFrame
  checkAnswer
  go to frame 1
end
```

Try it! The movie now stops when you click on the Yes Button of the MIAW.

But something's still not right. After you've played the movie and clicked on the Yes Button, bring out the Message Window and type:

```
put the windowList
```

The result is:

```
--[(window "AAlert.dir")]
```

This means that the window is still in memory, but since you can't see it, it is either closed or behind the stage.

The windowList, by the way, is like any list in Director and can be operated on by the list commands you investigated in Chapter 10. Note that the windowList is a list of lists. To extract the name of a window in a usable way, you'll have to use the same getAt, getOnet sequence you used in Chapter 10.

Windows are maintained in layers. Newly opened windows, by default, are "on top," but you can use the moveToBack and moveToFront commands to change the layering of windows.

Since you have no good reason to keep the Alert movie around after the user has clicked on the Yes Button, you should dispose of the movie. Open the Movie Script and edit your checkAnswer handler to read:

```
on checkAnswer
  global theAnswer
  if theAnswer = "Yes" then
    halt
  else
    forget window "AAlert.dir"
  end if
end
```

The forget window command disposes of the movie, releasing the RAM for other uses.

In this movie, the MIAW is forgotten only when the user clicks on the Yes Button. When the user clicks on the No Button, the window is closed, but the movie stays in memory so that the next time it is invoked, it appears quickly.

If you design a project using MIAWs, be sure to consider when a window should be maintained in memory and when it can be disposed of.

 Be careful using MIAWs. Large movies in a window will up the RAM requirements of your project significantly.

Active Communication

Global variables are fine for passing parameters from one movie to another, but you sometimes want to make one movie actually control another.

Lingo, as you might have guessed, possesses a command exactly for this purpose: tell.

Open MIAW2.dir from the Chap14 folder of the companion CD-ROM and play the movie. A small "control panel" window will appear. Click on the buttons on the control panel to move the circle. The buttons on the control panel are telling the stage what to do.

Open Panel.dir from the Chap14 folder of the companion CD-ROM. This is another movie with a tiny stage.

Each of the four button cast members is already programmed. Select cast 1 in the Cast Window and open the Script Window by clicking on the purple Script Button at the top of the window. Here is the handler:

```
on mouseUp
  tell the stage to moveLeft
end
```

The other buttons are similar except that the command being sent to the stage reflects the arrow direction: moveRight, moveUp, and moveDown. You can't try out this movie—the handlers that move the sprite are located in the main movie. So Director will report that the handler is not defined.

Open MIAW21.dir from the Chap14 folder of the companion CD-ROM. This is the main movie with only the standard loop programming in the Script Channel of frame 1.

The handlers you will define, as you've seen so often, belong in the Movie Script. Open the Movie Script and enter:

```
on startMovie
  set the puppet of sprite 1 to true
  set the windowType of window "Panel.dir" to 4
  open window "Panel.dir"
end
```

This handler establishes the ball (sprite 1) as a sprite, sets the proper window type for the control panel, and then opens the MIAW.

Now continue with the handlers that will be triggered by the buttons on the control panel:

```
on moveLeft
  set the locH of sprite 1 to the locH of ¬
  sprite 1 - 10
  updateStage
end

on moveRight
  set the locH of sprite 1 to the locH of  ¬
  sprite 1 + 10
  updateStage
end

on moveUp
  set the locV of sprite 1 to the locV of ¬
  sprite 1 - 10
  updateStage
end

on moveDown
  set the locV of sprite 1 to the locV of ¬
  sprite 1 + 10
  updateStage
end
```

These handlers use the tried-and-true animation technique of adding an offset to the current position of the sprite.

Once you've entered these handlers, you're ready to try the movie. The tell commands in the MIAW are activating the handlers on the stage of the main movie.

You can also send messages from the main movie to an MIAW using a command something like this:

```
tell window "Panel.dir" to command
```

where command is either a standard Lingo statement or a handler you've included in the Movie Script of the MIAW.

Before continuing, you might want to check to make sure that the windows we've created here aren't still hanging around. In the Message Window type:

```
put the windowList
```

If Director reports an empty list ([]), your windows are properly disposed of. If there are windows still on the list, dispose of them by typing:

```
set the windowList = []
```

Checkboxes

Checkboxes and Radio Buttons

These two common controls are supported by the Tools Menu: checkboxes and radio buttons.

Checkboxes are used to set parameters that are not mutually exclusive. For example, in this movie, the user can set both Smoothing and Hilights on; the state of one does not affect the other.

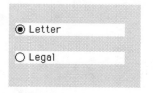

Radio buttons

Radio buttons, on the other hand, are used to set parameters that are mutually exclusive. For example: In this movie, the user can set Letter or Legal, but not both.

Both checkboxes and radio buttons default to auto hilite, meaning when the movie is playing, the user can click on the box or button and it will properly hilight. So checkboxes just work—draw them on the stage and you're pretty much done.

However, this is not the correct way for radio buttons to behave. Turning one radio button on should turn the other (or others) off. So to use radio buttons properly, you must do a little scripting.

Make a new movie and draw two radio buttons on stage. Label one "Letter" and the other "Legal." Enter these names into the Cast Information Window also.

Don't forget to make a loop so your movie won't stop. Open the Script Channel of frame 1 and enter:

```
on exitFrame
  go to the frame
end
```

Select the Letter Button in the Cast Window and open its Script Window. Enter the following script:

```
on mouseUp
  set the hilite of cast "Legal" to false
end
```

Select the Legal Button in the Cast Window and open its Script Window. Enter the following script:

```
on mouseUp
  set the hilite of cast "Letter" to false
end
```

Try it! The hiliting should be correct now. If there were three buttons in a group of radio buttons, each button should set the hilites of the other two buttons. And so on.

Don't use checkboxes or radio buttons arbitrarily. Their use is clearly defined in both the Macintosh and Windows interfaces.

Using the parameter that's been set by the checkbox or radio button most often requires setting a global variable in the box or button script, something like this handler on a Letter Button:

```
on mouseUp
  global pageSize
  put "Letter" into pageSize
  set the hilite of cast "Legal" to false
end
```

Sliders

Director has no built-in support for sliders, although a lot of movies use them.

Open Sliders.dir from the Chap14 folder of the companion CD-ROM. I've programmed this slider to report one of eight levels, such as you might use to set the sound volume in a movie. Play the movie and drag the slider. You'll see a number reported between 0 and 7.

Let's make your own slider.

Open Sliders1.dir from the Chap14 folder of the companion CD-ROM. This is the slider movie without the programming.

In the Score Window, note that sprite 2 (the slider itself) is set to moveable. As you know, this could also have been accomplished through Lingo.

Let's start with the Movie Script. Open it and enter:

```
on startMovie
  set the constraint of sprite 2 to 1
end
```

Setting the constraint property of a sprite to another restricts movement of the constrained sprite. In this case, the slider's (sprite 2's) movement is restricted to sprite 1. Sprite 1 is a thin line drawn with the Tools Menu.

Try it! You can drag the slider, but only as long as its registration point remains within sprite 1.

The idea behind the algorithm to report a value is similar to the algorithm you used to make the gun move in the arcade game project. We're essentially going to divide the full horizontal range of the sprite into eight sections. If the slider is in the first "segment," report a value of 0; in the second segment, report a value of 1, and so on.

Let's put a utility handler in the Movie Script to help figure out what values we'll need for the segments. Open the Movie Script and add this handler:

```
on idle
  put the left of sprite 2 into cast "Where"
end
```

Cast "Where" is a simple text cast member, on stage as sprite 3.

Try it! As you drag the mouse, the horizontal location is updated on stage. The lowest value, the left-most position, is 173, and the highest, the right-most position, is 474. This yields a full range of 301. Dividing this by 8 equals 37.6. So each "segment" of the slider's range is roughly 38 pixels long.

Edit the idle handler in the Movie Script to read:

```
on idle
  put the left of sprite 2 / 38 ¬
  into cast "Where"
end
```

Try it! Good start. This algorithm generates values of 4 to 11.

Why 4 and not 0? The slider is not positioned directly at the far left of the stage; in fact, it's 173 pixels from the right of the stage. The left property, then, evaluates to 173 at the far left position and 173 / 38 = 4 in Director's integer math.

So to force the algorithm to "start from 0," subtract this offset from the left of sprite 1 before dividing:

```
on idle
  put (the left of sprite 2 - the left of ¬
  sprite 1) / 38 into cast "Where"
end
```

Notice the parentheses to force Director to subtract before it divides. Further, instead of hard coding the offset into the handler, I've used a sprite propery. Using the property generalizes this handler so that it will work no matter where the slider is located on the stage.

Now that we have the algorithm that makes the slider work, let's put it where it belongs. Open the Movie Script, copy the algorithm, and delete the idle handler.

In the Cast Window, select cast 2, the slider, and open the Cast Script Window. Enter:

```
on mouseUp
  put (the left of sprite 2 - the left of ¬
  sprite 1) / 38 into cast "Where"
end
```

Try it! This location works OK, but it violates the important user interface principle of feedback. The user should know, as he or she drags the slider, what value is being represented.

Three Director messages are being constantly sent: idle, enterFrame, and exitFrame. Idle is not a good place for this type of script; you only want it to be executed when the slider is on screen. The best place is probably exitFrame. Open the Script Channel, frame 1, and add the following line:

```
on exitFrame
  put (the left of sprite 2 - the left of ¬
  sprite 1) / 38 into cast "Where"
  go to the frame
end
```

Try it! Better. You still have a use for that mouseUp script. How do you know that the user is happy with his or her slider selection? When the mouseUp message is sent! So open the Cast Script of cast 2 and change the script to read:

```
on mouseUp
  set the soundLevel to ¬
  (the left of sprite 2 - the left of ¬
  sprite 1) / 38
  beep
end
```

Try it!

There are several other ways to make sliders, but these algorithms work well for many uses.

Today's GUIs have many conventions, objects, and gizmos that you should incorporate into your movies where appropriate. Director supports a modicum of these features. But what if you must use a convention not supported by Director? Chances are you'll find an XObject to provide this feature, and that's Chapter 15.

Command Summary

close window *windowName*
Closes a window without removing it from memory.

Example:

```
close window "Control.dir"
```

Note: Use forget window to free the memory needed by the movie in a window.

forget window *windowName*
Closes a window and removes it from memory.

Example:

```
forget window "Control.dir"
```

installMenu cast *textCastMember*
Removes existing menus and creates menus defined in the specified text cast member.

Example:

```
installMenu cast "The Menus"
```

Menu: *menuname*
menuitem1 ≈ *instruction*
Defines the contents of and commands executed by a menu.

Example:

```
Menu: File
Quit ≈ Halt
Menu: Edit
Undo ≈ doUndo
```

Where doUndo is a handler defined in a Movie Script.

Note: Use (- to create a separator. See the checkMark and enabled menu properties in Appendix A.

open window *movieName*
Opens a new window and plays the specified movie in that window.

Example:

```
open window "Control.dir"
```

Note: Every window that you open occupies RAM. Use the forget window command to dispose of unneeded windows.

tell *object* **to** *instruction*
tell *object*
   instruction
   instruction
end tell
Sends the instruction to the specified object. The instruction can be a simple Lingo command or a handler name.

Example:

```
tell window "Control.dir" dimButtons
```

where dimButtons is a handler defined in that movie's Movie Script.

Note: If a dimButtons handler existed in the same script that contained the tell statement, the message would not be passed to window "Control.dir"; instead, the dimButtons handler in the local script would execute.

15 ◆ Beyond Director

Lingo can do amazing things, as you've seen, but no high-level language can do everything you might want to do. Director supports a software architecture called "XObjects," which enables Lingo to tap into routines written in other programming languages. You've already used one of these external objects in Chapter 11; here you'll see a bit more of the power of this feature.

This chapter contains the most machine-specific code in this book. Unfortunately, XObjects are written in a language like C and compiled to the machine language of a specific microprocessor and operating system. Therefore, XObjects written for the Macintosh won't work on the PC, and vice versa. Because Director was available on the Macintosh long before it was available as a development environment for the PC, there are many more XObjects available for Macintosh developers.

In this chapter, I'm using the term "XObjects" to refer to all external commands—commands that are not part of Lingo. Actually a diverse set of external commands is supported by Director including external commands written for HyperCard and DLL (Dynamic Link Libraries) written for Windows, in addition to XObjects written specifically for Director.

Unlike most of what we've done in this book, XObjects tie your movie irrevocably to a specific operating system. Carefully consider whether the feature offered by the XObject is really needed or whether you can improvise using standard Lingo to achieve an equivalent functionality.

Nonetheless, I felt that the features offered by XObjects were important to include here. The way the commands are used does not differ from platform to platform and, day by day, equivalent XObjects are appearing for the Windows. If you've followed the precepts I've encouraged you to follow, you'll isolate the machine-specific code and will need to modify only a handler or two to make your movie run on other platforms.

Finally, this chapter deals only with the XObjects distributed with Director or clearly in the public domain. There's a world of commercial XObjects out there—available to you for a licensing fee.

Identifying the Machine

Because I didn't want a lot of you to crash out sampling the movies on the companion CD-ROM, all of the movies in this chapter have code like this in their startMovie handlers:

```
on startMovie
  if the machineType > 255 then halt
  . . .
  . . .
end
```

For all Macintoshes, the machineType function returns a number less than 255; for PCs, the machineType function returns 256. For a PC movie, the equivalent code looks like this:

```
on startMovie
  if the machineType < 255 then halt
  . . .
  . . .
end
```

The Macintosh and PC movies are stored in folders Chap15M and Chap15PC, respectively.

If you have a PC, read through the Mac commands below (and vice versa), because although the XObjects themselves will not run on both platforms, the programming techniques used are similar.

Using XObjects

XObjects are always set up in a Movie Script using a well-defined algorithm. Most often, XObjects are stored as separate files, much like linked pictures or digital video. These files should be in the same folder as your movie or you must use a full path name to open them.

The first XObject is for the Mac only. PC users don't need this one, as the basic functionality of Rear Window is built into PC Projectors.

Rear Window

The Rear Window XObject floats the stage on a color or pattern of your choice—the Finder no longer appears behind the stage. The Finder is still there, but it is obscured by a screen-sized window that the XObject maintains behind the stage.

Open RW.dir from the Chap15M folder of the companion CD-ROM and play the movie. Click on the Stop Button on the stage and the black backdrop remains; click on the Stop Button on the Control Panel and the black backdrop disappears.

The Movie Script looks like this:

```
on startMovie
  global cover
  openXlib the pathName & "RearWindow.XObj"
  if objectP( cover ) = false then
    set cover = RearWindow(mNew,"M")
    set resultCode = value( cover )
    if resultCode < 0 then
      alert "System Error trying to create the ¬
      RearWindow" && string( resultCode )
      exit
    end if
  end if
  cover( mRGBColorToWindow,1,1,1 )
end
```

As you learned in Chapter 11, XObjects are handled as global variables. In this movie, I've called the reference to the Rear Window XObject "cover." Like the naming of all variables, this is arbitrary on my part; it could have been "junk" or "rearWindow." Use a name that makes sense to you.

A Digression on Programming Style

The examples distributed with Director use a different if statement to test for the presence of the XObject. For Rear Window, it looks like this:

```
global cover
  if objectP( cover ) then cover( mDispose )
    set myObj= RearWindow( mNew, "M" )
    set resultCode = value( cover )
  if resultCode < 0 then
    alert "System Error trying to create ¬
    the RearWindow" && string( resultCode )
  end if
```

This if statement functions almost like mine in that it assures that a second object is not created if one already exists. But it does so by disposing of the object (the "mDispose" command). When this code fragment is executed (it's part of a startMovie handler) for a **second** time, the Finder is seen briefly as the instance, cover, is disposed of, then recreated.

The flash bothered me. Therefore, I rewrote the if statement to check to see if an instance of Rear Window **does not exist.** A new instance is created only if the object doesn't exist.

Because my startMovie handler does not dispose of Rear Window, I had to create a stopMovie handler to do so.

This tiny difference explains the difference in behavior between the Stop Button on stage (which halts the movie without sending the stopMovie message) and the Stop Button on the Control Panel (which stops the movie and sends the stopMovie message).

I generally dislike coding for a negative test; I think it is harder to remember why you tested for "= false," but in this case inverting the logic makes the movie work to my liking.

When you look at someone else's code—mine included—first try to understand it and then make an effort to rewrite it in a style that's to your liking, or perhaps more important, to your sensibility. Computer programming is not exactly creative writing, but there are a surprisingly different number of ways to achieve the same goal.

If you've looked at the sample Rear Window examples that come on the Director CD-ROM, you'll note an important difference between my code and Macromedia's. See the sidebar "A Digression on Programming Style" for more information.

Play the movie, stop it using the on-stage Stop Button, and type the following in the Message Box:

```
put cover
-- <Object:7ab60c>
```

If the result you got was "<Void>," you probably stopped the movie using the Control Panel. This movie has a stopMovie handler in the Movie Script that disposes of the XObject.

The value is in hexadecimal (base 16) and will be different on your computer. Further, chances are the value will be different the next time you run the movie. The openXlib command loads the XObject into memory, and the value reported by the put command is the actual RAM address of the XObject.

It should be obvious that you don't want to open the XObject more than once—each openXlib command would create a new reference, and, soon, the RAM would be full of copies of the XObject. The if statement prevents that from happening.

The objectP() function evaluates to true if the object is in memory and false if it is not. Note that you check for *cover,* not *Rear Window*. In programmer's terminology cover is known as an "instance" of Rear Window. See the sidebar "In an Instance" for more information.

XObjects respond to a set of commands that are built into the XObject. All of these commands begin with "m." The command that actually establishes the connection between Lingo and the XObject is:

```
set cover = RearWindow(mNew,"M")
```

The command, or method—hence the "m," is mNew. All XObjects have this command; a statement like this one will *always* be found in the startMovie handler of a movie using XObjects. This command requires one argument, whether to cover the background of the monitor displaying the stage or to cover the background of all monitors connected to the Mac.

In an Instance

The term "instance" comes from object-oriented programming. I find object-oriented programming difficult because I first learned procedural programming (in FORTRAN—ugh!). The trend in computer science, however, is toward object-oriented languages and programming. The reason is simple—it's much more powerful. In procedural programming, you code everything step by step. The computer executes the code at the start and steps through it. In object-oriented programming, you create code segments, called "methods" in most languages.

If that were all there was to it, a method would be the same as a subroutine in procedural languages. The big difference is that you put your methods to work by sending messages to them. The messages tell the method **what** you want done, not **how** to do it. You can override the standard behavior of the system by overriding the method with a new one.

This shouldn't seem very unusual for you, as we've been doing just this for most of this book, in the handlers you've created. So you've already had a mini-introduction to object-oriented programming. But Director is not, at least yet, a true object-oriented environment. For example, you cannot override the routines called when the exitFrame message is sent: Director updates the stage and goes to the next frame.

True object-oriented programming languages offer far more than what I've described here. For example, to override a method you don't need to write it from scratch, you need only create a new instance. Do nothing and two instances behave identically; provide a new method and you'll get new behavior. In an accounting system, for example, the basic method to update a balance for either a withdrawal or a deposit is the same. Withdrawals, however, subtract from the balance, whereas deposits add to it. One method with two instances could accomplish this.

Lots of Director features are somewhat object-oriented, but two are strongly influenced by this trend: XObjects and Parent/Child scripting.

You can create additional instances of an XObject, and each instance operates **independently** of any others. There's little reason to do this for Rear Window, but for an XObject that controls the serial ports of your computer, you could create an instance for the Printer Port (COM1: on the PC) and another for the Modem Port (COM2: on the PC). Potent stuff for advanced programmers!

An "S" indicates a single monitor and an "M" indicates multiple monitors. You can use the "M" parameter even if you have only one monitor. The "S" parameter is useful in low memory situations where you have more than one monitor.

The next section of code in this startMovie handler is for error handling. What if there is not enough memory for Rear Window to do its thing? If the mNew command does not work, cover will be set to a negative number instead of the address of Rear Window.

The alert box error message created here is not particularly helpful to a user, but it is useful to you. I'm not sure what a good error message for users would be in this case—perhaps none, as there is really nothing a user can do if Rear Window doesn't work right. However, you can use the number to debug what went wrong. The value returned in this cast is a standard Macintosh system error value. Other XObjects have customized error messages that are explained in the documentation for the XObject.

If an error was found, when the user clicks on OK in the error alert, this handler is exited. If no error was found, the final line of this handler issues the Rear Window command to actually erase the background:

```
cover( mRGBColorToWindow,1,1,1 )
```

The command is "mRGBColorToWindow," and it requires three parameters: the values for Red, Green, and Blue. The higher the number, the more the color. Legal values are between 0 and 65535. In 8-bit color, the closest palette value to these settings is used.

Other RearWindow commands include:

```
mPatToWindow, n
```

where n can range from -1 to -5. This command fills the backdrop with a 1-bit pattern; intermediate values, such as -3, make dithered black-and-white patterns. You can also use -99 here to show the desktop pattern.

```
mIndexColorToWindow, n
```

where n is a number from 0 to 255. The command fills the backdrop with the specified color from the current palette. In 16- and 24-bit color, you cannot predict the color that will be produced.

```
mPICTToWindow, filename, n, m
```

where *filename* is the name of a PICT file, *n* can be either -1, 0, or 1, and *m* is a number from 0 to 255. You must specify a full path name if the picture is not in the same folder as the movie. The second parameter determines whether Rear Window stretches the picture to fill the whole screen, positions it in the upper-left corner of the screen, or positions it in the middle of the screen. The last parameter is the color to fill around the picture if it is not stretched to fit. This parameter works like mIndexColor-ToWindow.

```
mCastToWindow, the picture of cast ¬
whichCast, n, m
```

where whichCast is a bit-mapped cast member and n and m are the same as mPICTToWindow. Note that this command requires the picture **property** of a cast member.

The other place in this movie where the XObject is dealt with is the stop-Movie handler. It looks like this:

```
on stopMovie
  global cover
  cover(mDispose)
  closeXlib
end
```

The mDispose command is required in all XObjects. Its function is to release the memory being used by the instance created by the mNew command. Finally, the XObject is closed with the closeXlib command.

There are several other utility commands in the Rear Window XObject. One of these, for example, allows you to find out how much memory would be used by the window. How do you find out about these?

Self-Documentation

Because the specifics of particular XObjects are not described in the Director documentation, all XObjects are supposed to support a command that self-documents the XObject. (Of course, it's up to the developer of the

XObject to create this command, so it may not be available in all XObjects.)

Bring out the Message Window and type:

```
showXlib
```

You should see something like this:

```
-- XLibraries:
-- "*Standard.xlib"
--    XObject: FileIO           Id:1020
--    XObject: SerialPort       Id:200
--    XObject: XCMDGlue         Id:2020
-- "HD:Director:RearWindow.XObj"
--    XObject: RearWindow       Id:6213
```

If Rear Window is not open, it won't be listed here. You can reopen it by typing:

```
openXlib "RearWindow.XOBJ"
```

Then try the showXlib command again.

To access the documentation to Rear Window, type:

```
RearWindow(mDescribe)
```

And the Message Window will fill with the documentation.

PC users can try:

```
fileIO(mDescribe)
```

The Bottom Line

Every XObject you use requires a basic sequence of commands:

Declare global variable to store instance address

Open the XObject with OpenXlib

Check to see if instance exists with objectP()

If it does, do nothing

If it does not, use mNew to create instance

Check for error (value of instance < 0)

If error handle it

Call instance with proper command and parameters

Most of this should happen in your startMovie handler, but depending on the function provided by the XObject, you may call it from other places in your movie.

When you are finished with the XObject, you should:

Dispose of the instance with mDispose

Close the XObject with CloseXlib

Let's see another example in action.

Stage to Cast

In interactive movies, you cannot know what the user will do. The appearance of the stage, for example, in our arcade game from Chapter 8 depends upon alot of things—where the user positions the mouse, if he or she "fired" a bullet, where the duck was, the values of the scoring variables, and so on. If you wanted to "freeze frame" at the end of a game, using the stage as a backdrop for a frame asking the user if he or she wanted to play again, you'd have to know, in advance, what the stage looked like. This XObject converts the stage (or a portion of it) into a cast member, essentially freezing the frame.

This XObject is most useful if you have a large number of Lingo- or user-controlled sprites and require a stationary screen.

The fewer the sprites, the faster the movie can go.

Open StC.dir from the Chap15M or from the Chap15PC folder of the companion CD-ROM. Play the movie. Rewind and play the movie again. And again. If the Cast Window is not visible, bring it out. Watch cast 20. When the arrow stops, this cast member changes to show the current position of the arrow. If you have any windows overlapping the stage, they too become part of this picture (including the Cast Window!).

This movie should look familiar to you. You created a movie much like this in Chapter 6. There's a small difference here, though. Instead of always stopping at the same place, the arrow in this movie stops randomly.

The random stop feature was accomplished by the addition of a new global variable, stopPos, whose value is randomly chosen. Here's the revised Movie Script with the additions to the score shown in boldface:

```
on startMovie
  global whichCast, oldTempo, stopPos, done
  put 1 into whichCast
  put 60 into oldTempo
  put false into done
  set the puppet of sprite 1 to true
  puppetTempo oldTempo
  put random(8) into stopPos
end


on doRotate
  global whichCast, oldTempo, stopPos, done
  set the castNum of sprite 1 to whichCast
  updateStage
  put whichCast + 1 into whichCast
  if whichCast > 8 then put 1 into whichCast
  put oldTempo - 1 into oldTempo
  puppetTempo oldTempo
  if oldTempo = stopPos then put true into done
end
```

The new code simply creates a random stop position in the Movie Script and then, in doRotate called by exitFrame of frame 1, sets the done variable based upon stopPos (rather than the original "less than 5").

Here's the Movie Script for the Macintosh version of this movie with the addition of the StagetoCast.XOBJ (with the additions, again, in boldface):

```
on startMovie
  global whichCast, oldTempo, stopPos, done, ¬
  theStage
  openXlib "StagetoCast.XOBJ"
  if objectP(theStage) then theStage(mDispose)
  set theStage = StageToCast(mNew,0,0,480,640)
  if value(theStage) < 0 then
    alert "Error loading StageToCast"
  halt
  end if
  put 1 into whichCast
  put 60 into oldTempo
  put false into done
  set the puppet of sprite 1 to true
  puppetTempo oldTempo
  put random(8) into stopPos
end

on stopMovie
  global theStage
  theStage(mDispose)
  closeXlib
end
```

The doRotate handler is the same as above.

A global variable, theStage, holds the instance of the XObject. The start-Movie script additions and the stopMovie handler follow the guidelines given in this chapter for using XObjects. Notice the "pattern" of the code—it's identical with that used for Rear Window—it differs only in specifics.

The most important difference between this movie and the Rear Window movie is in the mNew command. Here, the XObject requires four para-meters, the Top, Left, Bottom, and Right of the area to be captured.

The code to activate StageToCast is not in the Movie Script here. You want to invoke this XObject when the arrow stops, so this code is located in the exitFrame handler for frame 1, like so (again with changes from the original shown in boldface):

```
on exitFrame
  global done, theStage
```

```
  doRotate
  if done then
  set the picture of cast 20 = ¬
  theStage( mGetHandle)
  go to frame 10
  else
    go to frame 1
  end if
end
```

The mGetHandle command returns the memory location of the piece of
the stage specified in the mNew command. By assigning this to the picture of cast 20, the specified stage rectangle becomes the cast member.
This instance, theStage, then always returns the entire stage area as mNew
defined theStage variable with parameters of 0,0,480,640.

The Movie Script for the PC version of this movie looks remarkably similar to the Macintosh version:

```
on startMovie
  global whichCast, oldTempo, stopPos, done, ¬
  theStage
  openXlib "MovUtils.dll"
  if objectP(theStage) then theStage(mDispose)
  set theStage = MovUtils(mNew)
  if value(theStage) < 0 then
    alert "Error loading MovUtils"
    halt
  end if
  put 1 into whichCast
  put 60 into oldTempo
  put false into done
  set the puppet of sprite 1 to true
  puppetTempo oldTempo
  put random(8) into stopPos
end
```

The stopMovie script is identical to the Macintosh version shown on the
opposite page.

A global variable, theStage, holds the instance of the XObject. The start-
Movie script additions and the stopMovie handler follow the guidelines

given in this chapter for using XObjects. Notice the "pattern" of the code—it's identical with that used for Rear Window—it differs only in specifics.

Unlike the Macintosh XObject, the mNew command for MovUtils requires no parameters. This DLL contains many commands so instead of feeding the mNew command arguments, you give them to the individual commands.

Because of this, I decided to isolate the call to the XObject, so the exit-Frame handler for frame 1 in the PC version of this movie looks like:

```
on exitFrame
  global done
  doRotate
  if done then
    getPicture
    go to frame 10
  else
    go to frame 1
  end if
end
```

The getPicture handler (in the Movie Script) does the work:

```
on getPicture
  global theStage
  put theStage( mStageToCast,¬
  the rect of window "STC.dir") into picture
  set the picture of cast 20 to picture
end
```

The global variable theStage contains the instance of the MovUtil DLL XObject and is invoked with the command "mStageToCast" followed by a rect that represents the area of the stage to be captured—in this case, the entire stage.

In this sample movie, capturing the stage with only one moving sprite is probably more trouble than it is worth. But if you had 20 moving sprites, you'd save yourself 19 sprites by combining all of those into 1. Conserving sprites is an important speed consideration in complex movies.

Audio CD Control

The trend in multimedia is toward all digital media—like the digital video you worked with in Chapter 13. Many multimedia projects, however, must control external devices, including the playing of audio CDs and videodiscs.

The AppleCD XObject offers commands to control audio CDs playing in Apple-branded CD-ROM players. If you do not have an Apple CD-ROM player, try this movie anyway—chances are it will work. Most modern CD-ROM players conform to Apple's API (Application Programming Interface) for CD-ROMs. This XObject supports only the first CD-ROM player in your SCSI chain. If you have more than one CD-ROM player, place the audio CD in the drive with the lowest SCSI ID number.

> *If this movie does not work with your CD-ROM player, consult the documentation that came with the hardware. There's a good chance that some sort of external command module has been provided and can be used in place of the XObject, with only minor changes to the programming.*

If you have not already done so, copy the Chap15M folder from the companion CD-ROM and open AudioCD.dir from this folder. Put an audio CD into your CD-ROM player. It should appear on the desktop labeled Audio CD 1 or somesuch. If it does not appear, this movie won't work as your system, apparently, cannot play audio CDs. Check the documentation that came with the CD-ROM drive.

If the audio CD appears on the desktop, play the movie. Click on the Track Buttons to play a track. Click on the Stop Button to stop playing. As you play the movie, two text fields are updated to show you the current timing and the current status.

> *Audio CDs are addressed by minutes, seconds, and frames. (Each second is divided into 75 frames.) You can access an audio CD, then, in units of 1/75th of a second.*

This XObject supports a wide variety of commands to allow you to do pretty much anything you might want to do with audio CDs. We're only going to use a small subset of these commands in this movie. Use the mDescribe command to reveal this XObject's entire command set.

The startMovie handler should, by this time, look very familiar to you:

```
on startMovie
  global CDSound
  if objectp(CDSound) then CDSound(mDispose)
  set CDSound = AppleAudioCD(mNew)
  if objectp(CDSound) = false then
    alert "There is no Apple CD-ROM drive ¬
    connected."
  else
    if CDSound(mStatus) = ¬
    "No Audio CD Status" then
      alert "There is no disk in the CD-ROM ¬
      drive."
    end if
  end if
  put empty into cast "The Time"
  put empty into cast "CD Status"
end
```

The only major difference between this startMovie handler and the others in this chapter is a second if statement to check to see if an audio CD is in the CD-ROM drive. This is accomplished through the mStatus command. The message checked for here, "No Audio CD Status" is, incidentally, not listed in the documentation for this XObject. I discovered it by putting the CDStatus in the Message Window when there was no CD in the drive.

Checking for absolute error messages like this is not a good idea, as the message strings may change with newer versions of the XObject. There's no real alternative in this case, however, as no XObject command exists to determine if an audio CD is mounted.

As in our other XObject movies, this one has a stopMovie handler to dispose of the instance of the XObject and close the file. Like so:

```
on stopMovie
  global CDSound
  stopCD
  CDSound(mDispose)
end
```

Any movie that drives a device, be it an audio CD or a videodisc, will probably have to manipulate lots of numbers, so it's wise to make utility handlers to do the dirty work, calling these where needed from the frame or button scripts of your movie. This movie has two such utility handlers, playTrack and stopCD. Here they are, from the Movie Script:

```
on playTrack whichTrack
  global CDSound
  CDSound(mPlayTrack,whichTrack)
end

on stopCD
  global CDSound
  CDSound(mStop)
end
```

The playTrack handler is called with one parameter, the track number to be played. This is passed to the mPlayTrack command from the button scripts (on cast members 5–8) that play specific tracks of the movie.

The stopCD handler simply sends the mStop command. Calls to this handler, in this movie, come from both the Stop Button and the stopMovie handler.

You could easily scatter such simple commands throughout your movie without using utility handlers. However, by using utility handlers, you are isolating the code that is potentially specific to a particular brand of CD-ROM player. Simple if statements could make these handlers operate on different drives.

The final handler in the Movie Script of this movie is for development purposes only. An idle handler, at least one like this, wouldn't normally be found in a CD audio application:

```
on idle
  global CDSound
  put CDSound(mStatus) into cast "CD Status"
  if CDSound(mStatus) = ¬
  "Audio play in progress" then
    put CDSound(mCurrentTime) into ¬
    cast "The Time"
  end if
end
```

This handler puts the current CD status into a text cast member continuously as your movie plays. The if statement puts the current playing time of the audio CD when the CD is playing—that is, only if "Audio play in progress" is returned as the message string from mStatus.

> *Recall that it is dangerous to code for a specific error string. We've no choice here.*

If you think you might want to work with device control, print out the mDescribe documentation for the AppleAudioCD XObject. You'll find a myriad of commands, including one to let you play only a small segment of the CD—not just a whole track. You could, for example, key an audio segment to visuals, as you did in Chapter 13 with digital video, or you could place lyrics on screen to correspond to what's being sung on the audio CD, or, well, the possibilities are endless.

Videodisc XObjects work much in the same way except that you access the device by frames rather than by time.

Under Windows, external devices are accessed through the mci command. This instruction sends a command string to Window's media control interface. The command to play track 1 of a mounted audio CD, then, is:

```
mci "play cdaudio track 1"
```

Command strings are always structured like so: command, device, arguments. You do not have to create a global variable to reference the instance of the XObject—the mci command is built into Director. When played back on a Macintosh, these commands are simply ignored.

The movie CDAudio.dir in the Chap15PC folder of the companion CD-ROM contains the basic code to get you started controlling audio CDs from Director. It's functionally identical to the Mac version described above but uses the mci command instead of the baroque XObject command syntax.

As digital video and audio gets better and better, the use of external devices will become less important. However, for now, device XObjects are an important part of commercial multimedia and are worth exploring.

Command Summary

CloseXlib

Closes all external XObjects.

Example:

```
closeXlib
```

mci *"commandString"*

Sends the command string to Windows media control interface processor.

Example:

```
mci "open cdaudio"
```

OpenXlib *fileName*

Opens XObject file name. Unless you provide a full path name, the XObject must be located in the same folder or subdirectory as the movie.

Example:

```
OpenXlib "PopUp"
```

ShowXlib

Lists the currently open XObjects in the Message Window.

Example:

```
ShowXlib
```

16 ◆ Lingo Potpourri

This chapter explores important Lingo features and commands that didn't easily fit into the sample movies and projects of other chapters: event handling in depth and property lists.

Event handling is at the core of many interactive Director movies. As you've learned, Lingo scripting is based upon creating handlers to respond to events. The arcade game in Chapter 8 required the when command to trap and act on the mouseUp event. The usefulness of the when command, however, extends far beyond arcade games.

Recall that there are 10 system messages being sent by Director: start-Movie, stopMovie, enterFrame, exitFrame, mouseUp, mouseDown, keyUp, keyDown, idle, and timeOut. In the movies you've created, you've programmed a response to most of these messages.

Director, version 3, had a system message called "stepMovie" that functioned like enterFrame. Version 3 lacked the enter/exitFrame messages.

You've also written your own handlers and called them by using their names in another handler. One way or another, your handlers are always tied to one of the system messages—most often to the time-based events, enterFrame and exitFrame, or to the button events, mouseUp and mouse-Down.

The when command allows you to call a handler without tying it to a specific location in the score. In the arcade game, you saw the mouseUp event trapped to trigger the firing of the bullet. Here, we'll use it very differently.

Open When.dir from the Chap16 folder of the companion CD-ROM. Play the movie. Click on the buttons and on the stage. Open the Cast Window. Note that the buttons don't have scripts. Here is the Score Window, shown in script view. Note that only the Back Button is scripted (channel 1, script 7).

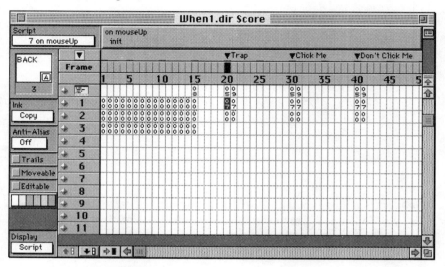

The key to this movie is its Movie Script:

```
on startMovie
  init
end

on init
  when mouseUp then doMouseUpCheck
end

on doMouseUpCheck
  if the mouseCast = -1 then
    go frame "Trap"
  else
    if the mouseCast = 1 then go frame ¬
    "Click Me"
    if the mouseCast = 2 then go frame ¬
    "Don't Click Me"
  end if
end
```

The startMovie handler calls the init handler, which sets up the when trap. The mouseCast function returns the castNum of the object under the pointer when mouseUp occurs. MouseCast returns a -1 if nothing is underneath the pointer (i.e., the pointer is on top of the stage).

Compare mouseCast with the clickOn. Both are activated by mouseUp, but mouseCast returns the cast *number, while the clickOn returns the* sprite *number. This script could easily be rewritten using the clickOn. See WhenAlt.dir in the Chap16 folder of the companion CD-ROM.*

The problem with the when command is that once you set up the trap, it's active for the duration of the movie. The Script Channel scripts in frames 20, 30, and 40 take care of this problem by turning the event trap off. Note that this is an enterFrame script. Like so:

```
on enterFrame
  when mouseUp then nothing
end
```

The scripts on the Script Channel of frames 21, 31, and 41 simply loop:

```
on exitFrame
  go loop
end
```

The Score Script of the Back Button channel reactivates the event trap.

```
on mouseUp
  init
  go frame 1
end
```

This script could have been placed in the Cast Script of the Back Button cast member to achieve the same effect.

Because I knew I had to reactivate the trap elsewhere in the movie, I created a separate init handler rather than directly including it in the start-Movie handler.

Event Scripts

The when command is only one way to assign an event to an action. The keyboard, mouse, and timeOut events can have scripts directly attached to them, making that script the primary event handler for the event and, therefore, the first to receive event messages.

Open Event.dir from the Chap16 folder of the companion CD-ROM. Play the movie. (Your key presses will be gobbled up by the Message Window if it is active. Close it.) Use the arrow keys on your keyboard to move the circle around the stage.

If the circle doesn't move, read on. Your keyboard may be reporting values different than those mine did. This situation is easy to fix.

The circle is a puppet, and the arrow key control is accomplished by assigning a handler to the keyDownScript property. Here is the Movie Script:

```
on startMovie
  set the puppet of sprite 1 to true
  set the keyDownScript = "checkArrows"
end
```

The string assigned to the keyDownScript property can be any legal Lingo command. Here, it's my own handler, checkArrow. Also in the Movie Script, it looks like this:

```
on checkArrows
  put the keyCode into keyValue
  put 0 into vMove
  put 0 into hMove
  if keyValue = 126 then put -10 into vMove
  if keyValue = 125 then put 10 into vMove
  if keyValue = 123 then put -10 into hMove
  if keyValue = 124 then put 10 into hMove
  set the locV of sprite 1 to the locV of ¬
  sprite 1 + vMove
  set the locH of sprite 1 to the locH of ¬
  sprite 1 + hMove
  updateStage
end
```

The keyCode function returns a numerical code for the key that was last pressed. The code is not the ASCII value of the key, but the actual numeric value of the key. The operating system translates this value into a character. In Chapter 9 you used the key function that returns the ASCII character of the last keypress. On my system, pressing the letter "A" results in this:

the keyCode   0

the key   A

You can determine the keyCode returned for your keyboard by adding this line to the checkArrows handler:

```
on checkArrows
  put the keyCode
  put the keyCode into keyValue
  put 0 into vMove
  put 0 into hMove
  if keyValue = 126 then put -10 into vMove
  if keyValue = 125 then put 10 into vMove
  if keyValue = 123 then put -10 into hMove
  if keyValue = 124 then put 10 into hMove
  set the locV of sprite 1 to the locV of ¬
  sprite 1 + vMove
  set the locH of sprite 1 to the locH of ¬
  sprite 1 + hMove
  updateStage
end
```

Open the Message Window, but make sure that the Cast or Script Window is active. Run the modified movie. The keyCodes will be placed into the Message Window.

If this movie didn't work on your computer, you can edit the if statements in the checkKey handlers to include the proper code for the up, down, left, and right arrow keys, respectively.

The updateStage command is, strictly speaking, not necessary in this movie as it is looping—the frame 1, Script Channel script is our typical go loop command. Recall that the stage is updated upon exitFrame.

As with the when command, you may want only a part of your movie to respond to the keyDown event. To remove the event handler, set the key-DownScript property to empty:

```
set the keyDownScript to empty
```

You can also attach scripts to the keyUp as well as mouseUp and mouse-Down messages and timeouts.

Timeouts

Many applications of Director benefit from the timeOut event. For example, in a kiosk program, the movie may play an "attract loop" when no one is using it. The purpose of the attract loop is just as it sounds—to attract a viewer. When the attract loop has seduced a user, the movie jumps to a menu or another introductory screen. If the user then leaves and there's no activity on the computer, the movie should jump back to the attract loop. This is called a timeout.

You've already used the timer function to create a wait handler in Chapter 8. Recall that Director's bottom-line timing is based on ticks, 1/60th of a second each. There are properties that can be tested to determine if a timeout has occurred, and if it has, you can act on it.

Open Attract.dir from the Chap16 folder of the companion CD-ROM and play the movie. Don't click on the button (it only stops the movie) or press a key. Just wait. In 600 ticks—10 seconds—the attract loop will activate. To return to the button screen, move the mouse. If you have the Message Window open, you'll see a lot of numbers scrolling by as this movie is running.

The startMovie handler sets up the timeout:

```
on startMovie
  set the timeOutLength to 600
  when timeOut then go to frame "Attract"
end
```

The timeOutLength property controls the length of the wait before a time-Out event is generated and the when command sets up the event trap. As usual with when, the command can be only one line long, but you can call your own handler. Therefore, if you had a lot of "housecleaning" to do (such as emptying text fields, saving data, or unpuppeting sprites) before the attract loop can begin, you could call your own handler here.

The code that moves the sprites is also in the Movie Script:

```
on attract
  set the puppet of sprite 1 to true
  set the locH of sprite 1 to random(500)
  set the locV of sprite 1 to random(400)
end
```

You've seen code like this in several movies. This handler is called in the Script Channel of frame "Attract." Which looks like this:

```
on enterFrame
  global oldH, oldV
  put the mouseH into oldH
  put the mouseV into oldV
end

on exitFrame
  global oldH, oldV
  attract
  if the mouseH <> oldH or ¬
  the mouseV <> oldV then
    set the puppet of sprite 1 to false
    go frame "Opening"
  end if
  go loop
end
```

This frame has both an enterFrame handler and an exitFrame handler, because I wanted the event that signaled activity to be movement of the mouse. Keyboard events and mouse events automatically reset the internal timeout counter, but mouse movements do not.

The enterFrame handler here saves the horizontal and vertical position of the mouse when the frame is entered in a global variable. The exitFrame handler then compares these values with the current position. If either the horizontal or vertical position has changed, jump back to frame "Opening" and unpuppet sprite 1; otherwise, keep going.

There's an interesting bug in this movie. Oh, the movie works OK, but it works because of a side effect. To illustrate this bug, edit the exitFrame handler in the Script Channel of frame "Attract" to read:

```
on exitFrame
  global oldH, oldV
  attract
  if the mouseH <> oldH or ¬
  the mouseV <> oldV then
    set the puppet of sprite 1 to false
    go frame "Opening"
  end if
  go to frame "Attract"
end
```

Close the window and run the movie. Ugh!!! Once you gain sufficient skills with Lingo's commands and start struggling with really interesting problems of making an algorithm work, errors like this may start creeping into your scripts. It's so simple—handlers execute line by line. Be a dumb computer here and read this handler as though you've never seen it. Whether the mouse was moved or not, it always loops back to frame "Attract." Yes, I know, it says go frame "Opening," and the movie does; but then, two lines later, this script is ordering Director to jump back to "Attract." The original code "go loop" worked because go loop jumps to the closest marker, which was "Opening."

So what? It worked, so why should you fix it? Well, if you wanted to expand the attract loop over many frames—as most attract loops would be—and if you put some markers in that loop to delineate segments, you'd be in trouble. Try this:

```
on exitFrame
  global oldH, oldV
  attract
  if the mouseH <> oldH or ¬
  the mouseV <> oldV then
    set the puppet of sprite 1 to false
    go frame "Opening"
    exit
  end if
  go to frame "Attract"
end
```

And it works again. This is robust code. That is, it does not depend on a side effect of how a command works.

The numbers that appear in the Message Window arise from the script in the Script Channel of frame 1:

```
on exitFrame
  put the timeOutLapsed
  go loop
end
```

The timeOutLapsed property returns the current state of the timeout timer. If you play this movie and click on the mouse button or press a key, you'll notice that the timer resets itself. This frame is not programmed to accept a mouse movement as a valid event.

Similarly, the "Attract" frame is not programmed to accept keyboard or mouse click events. Were this a real application, I'd include these events too.

Timeouts can also be assigned scripts using the "set the timeOutScript" property. Whether you do it via the when command or as a timeOutScript is largely a matter of programming style—both achieve the same end.

Passing Events

In all of the movies in this book, so far, when a script has responded to an event, that event is discarded. Lingo possesses a command to allow you to specifically pass an event.

Open the movie Pass.dir from the Chap16 folder of the companion CD-ROM. Play the movie. Click on the black box. One beep. Click on the red circle. Two beeps.

The Cast Scripts of the box and the circle are almost identical. Here's the black box:

```
on mouseUp
  beep
end
```

and the red circle:

```
on mouseUp
  beep
  pass
end
```

The second beep when you click on the red circle comes not from the black box but from the Movie Script, which looks like this:

```
on mouseUp
  beep
end
```

The mouseUp message is not passed from the red circle to the black box because they are on the same level of the message hierarchy—the pass command sends the message to the **next** level of the hierarchy. Besides, you clicked on the red circle, **not** on the black box. (See the sidebar "Message Central" in Chapter 1 for a description of the message hierarchy.)

Here's a practical application of the pass command. Open Pass2.dir from the Chap16 folder of the companion CD-ROM. Play the movie. This is a simple menuing system much like those you created in Chapter 1.

The click you hear when you make a selection is not programmed into the buttons. They all look something like this:

```
on mouseUp
  go frame "One"
  pass
end
```

Instead, passing the mouseUp triggers this handler in the Movie Script:

```
on mouseUp
  if the clickOn <> 0 then puppetSound "Click"
end
```

This technique means that the puppetSound command does not have to be repeated in each button. If there were lots of buttons and the button scripts were longer, you'd save considerable scripting.

There is a companion dontPassEvent command that squelches the passing of messages. This command is useful if you have used the script property of a keyboard, mouse, or timeOut events to designate a primary handler and want the event to stop there.

As you grow more sophisticated in your Lingo programming, you'll find that event trapping and passing can simplify many projects.

Property Lists

You worked with simple, linear lists in Chapter 10. Lingo supports a second type of list, a property list. Each item of a property list has two elements: a property name and its value. Like this:

```
[color:151,vloc:200]
```

This list has two properties: color and vloc. The value of color is 151, and the value of vloc is 200. A series of commands, much like those you used for linear lists, allow you to manipulate property lists. So instead of getOne, with a property list, you getProp.

Open PropList.dir from the Chap16 folder of the companion CD-ROM. Play the movie. Click on the Go Button to start the action. This movie allows for four moving balls. On the fifth click on the Go Button, the balls will stop.

The property list for this movie contains two entries, one for the horizontal increment and one for the vertical increment. Each of the four sprites has a different value associated with these properties, which is why the balls move at different speeds and directions.

This one frame movie looks like many others you've made. The frame 1, Script Channel script makes a call to the main animation handler in addition to looping. Like this:

```
on exitFrame
  moveIt
  go loop
end
```

MoveIt is, of course, in the Movie Script. In addition to moveIt, the Movie Script has a startMovie handler to set up this animation.

```
on startMovie
  global attributes, nSprites
  set the puppet of sprite 1 to true
  set the puppet of sprite 2 to true
  set the puppet of sprite 3 to true
  set the puppet of sprite 4 to true
  put [[hInc:5,vInc:10] , [hInc:-10,vInc:15],¬
  [hInc:10,vInc:-15] , [hInc:-5,vInc:-10]] ¬
  into attributes
  put 0 into nSprites
end
```

First, you'll need two global variables. The property list is assigned to attributes, and nSprites holds the number of moving sprites (0–4).

Then make sprites 1–4 puppets.

Finally, initialize the variables. Sprite 1, then, will have an initial horizontal increment of 5—meaning it will start moving in steps of 5 pixels and it will move to the right. (An hInc of -5 would make it move to the left.) Sprite 2, however, has an initial hInc of -10—meaning it will move to the left in steps of 10 pixels. Start the movie with no sprites moving by assigning 0 to nSprites.

MoveIt does all the work. While this may look complicated, you've already worked through most of the logic in this handler in other movies in this book.

```
on moveIt
  global attributes, nSprites
  repeat with i = 1 to nSprites
    put getaProp(getAt(attributes,i),#hInc) ¬
    into hInc
    put getaProp(getAt(attributes,i),#vInc) ¬
    into vInc
    set the locH of sprite i to the locH of ¬
    sprite i + hInc
    set the locV of sprite i to the locV of ¬
    sprite i + vInc
```

```
      if the locH of sprite i > 630 or ¬
      the locH of sprite i < 10 then ¬
      setaProp(getAt(attributes,i),¬
      #hInc,hInc * -1)
      if the locV of sprite i > 440 or ¬
      the locV of sprite i < 10 then ¬
      setaProp(getAt(attributes,i),¬
      #vInc,vInc * -1)
    end repeat
  end
```

You must declare the globals so that moveIt can access them. Then repeat everything for the current value of nSprites. (So if one sprite was moving, the repeat loop would happen only once, and so on. The loop variable, i, is identical to the sprite number.)

Next, the two put statements pull out, from the attributes list, the specific properties associated with sprite i. You used an identical algorithm with linear lists in the Chapter 10 Match Game movie.

Start reading from the interior parentheses outward. The getAt command extracts the attributes for a particular sprite (sprite i, the loop counter) from the full attributes property list. So if i was 1, this command would evaluate to:

```
put getaProp([hInc:5,vInc:10]),#vInc) into ¬
vInc
```

Then, the getaProp command extracts the particular property you require—in this case, the vInc:

```
put 10 into vInc
```

The power of the getaProp command becomes clear here. Instead of indexing by value or by index number as you did with linear lists, here the list index is "#vInc," the name of the desired property. The pound sign is the Lingo sign that the word is a symbol instead of a command, keyword, or variable.

After these put commands, then, the value of the variables vInc and hInc has been extracted from the property list. A pair of set statement moves the puppet sprites to a new location, just as we've done time and again.

Finally, a pair of if statements checks to see if the sprite is touching the edge of the stage. If it is, it multiplies vInc or hInc by -1 to cause the ball to bounce—the same algorithm you used in Brickout, Chapter 7. The difference here is that instead of directly changing the sprite, these if statements change the property list to reflect the new direction using the setaProp command.

This command, setaProp, is parallel to the setAt command used with linear lists. Like getaProp, setaProp indexes the property list using a symbol to represent the specific property being altered (#hInc or #vInc).

To demonstrate the effect of this command, rewind the movie and then play it. Before clicking on the Go Button, type in the Message Window:

```
put attributes
-- [[#hInc: 5, #vInc: 10], [#hInc: -10, #vInc:
15] ...
```

Click on the Go Button a couple of times. Give the balls a chance to bounce a few times and then stop the movie. Once again, in the Message Window type:

```
put attributes
-- [[#hInc: 5, #vInc: -10], [#hInc: 10, #vInc:
15] ...
```

Examine the two lists. The starting list is the same as in the startMovie handler, but the second list, assuming you let the balls bounce, has different numbers for several of the sprites.

Command Summary

getaProp(*propertyList, property*)
Returns the specified property from the property list.

Example:

```
getaProp([height:10,width:50],#width)
```

the keyCode
Returns the numeric value of the key last pressed.

Example:

```
put the keyCode into whichKey
```

Note: This function does not return the ASCII value of the key.

pass
Sends the message onto the next level of the message hierarchy.

Example:

```
pass
```

setaProp(*propertyList, property, value*)
Changes the property to the specified value on the specified property list.

Example:

```
setaProp([height:10,width:50],#width,20)
```

Coda

The movies and scripts in this book have only touched the surface of what you can do with Lingo. There's no better way to learn the tricks of the trade than reading code. Beg, steal, or borrow the source movies. (Projectors won't do you much good, although they can provide inspiration.) Well, maybe not steal—that's piracy. Read the code, modify it, trace it. You'll find surprisingly few structures—many of them you've experienced in this book.

With the foundation you now have in Lingo and programming, you're ready to make magic.

The problem with programming a multimedia presentation is:
If you're a rookie, it will take you forever to put a program together—
and if you know your way around, you never stop adding things.

— Ken Willis, 16 years old, as quoted in
CD-ROM Today magazine

Appendix A ◆ Objects and Properties

As we've seen in many of the movies in this book, manipulating an object's properties is one of the most common things Lingo programmers do.

In the following table, the properties are listed by object. In all cases, you must specify the object (if any) when setting or putting a value. A fairly large number of properties do not refer to a specific object but, instead, refer to the movie at run time. The set command is used to specify a property and the put command is used to retrieve a property.

Here are some examples:

```
set the buttonStyle to 1
set the castNum of sprite 1 to 32
set the startTime of cast 10 to 100
put the timeOutLength
put the trails of sprite 2
```

OBJECT	PROPERTY	LEGAL VALUES
run-time environment	the buttonStyle	0,1
	the centerStage	true, false
	the checkBoxAccess	0 – 2
	the checkBoxType	0 – 2
	colorDepth	1, 2, 4, 8, 16, 32
	the colorQD	true, false*
	the exitLock	true, false
	the itemDelimiter	character string
	the keyDownScript	string
	the keyUpScript	string

* Can be put but not set.

OBJECT	PROPERTY	LEGAL VALUES
run-time environment	the lastFrame	number*
	the mouseDownScript	string
	the mouseUpScript	string
	the number of castMembers	number*
	the preLoadEventAbort	true, false
	the preLoadRAM	true, false
	the randomSeed	number
	the romanLingo	true, false
	the selEnd	0 — number chars in field
	the selStart	0 — number chars in field
	the soundEnabled	true, false
	the soundLevel	0 — 7
	the stage	n/a
	the stageColor	0 — 255
	the switchColorDepth	true, false
	the timeOutLapsed	true, false
	the timeOutLength	number
	the timeOutMouse	true, false
	the timeOutPlay	true, false
	the timeOutScript	string
	the timer	n/a
	the trace	true, false
	the traceLoad	0 — 2
	the traceLog	string
	the upDateMovieEnabled	true, false
	the windowList	[ ]
	timeOutKeyDown	true, false
Button	the hilite	true, false
Cast	the backColor	0 — 255
	the castType	symbol*
	the depth	number*
	the fileName	legal file name
	the foreColor	0 — 255
	the height	number*
	the loaded	true, false*
	the modified	true, false
	the name	string
	the number	1 — 32K
	the palette	number
	the picture	1 — 32K
	the purgePriority	0 — 3

OBJECT	PROPERTY	LEGAL VALUES
Cast	the rect	rect*
	the regPoint	number
	the scriptText	0 — 32K
	the size	number
	the text	string
	the width	number*
Digital Video	the directToStage	true, false
	the duration	number*
Field	the textAlign	left, center, right
	the textFont	string
	the textHeight	number
	the textSize	number
	the textStyle	plain, bold, italic, underline, shadow, outline, condense, extend
Frame	the frameLabel	string*
	the framePalette	number*
	the frameScript	string*
	the frameTempo	number*
Menu	the name	string
	the number of menuItems	number*
	the number of menus	number*
MenuItem	the checkMark	true, false
	the name	string
	the script	string
Movie	the beepOn	true, false
Sound	the volume	0 — 255
Sprite	the backColor	0 — 255
	the blend	0 — 100
	the bottom	number*
	the castNum	1 — 32K
	the constraint	0 — 48
	the cursor	number
	the editableText	true, false
	the foreColor	0 — 255
	the ink	0 — 9, 32 — 39
	the left	point*
	the lineSize	0 — 14
	the locH	-32K — 32K
	the locV	-32K — 32K
	the moveableSprite	true, false

OBJECT	PROPERTY	LEGAL VALUES
Sprite	the puppet	true, false
	the right	number*
	the scoreColor	0 – 5
	the scriptNum	1 – 32K*
	the stretch	true, false
	the top	number*
	the trails	true, false
	the type	0 – 10, 16
	the visible	true, false
	the width	number
Video Cast	the center	true, false
	the controller	true, false
	the crop	true, false
	the frameRate	-2, -1, 0 – 255
	the loop	true, false
	the pausedAtStart	true, false
	the preLoad	true, false
	the sound	true, false
	the video	true, false
Video Sprite	the movieRate	-1, 0 , 1
	the movieTime	1 – 48
	the startTime	number
	the stopTime	number
	the volume	-256 – 256
Window	the drawRect	legal rect
	the fileName	legal file name
	the modal	true, false
	the rect	rect
	the sourceRect	rect*
	the title	string
	the titleVisible	true, false
	the visible	true, false
	the windowType	0 – 8, 12, 16

Appendix B ◆ Real-World Production Considerations

It's a big leap from creating a movie for your own amusement to creating a movie to be distributed to others. This appendix describes the most important issues involved in creating movies that will work on another computer.

Stage Size

It's amazing how few of my students consider stage size, perhaps the most important parameter, as they create their projects. The standard business computer monitor is 640 x 480 pixels. However, many computers cannot display a stage this size without chopping off the sides. (How Director crops is determined by the Always Center option in the Preferences dialog box.)

All sprites are locked to a specific locH and locV. Director does not consider the stage size when putting a sprite on the stage. A sprite at locV of 425 would not be displayed on a monitor that could display only 400 vertical pixels.

Consider the market for your movie carefully when choosing a stage size. If you want your movie to run well on all computers, you'll have to settle for 512 x 342—the size of the original Macintosh screen. Research your market and choose an appropriate stage size.

Because fixing a movie with a wrong stage size is a painful experience, decide on the stage size early on.

Speed

The playback speed of Director movies is tied to the speed of the host computer and of the storage device the movie is running from.

If you are creating your movie on a fast computer, be sure to play it on the slowest machine you are targeting. You can lock the playback speed on the slow computer; it will run at that speed, then, on faster machines.

If you are developing on a slower computer, be sure to test your movie on the fastest machine you are targeting — especially if you have arcade game elements.

If you are developing for CD-ROM, beware that even very fast CD-ROM players do not begin to approach the speed of hard disks. Your movie, played from CD-ROM, will load cast members more slowly than from a hard disk. With the price of CD-R drives dropping, it seems, almost daily and with most multimedia service bureaus offering quick "1-offs," you can easily burn a CD-ROM and test your product several times.

Beyond your hardware, many factors interact to determine maximum playback speed. The most important are: the number of sprites, the size of the sprites, the ink mode of the sprites, and the color depth.

Use as few sprites as possible. Animate only the moving part of a sprite — not the entire object. Use copy, matte, background transparent, or transparent ink. Use 1-bit, 4-bit, or 8-bit cast members rather than 24-bit.

If you have a stage with lots of sprites, but only a few moving, set the visible of the moving sprites to false, save the stage as a picture, and import it into the cast. Put this picture on the stage and eliminate all non-moving sprites from the score.

Be careful stretching sprites. You'll get better speed (and image quality) if you create new cast members at different sizes.

Be careful programming idle. This message is sent often — a long idle script is a sure way to slow down your movie.

Movies with large bit maps, digital video, or sounds may pause while these cast members are being loaded from disk. The Lingo property traceLoad will display the names of the cast members in the Message

Window as they are loaded. Use this command by typing in the Message Window:

```
set the traceLoad to true
```

You can also set traceLoad to true in a handler, such as a startMovie handler. Set the traceLoad to false to stop the trace. Use the preLoad command in conjunction with the purge priority properties in the Cast Information Window to load needed cast members when a normal pause occurs in your movie—for example, when a menu frame appears.

If there must be a delay, set the cursor to a watch or an hourglass, put up a message, or otherwise inform the user that the movie is doing something and hasn't crashed.

Memory Requirements

Director must have enough memory to load all sprites on stage for the frame of the movie currently being shown. A 640 x 480, 24-bit picture occupies 900K, whereas the same picture at 8 bits occupies only 300K. Therefore, if you have a full-stage backdrop at 24 bits, Director needs at least 1800K—900K for the cast member and 900K for the screen buffer.

You can use the About Director command from the Apple Menu (Mac) or the Help Menu (PC) to monitor the amount of memory Director requires.

Director on the Mac can use pictures that have been JPEG compressed with QuickTime. These pictures may be tiny—32K for a full-screen picture. When imported into the cast, whether linked or not, these pictures will be expanded to 900K for display.

You can determine the size of individual cast members by typing the following command into the Message Window:

```
put the size of cast castNameorNumber
```

Link pictures rather than importing them into the cast. This makes your movie smaller but doesn't ease RAM requirements.

Break a long movie into manageable segments based upon natural divisions in its design.

When your project spans over several movies, use the Shared.dir movie to store the common elements.

Stick to 8-bit graphics and 11-kHz sounds (see below).

File Names and Folders

Unless you specifically use full path names in many Lingo commands, Director will look only in the current folder (the same folder as the movie) for linked pictures, sounds, and digital video files.

If you want your main movie to run off a hard disk, but submovies or other elements to be stored on a CD-ROM or other such media, create a global variable to contain the volume and folder names and use these for go to movie commands. For example:

```
global theMovies
put "CDROM:Data:SubMovies" into theMovies
```

If your project is cross-platform, use DOS-style folder (subdirectory) names and file names, unless you want your movie to run only on the Macintosh and on Windows 95.

Fonts

Text created from the Tools Menu, either fields or buttons, is "real" text. That is, Director is saving the ASCII values of the characters and displaying them using the operating system's text routines. Therefore, the typefaces you use must be carefully chosen — the users of your movie must have the same faces installed on their machines.

On the Macintosh you can install a typeface into a projector using a resource utility like ResEdit (install both the FONT and NFNT resource), but you cannot do this on the PC.

> *Do not install a typeface into a movie. Apple strongly recommends that font resources not be installed into* documents. *Projectors are* applications.

If your project is cross-platform, use the FONTMAP.TXT file to assure that a desirable substitute font or character is used.

Colors

As a graphics maven, you may have access to 16- or 24-bit color but 256 colors (8-bit) is more likely to be the norm. Further, Director for Windows does not currently support greater than 8-bit color. If your movie must display accurate skin tones or other subtle colors, require your users to have a Macintosh and have true color, but for most Director movies, develop in 8-bit color.

Invest in a utility like DeBabelizer, which allows you to optimize palettes — either by creating a custom palette or by dithering to the System Palette.

If your project is cross-platform, check all of the graphics on both systems. The default palette of the Mac differs from that of Windows. You can start a movie in the **other** platform's palette by using the Palette Channel.

Digital Video

On the Macintosh, Director will play only QuickTime movies, whereas on the PC, Director will play both QuickTime and AVI movies (assuming QuickTime has been installed). Because of this and because Quick-Time offers several technical advantages over AVI, stick to QuickTime.

If you are developing a commercial product, you can get a license from Apple to distribute QuickTime with your product for a surprisingly reasonable fee.

Macintosh QuickTime movies must be converted to play back on the PC. The converted movie will also play back on the Macintosh.

Director for Windows always plays digital video direct to stage, so don't animate on top of digital video (it's probably not a good idea, anyway).

If playing digital video is optional (e.g., it's used to display menu items), as you did in Chapter 13, consider saving a frame and using this still picture on the stage. Load and play the movie only if the user chooses it.

If your video is to be played back from CD-ROM, use a utility to optimize it for playback.

Sound

Because the basic specifications of PCs do not include hardware to produce much more than a simple beep, don't require sound (e.g., don't give instructions **only** via a sound track). Even on a Mac or a sound-equipped PC, the user may have the sound turned off.

You can get and set the volume level. Be careful on PCs, as high volume levels tend to distort the sound. You can check for machine type and then set it high for Macs and lower for PCs. Better to let the user set the sound level.

"The user is in control" is user interface principle number 1.

Director for Windows supports both the WAV and AIF formats, whereas Director for Mac supports only AIF. Most sound utilities on either platform can convert these sound file formats.

The most common sound sampling rate is 22 kHz. Try down sampling it to 11 kHz. The file will be much smaller and the quality may be adequate, especially if it is speech.

Keep sound files small. If you have a long narrative section, break it up and synch it with events in the score to cover the load time.

Consider playing sounds from disk with the sound playFile command rather than importing them into the cast. This will make your movie smaller and will make playback begin immediately rather than waiting for the entire sound to load.

If you are playing sound to cover a go to movie command or if Director is loading cast members, **do not** use sound playFile or linked sound cast members. Such sounds should be imported into a Shared.dir movie so that they stay in memory and continue to play while the other information is loading into RAM.

If you are attempting to synchronize sound and animation, consider making an audio-only digital movie and use the synchronizing techniques you learned in Chapter 13.

XObjects

There is no cross-platform compatibility between XObjects, so isolate your references to them in clearly identified handlers.

Many Macintosh multimedia XObjects are unneeded on the PC. Microsoft's MCI (media control interface) commands, included in Windows 3.1, provide a simple, consistent substitute.

Monitor MacroMedia's WWW site or the forums it maintains on America Online or eWorld for the latest XObjects both from MacroMedia and from third-party developers.

A Final Word

Test, test, test. Whether you are creating an interactive résumé or a large commercial product, if you want your Director movie to run reliably on other computers, you must play it on other computers.

Appendix C ◆ Bibliography

The following books, magazines, and newsletters have provided me with inspiration, solutions to problems, and challenges. Especially challenges. You cannot read Bruce Tognazzini and not want to "raise the bar." I don't pretend that this is an exhaustive list, but these are the sources I return to time and again. Check them out!

On Interface Design

Apple Computer. 1989. *HyperCard Stack Design Guidelines*. Reading, MA: Addison-Wesley.

Apple Computer. 1992. *Macintosh Human Interface Guidelines*. Reading, MA: Addison-Wesley.

Barrett, Edward. 1992. *Sociomedia: Multimedia, Hypermedia and the Social Construction of Knowledge*. Cambridge, MA: MIT Press.

Barrett, Edward and Marie Redmond, eds. 1995. *Contextual Media: Multimedia and Interpretation*. Cambridge, MA: MIT Press.

Bauersfeld, Penny. 1994. *Software by Design*. New York, NY: M&T Books.

Carroll, John, ed. 1991. *Designing Interaction*. New York, NY: Cambridge University Press.

Cooper, Alan. 1995. *About Face: The Essentials of User Interface Design*. Foster City, CA: IDG.

Heckel, Paul. 1991. *The Elements of Friendly Software Design*. 2nd ed. San Francisco, CA: Sybex.

Horton, William. 1991. *Illustrating Computer Documentation*. New York, NY: Wiley.

Kristof, Ray and Amy Satran. 1995. *Interactivity by Design*. Mountain View, CA: Adobe Press.

Laurel, Brenda, ed. 1990. *The Art of Human-Computer Interface Design*. Reading, MA: Addison-Wesley.

Laurel, Brenda. 1993. *Computers As Theater*. Reading, MA: Addison-Wesley.

Tognazzini, Bruce. 1992. *TOG on Interface*. Reading, MA: Addison-Wesley.

On Graphic Design and Software Techniques

Cohen, Luanne Seymour, Russell Brown and Tanya Wendling. 1993. *Imaging Essentials*. Mountain View, CA: Adobe Press.

Cohen, Luanne Seymour, Russell Brown and Tanya Wendling. 1995. *Design Essentials*. 2nd ed. Mountain View, CA: Adobe Press.

Dayton, Linnea and Jack Davis. 1995. *The Photoshop 3 Wow! Book*. Berkeley, CA: Peachpit Press.

Spiekermann, Erik and E.M. Ginger. 1993. *Stop Stealing Sheep*. Mountain View, CA: Adobe Press.

Weinmann, Elaine and Peter Lourekas. 1995. *Photoshop Visual Quickstart Guide*. Berkeley, CA: Peachpit Press.

White, Jan. 1982. *Editing by Design*. 2nd ed. New York, NY: Bowker.

Williams, Robin. 1990. *The Mac is not a typewriter*. Berkeley, CA: Peachpit Press.

Williams, Robin. 1991. *The PC is not a typewriter*. Berkeley, CA: Peachpit Press.

Williams, Robin. 1994. *The Non-Designer's Design Book*. Berkeley, CA: Peachpit Press.

On Programming and on Director

Dijkstra, Edsger. 1976. *A Discipline of Programming*. Englewood Cliffs, NJ: Prentice-Hall.

Foley, J.D. and A. Van Dam. 1982. *Fundamentals of Interactive Computer Graphics*. 2nd ed. Reading, MA: Addison-Wesley.

Knuth, Donald. 1968. *The Art of Computer Programming, vol. 1: Fundamental Algorithnms*. Reading, MA: Addison-Wesley.

Roberts, Jason. 1995. *Director Demystified*. Berkeley, CA: Peachpit Press.

Thompson, John and Sam Gottlieb. 1995. *MacroMedia Director Lingo Workshop*. Indianapolis, IN: Hayden.

Tognazzini, Bruce. 1996. *TOG on Software Design*. Reading, MA: Addison-Wesley.

Wirth, Niklaus. 1976. *Algorithms + Data Structures = Programs*. Englewood Cliffs, NJ: Prentice-Hall.

Magazines and Newsletters

DV magazine. IDG.
InterActivity magazine. Miller-Freeman.
MacroMedia Director User Journal. Hypermedia Communications.
NewMedia magazine. Hypermedia Communications.

Index

Marker Channel, 14
Mask, making, 38
Match.dir file, 188
Match1.dir file, 188
Matching game, 188–189
    answer checking in, 195–200
    code for, 190–195
    logic behind, 189
Mathematical operators, 88
mCastToWindow command, 280
mci command, 290, 291
MCI (media control interface), 321
mDispose command, 206, 215, 280
Memory
    conserving, 282, 317–318
    direct access to, 285
Menu
    creating, 253–257
    properties of, 313
Menu button, creating, 12–14
Menu system, 3, 186–187
Menu.dir file, 186
Menu: keyword, 253, 270
Menu1.dir file, 255
menuItem, properties of, 313
Message Window, using, 56–57
mGetHandle command, 285
MIAW1.dir file, 258
MIAW2.dir file, 262
mIndexColorToWindow command, 279
mNew command, 206, 214, 277, 284
mod operator, 148
modal property, 314
modified property, 312
Modular construction, 18–21, 317
Motion, diagonal, 146
Motion
    of game ball, 120–125
    of objects, 125–129, 143–149
Mouse events, 6
mouseCast function, 295
mouseDown event, 6, 12
mouseDownScript property, 312
mouseH property, 96
mouseUp event, 6, 12, 293
mouseUpScript property, 312
mouseV property, 96

mouseWord command, 231–232, 237
Moveable option, 47
moveableSprite property, 313
Movie
    ending, 106
    properties of, 313
    speed of, 106–112
Movie events, 6
Movie in a Window (MIAW), 258–262
movie keyword, 26
movieRate property, 243, 244, 314
movieTime property, 244–245, 314
mPatToWindow command, 279
mPICTToWindow command, 280
mReadFile command, 206
mRGBColorToWindow command, 279
mStop command, 289

N

name property, 312, 313
Nested if statements, 164
next keyword, 26
not equal to condition, 166
nothing command, 140, 152
Null string, 161
number of castMembers property, 312
number of menuItems property, 313
number of menus property, 313
number property, 312
numToChar function, 212, 218

O

Object cast members, registration points of, 84
Object-oriented programming, 278
objectP function, 277
Objects, list of, 312–314
on keyword, 5
open window command, 259, 271
openXlib command, 275, 281, 291
Operators, mathematical, 88
Order of execution, 111

Index